When the
Light
Turns
Green

A Handbook of Motorcycle Drag Racing

TOM MURPHY

A Tech Series Book
Whitehorse Press
North Conway, New Hampshire

Cover photo by Matt Polito (Fred Collis lights up his Star Performance
AMA/Prostar bike)

Back cover photo by Matt Polito (Larry "Spiderman" McBride rode the
first Top Fuel bike below six seconds in the quarter-mile)

We recognize that some words, model names and designations
mentioned herein are the property of the trademark holder. We use
them for identification purposes only.

Whitehorse Press is a trademark of Kennedy Associates.

Whitehorse Press books are also available at discounts in bulk quantity
for sales and promotional use. For details about special sales or for a
catalog of motorcycling books and videos, write to the publisher:

Whitehorse Press
P.O. Box 60
North Conway, New Hampshire 03860-0060
Phone: 603-356-6556 or 800-531-1133
E-mail: Orders@WhitehorsePress.com
Internet: www.WhitehorsePress.com

ISBN 1-884313-29-9

5   4   3   2   1

Printed in the United States of America

This book is dedicated to all of you out there who labor hard to ride your motorcycle one quarter-mile at a time.

Some of the important people who aided and abetted my work, and who made sure all the errors were mine:

George & Jackie Bryce
J.D. & Bev Davis
Mike Davis
Jean Grandy
Dan Kennedy
Matt Polito
Puppet
John Stein

Contents

Preface

Motorcycle drag racing in the United States is turning into a huge sport. If you want to race a motorcycle, whether it's stock or burns nitro, there are literally hundreds of races all over the country where you and your bike will be more than welcome. Sanctioning bodies—those groups who organize and put on drag races—abound. Just some of them are: NHRA (National Hot Rod Association), Prostar (The AMA's group), IDBA (International Drag Bike Association), ADBA (American Drag Bike Association), AHDRA (All Harley Drag Racing Association), AMRA (American Motorcycle Racing Association), IHRA (International Hot Rod Association), and a few others I have probably forgotten.

Each of these organizations has slightly different rules for how a bike is prepared, and some organizations, such as NHRA, limit the number of classes that are run. However, if you have enough desire to run a motorcycle down a 1/8- or 1/4-mile track, there is a place for you.

I got my start making long black lines on asphalt at a race track known way back in the 1960s as Pacific Raceways in Kent, Washington. Today you know it as Seattle Raceways. I started out on a 1965 Triumph 500, bog stock, and with whatever passed for "tyres" at the time. All races were started by a flagman for the first few years, but after a bit, timing lights came into the picture, right about the time I decided to play around with my bike in search of a little better elapsed time (ET) and speed. If memory serves, I started out turning ETs around 16.3 seconds (*Cycle World* tested it at 14.9 and 90 mph) and through determination and closing my ears to loud noises, managed to get into the fifteens by the end of my first season.

Why so fast, you sarcastically ask? Well, a lot of the lack of go had to do with the way I launched off the line—no burnouts, no wheel spin, lots of clutch slip—but most of it came from the bike itself. The Triumph T100R Daytona came with a screaming 41 hp at 7,200 rpm. Mine felt like about 35 hp and I'm fairly sure the one *Cycle World* tested had a few more than normal. Even with another season of racing and learning how to burn out (which I couldn't do much of with 41 hp) I don't think there was another tenth of a second in the bike.

Time passed and I found a number of different drag bikes under me: two-cylinder Harleys, three-cylinder Kawasakis, four-cylinder Suzukis, and others. Now, however, the years, beers and good living have slowed my reflexes while adding a lot more road-hugging weight, so most of my racing is done with a computer.

Now it's your turn to smoke the tires. Take a walk through this book, go to some races, then let's see how fast you are when the light turns green.

From the air, Atlanta Dragway shows the general layout of a drag racing track. The owners's suites are on the second floor and the officials (timers scorers, and the announcer) work from the top of the operations building.

Introduction

Drag racing really got its start after the end of World War II in 1945. It started on Main Street America with one man trying to prove his bike was faster than the next guy's. (Sorry ladies, but it was a man's game back then.) America was pretty much the stronghold of drag racing. The Europeans and British never quite understood the fascination with just racing in a straight line—and usually for much less than a mile. A great part of our fascination came from our roads. The layout of the continental highway system in the U.S. consisted of mile upon mile of die-straight roads. Covering those roads in the shortest time took a machine that was a lot like its rider: simple, single-minded and strong. And it took engines—big, healthy, and usually loud—to haul our heavy bikes down the road.

Racing down a straight road for a fixed distance was all about engines. Handling, other than staying upright and relatively straight, was not a concern; lots of pure power was. Rider skill played a much smaller part in straight-line speed contests than did horsepower.

Power begot more power and the long chase for higher speed began with increased displacement, bigger cams, higher compression and higher revs. However, the motorcycles generally available in the 1950s and 60s really didn't lend themselves to massive increases in power. Consider the Triumph 500cc Speed Twins and 650cc Thunderbirds of the era. They were smooth, tractable, fairly reliable engines when used within their limits, which were 40 hp and 70 mph cruising. When asked to run with double the horsepower and wildly increased revs, their foibles and faults became evident. What had been a comfortable, low-vibration motorcycle in stock form turned into a vibrating beast with the half-life of a fruit fly. Race tracks the country over were filled with soft thuds as the two-main-bearing engines spit their crank through the cases.

American motorcycles fared a bit better at the horsepower race. First, they were very understressed by design because American manufacturers knew that the average Harley or Indian rider was likely to pick the shortest and straightest distance between two pints and head in that direction with the throttle pinned. Not that U.S. bikes were of higher quality than their British

Here's where it all starts. This is called the "tree." Most races are won—or lost—right here.

Above and Opposite Here's a complete run from staging in the burnout box, to warming the tire, through the launch and down the track. Note how the rider's feet are out for balance.

counterparts, but they were built with durability in mind and the builders knew that a big, simple, slow-turning engine with modest compression would be around long after a 500cc vertical twin shook itself to death.

Some manufacturers, however, designed their machines to hold together while doing as they were expected. BMW, Zundapp and NSU had to rebuild their factories from scratch after the great Allied European Redevelopment and Renovating Process of 1941–45 (World War II), and they took advantage of this to go back into production with new machinery and new ideas. The German idea of "new" went way beyond just producing another version of the same model they were building before World War II. They, more than anyone else, took seriously the challenge of building transportation machines. The new owner of a German bike could be sure that from delivery on, their new machine would give thousands of miles of trouble-free riding. The bikes may not have had much soul, but they were reliable and dependable.

Americans never saw their motorcycles as transportation implements. Sure, they would take a young man to work day in and day out. They would even haul a small amount of baggage if one could be persuaded to stop at a store on the way home, but they were never seen as a replacement for the car. Transportation in America was considerably cheaper than in war-torn Europe for many years after World War II. Cars

were, if not exactly cheap, then not expensive. They could haul a lot of people, were easy to repair, and usually had a back seat—an important feature in the courtship habits of young males.

So, motorcycles were seen mostly as an extension of the male ego. Compared to most cars, they were much faster, louder, and put the rider right out in the public eye while being faster and louder—which was right where many 20-year-old men wanted to be.

Bikes in Europe were usually smaller in displacement and much quieter than their American cousins. Motorcycles never did acquire the negative cachet in Europe that they did in the U.S. They were seen by Europeans as transportation, with a little fun thrown in. Engine size reflected this, with a medium-engined bike being right around 250cc. A big bike was a 500 and only the rich owned 650cc monsters.

American riders never got attached to the tiddler-for-transportation idea of motorcycles. A fast motorcycle was for one purpose and one purpose only: to sit side-by-side at the last light in town and rail it when the light turned green. The next 30 seconds or so decided who had the really fast bike and who should stay in the sandbox. Having enough top end to leave any other bike or hot rod car like they were painted on the road didn't hurt either.

However, it was the brutal, visceral thrill of acceleration that provided the reason for building faster bikes. America became the home of

the fastest, strongest British bikes in the world because of this demand for acceleration. If a part broke while racing, just weld three more pounds of metal on it until it quit breaking. But quit breaking it would. Where the English were happy increasing power by a whole two to three horsepower per year, Americans weren't happy unless a nice smooth 40 hp engine could be whipped into a 75 hp screaming, bone-rattling, racer. After a while there would be more speed tuners' parts on the speed junky's bike than factory stuff—a tradition that carries on today.

Things got a little out of hand when cars and bikes began running at serious speeds on the street. Midnight racing was popular because of the empty streets at the time, but 100 mph in a 40-mph zone would earn the zealous racer a healthy ticket; with the installation of radios on cop cars, evading arrest became much harder.

If you're reading this, you are probably having some of the same thoughts I did about street racing, and now think it's time to take it to a track. The purpose of this book is to make your venture into drag racing a little easier. When I started, I had to learn everything the hard way. I hope this book will save you from making some of the more expensive mistakes.

I could have filled this book with a lot of numbers, recited names, and detailed exactly what went into each bike. However, that's not what this book is all about. Machines come and machines go. Records are made; records are broken. By the time this book hits your doorstep, all the current records could easily be ancient history. After all, just a few years ago, who would have thought that a Top Fuel, four-cylinder bike would go into the fives? And, if you think that's as fast as they are going to go, let's get some money on the table.

Personally, I think that in the motorcycle drag racing game there's a bunch of certifiably crazy nice people running on the tracks, and it's sure fun to watch them in action. If by looking at these smoke-filled, nitro-burning photos, you get the burning desire to go turn fuel into noise at a sanctioned dragstrip, then this book has served one of its purposes.

So come along, look at the pictures first if you must, but be sure to read every word in the book. I've packed a lot of information in here, so you'll probably want to read the book several times to be sure you've absorbed it all.

Let's go make a run!

Top   Sure as there's snow in the mountains, these guys will race anywhere. Well, what else do you do with your sled when the temp's above 80? They turn in the 8 second bracket. Fast, damn fast. Think about how fast those little bitty front wheels are spinning at 150 mph!

Right   Anybody and any type of bike can race. This rider pulled the front end so high that the Harley dresser is literally riding on the rear wheel and exhaust pipes. It put on quite a show; went pretty well, too.

Bottom   Air pollution. This type of burnout is why spectators like Top Fuel bikes. It's also hard on the fool photographer standing next to the rear wheel.

CHAPTER 1

What's It All About

What Exactly is a Drag Race?

To better explain the concept of drag racing, here's an excerpt from the AHDRA's (All Harley Drag Racing Association) information sheet on drag racing.

"In basic terms, a drag race is an acceleration contest from a standing start between two vehicles over a measured distance. The accepted standard for that distance is either a quarter-mile or an eighth-mile. These contests are started by means of an electronic device commonly called a "tree" (or sometimes "Christmas tree"). Upon leaving the starting line, each contestant activates a timer, which is, in turn, stopped when the same vehicle reaches the finish line. This start-to-finish clocking is the vehicle's ET (elapsed time), which serves to measure performance and often helps to determine handicaps during competition." More on this later.

All right, what does all that mean?

It means that you are going to race against another competitor to see who cuts the lights first at the other end of the track. It doesn't mean that your bike is faster than theirs, though. Through handicapping by controlling the lights at the start, both vehicles—cars or bikes—ideally should hit the other end of the quarter at exactly the same time, even if you're running a Suzuki 600 and the other dude's pushing a stretched-frame Suzuki Hayabusa 1300cc with nitrous oxide and turbo.

Junior draggers take racing just as seriously as the pros. I was told, "I've been racing for five years, and I'm running second in class. Need more power, though." He's 12!

Who Can Compete?

If you own a motorcycle and can fill out the entry forms without help from a friend, you can race. Most sanctioning bodies want you to have a competition license of some sort, but they will have a training program in place to let you get one. Sometimes all it takes is possession of a valid driver's license with a motorcycle endorsement to get on the track. Usually there will be a procedure to work up through the ranks to obtain different levels of a racing license. No group is going to let a novice loose on a Top Fuel bike until a high level of competency can be shown.

At minimum, riders will have to exhibit the ability to handle a motorcycle safely and competently. The bike itself must pass a technical inspection that covers safety items and proper setup. Things like safety wiring all drain plugs, providing a properly installed catch can to contain any oil that escapes through the breather, good tires, working brakes, and so on, will be checked.

There are lots of last minute adjustments right at the starting line. The electronics have to be set for the run just before the race.

Basic Requirements

It is very important that your bike is oil-tight and in good enough mechanical condition to stay together while on the track. If something goes very wrong and you end up oiling down the track due to a blown engine or some other fault, the organizers are going to be a smidgen unhappy with you. If you do it repeatedly, they may ask you to confine your racing to dirt roads where the oil will help combat dust.

It's important to ensure that your bike is in the best possible condition for other reasons, too. First, it costs a bunch of money to race, and there's nothing more embarrassing than showing up at a race and not being able to make it past the burnout box. Second, nothing is tougher than trying to build the bike in the pits. I can't begin to tell you how many times I've seen a competitor show up at the track, immediately lay out his tools and proceed to tear down his bike. In classes such as Top Fuel, this is normal, but in the lower classes the bike should be ready to run when it comes off your truck.

It's a Busy Place

You will learn that there are too many other things to occupy your mind at the track without having to worry about the machine being ready. There's always another race. Sometimes, too, Murphy's Law will take over. (Yeah, I know—I'm a Murphy, but it still gets me at times, too.) I've shown up at a race with schedule in hand showing that my class doesn't run until 11:30 a.m. just to hear the announcer say that everything's been moved up by a half-hour. Usually I hear this less than 60 minutes before it is my turn to run. Last time this happened, I hadn't had time to get the bike weighed due to sponsor commitments and had to jump around like an Armenian saber dancer to be ready on time. Try putting on leathers fast on a hot sweaty day. Once was enough.

Pay attention to my preaching about safety, 'cause it's going to be a major theme throughout this book. You don't want to get a helicopter ride from the track. I can tell you from personal experience, it's real hard to ride a motorcycle with a plaster cast extending from your little toe to your

Your bike and your gear must be in top condition. This setup's clean and easily passed the tech inspection. A dirty bike might be safe, but it shows a lack of care for the equipment and will be scrutinized much more critically.

reproductive organs. (I didn't say it *can't* be done, just that it's real tough.)

As you move up through the ranks from street bikes to faster all-out race bikes like Pro Stock, Funny Bike and any fuel/alcohol classes, rules will become much more demanding of your qualifications and vehicle construction. Here's one reason why.

Up Against the Wall, Angelle!

On the weekend of August 18–20, 2000, I was at the NHRA Nationals at Brainerd, Minn. to shoot some photos of Pro Stock bikes. The bikes were supposed to run at 1:45 p.m., but were moved up a bit and things were a bit busy in the pit area. In the first round of qualifying, Angelle (Seeling) Savoie made her initial run from about the fourth position in the staging area. The first three pairs of Pro Stock bikes made fast, but uneventful runs. Then it was her turn.

If you have never had the pleasure of watching Ms. Savoie race, you owe it to yourself to do so. More about her later. Her run went off flawlessly until the last 100 feet before the finish line, when the rear tire lost its bead on the rim and all the air pressure left the tire. I can't speak for her, but I would imagine that life became a bit busy right about then.

Her bike started swerving from side to side, covering 20 feet in each jump and getting bigger each time the rear end passed centerline. Remember, this was all happening at 160+ mph and took a lot less time to transpire than tell.

She was headed for a major laydown when the bike hit the right wall. Clouds of white dust flew, obscuring her from our view at the starting

Angelle earns her championship. This is the type of concrete wall she hit when her tire lost its bead.

Right Angelle's right bar took a lot of the load when she hit the wall. She kept the bike straight and rode it out.

Far Right This tire popped off its bead, but then went back on as the bike was being towed back to the pits. All Angelle wanted to do was go run again.

line. After the cloud cleared, we could see the bike still upright and slowing rapidly. She had managed to ride it down just fine, but it wasn't until I got into the Star Performance pits and spoke with George Bryce that I could see exactly what had happened.

When the tire lost pressure and started walking around, the bike started moving in ever increasing swings. Only hitting the wall could have stopped the oscillations and forced the bike to run straight. However, if the bars had been free to turn, the bike could easily have tucked under and flipped. Angelle managed to hold the bars straight while the bike ran down the wall, and this saved her. It also ground an inch-and-a-half off the end of the right bar—at an angle. This meant the bars were cocked during part of the time the bike was doing some high speed wall renovating. The right footpeg and the header pipe also spent their share of time grinding away the wall and showed the same type of damage.

I firmly believe it was her skill and familiarity with the 300+ hp bike that made the event almost anti-climactic. Most people in the stands didn't even know something had happened. Back in the pits, the crew applied a little air pressure and the tire walked right back onto the rim. With the footpeg and megaphone removed, it was hard to find any damage at all.

Could you do the same?

Angelle's only comment? She couldn't wait to get back on the track.

Number One

Angelle took the number one spot in the NHRA Pro Stock Championship in 2000 and in 2001. She also became the second woman to take an NHRA title (the first being Shirley Muldowney who won Top Fuel Dragster a few years ago.)

Angelle ran her milestone 2000 season with five victories, for a career total of 15. She had these reflections: "I learned a lot last year (1999). I thought winning was the only thing. That's not true. It's how you experience the journey along the way. Last year, I almost killed myself trying to win. This year I enjoyed myself. I realized if I lost, I wasn't going to die."

Winning Your Class

Initially, most people race strictly for the pleasure of racing. It's great fun to win, and the adrenaline rush is the best high in the world. Eventually, if you continue in the sport and start getting serious, winning your class becomes more important than simply winning a race.

In *elimination* racing, competitors are paired against each other with the winner moving up into succeeding rounds of racing and the loser hitting the trailer, until only two racers are left. The final run between the two determines the overall class winner.

Handicap Racing

Another type of racing matches potentially unequal competitors against one another, with each rider assigned a handicap to equalize results (see sidebar on the next page).

Let's say you have elected the 15.25 dial-in described in the sidebar. (First, better get a faster bike, 'cause my granny in her '83 Buick will leave you for dead.) Okay then, how 'bout a 10.77—sound fast enough? Now you stage and run against another bike running right around your dial-in. You know exactly how hard to run to stay above 10.77, but he's starting to pull you. "Huh, I think not," says you and slam goes the throttle. You win by a tire width—.01 seconds ahead of him. Why you just went 10.76! Great—except now you're disqualified because you ran under your dial-in time of 10.77. "Damn, damn, damn." You don't even look at the timing board to see who won.

Back down the return road, you pull in behind him at the timing booth to get your ET slip. What's this? He takes his, shakes his head and wads up the slip, and throws it over his shoulder. Funny way for a winner to react. You pull up and get your slip. Over in the top right corner it says "win." Uuuh? Howdidthathappen?

Easy. While you were busily beating your fellow competitor, he wasn't exactly waiting for you to pass. He saw you moving up when you pinned the throttle and—foolish him—he went for the win instead of the ET. Guess what? He went under his dial-in by .02 seconds. Guess what else? You do win!

Sometimes it's better to be lucky than good.

Let's Race!

The Most Important Moment: The Start

The key to making a good run is in how you leave the line after the lights run down. Notice I didn't say after the green lights, because if you see a green light before your bike is moving, you've already lost the race between two equal bikes. Even if you are a bit faster than the other racer, should he cut a better reaction time and leave before you, the chances are good that you won't be able to come from behind hard enough to win.

Above and Below Angelle Seeling Savoie went from Frank Hawley's Motorcycle Drag Racing School to being NHRA #1 Pro Stock champion in 2000 *and* 2001.

ET Handicap Racing

Here's how the AHDRA explains ET Handicap racing.

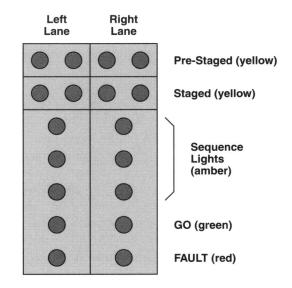

Left Lane / Right Lane

Pre-Staged (yellow)
Staged (yellow)
Sequence Lights (amber)
GO (green)
FAULT (red)

While some racers choose to race vehicles they build to certain specifications to fit into a certain class, an ever-growing number of racers choose to race on a local level in categories divided on the basis of performance or ET brackets. This is known as Bracket Racing. This form of drag racing offers a good starting point for the novice wishing to become involved in the sport. However, thousands of drag racers enjoy ET Handicap Racing so much that they have participated in it for years.

In this form of racing, two motorcycles of varying performance potentials can race on a potentially even basis. The anticipated elapsed times for each motorcycle are compared, with the slower motorcycle receiving a head start equal to the difference between the two. With this system, virtually any two motorcycles can be paired in a competitive drag race.

For example: Motorcycle "A" has been timed at 17.87, 17.74 and 17.76 seconds for the quarter-mile and the rider feels that a "dial-in" of 17.75 is appropriate. Meanwhile the rider of motorcycle "B" has recorded elapsed times of 15.27, 15.22 and 15.26 on the same track and he has opted for a dial-in of 15.25. Accordingly, motorcycle "A" will get a 2.5-second head start over motorcycle "B" when the tree counts down for each lane's green light. If both motorcycles cover the quarter-mile in exactly the same predetermined elapsed time, the win will go to the rider who reacts quickest to the starting signal. That reaction to the starting signal is called the "reaction time." Both lanes are timed independently of one another, and the clock doesn't start until the motorcycle actually moves. Because of this, a vehicle may sometimes appear to have a mathematical advantage in comparative elapsed times but actually lose the race. This fact makes starting line reflexes extremely important in drag racing. ■

So how you play the lights is most important. Here's how it works. The "tree" displays a vertical array of lights that control the start. At the top are four pairs of small yellow lights. These are staging lights. The two pairs on the left control the left lane and the two on the right handle the right lane. Below the staging lights are three large amber lights, with a green one below them.

When a vehicle comes to the line, its front wheel will break a beam, causing the top two staging lights to illuminate. As the bike rolls into the starting box a bit farther, the lower two staging lights will also come on. After both bikes have cut both sets of staging lights, the starter, who stands in the middle of the track behind the two competitors, will cause the amber lights to sequence by pushing a button. From the time both bikes are staged, to the instant the first amber comes on, is totally at the discretion of the starter. Usually he will hit the switch pretty rapidly after staging, so you have to be ready to run just as soon as the staging lights are lit.

The progress of the three amber lights down the tree can be set up in numerous ways. Normal track procedure is to dial in a half-second delay in the countdown for Sportsman or Handicap. For some types of pro events, the delay is four tenths of a second. One more setup is to have all three lights come on at once, then after a preset delay the green comes on.

Left The starting lights can be set up to start different classes of bikes at different times. The 13.85 ET bike will get a green after the 14.40 bike. This handicapping is supposed to make the competition dead equal.

Below With handicapping, the bike in one lane gets the lights before the other. In this case, the right bike got a green before the left lights even started down.

One light I've left for last is that red one down at the very bottom. That's the "tow" light, because if you see it, you get to tow home right afterwards. The red light means you anticipated the green too eagerly and your front tire let the back staging light extinguish before the green came on. The red light means you're disqualified. In Eliminations this usually means your racing is over for the event. If both competitors get a red, depending on the class of racing, the winner will be the first bike at the finish, or both bikes are out.

Let's look more closely at the different methods of sequencing the starting tree.

Pro Tree

Most Pro classes have what's called a .4-second (four-tenths) tree. That means that all three amber bulbs are lit at the same time when the starter pushes the GO button. Four-tenths of a second later the green light comes on. the rider has .4 seconds to react to the amber bulbs (sometimes called "yellow") and launch exactly as the green comes on. If the rider leaves before the .4 seconds are up, the red light comes on and he's disqualified.

The rider has .4 seconds to react. If his reaction time is .467, it took .467 of a second to move the front wheel out of the pre-stage (rear) light beam, or .067 after the green came on. Reaction times will usually win events between evenly-paired bikes. A good rider will react before he sees the green light. Any reaction times above .500 indicate the racer was either asleep at the line, or there was a problem getting the bike to move. How much time it takes for the machine to move after the rider decides to go is somewhat dependent upon the amount of slack in the drivetrain as much as his physical reaction time.

Street Tree

In some classes such as Street and non-Pro classes, the tree runs in a different sequence, usually with a .5-second (five-tenths) time progression. Once staged, the three amber lights will come on and off successively each half-second, progressing downward, and then there is a .5-second delay between the last amber light going off and the green light coming on. This system is much better suited for street bikes and riders whose reaction times aren't quite up to Pro ability. Some classes use this same sequence but on a .4-second time progression.

Left This is heads-up racing. Both bikes get the green at the same time. The rider has anticipated the lights just right and you can see the wheelie bars just touching the track as the engine loads the suspension.

Right The first rider just got the green light and is about six feet out while the second rider moves up to stage in the burnout box. The right lane hasn't got the green yet.

Anticipation

More than half of all drag races are won or lost on the starting line. How you react to the tree is all-important. For example, with a Street Tree most riders try to get underway between the last amber going out and the green turning on. A perfect start would have the green light just barely appear in your peripheral vision as the bike moves out. Learning to cut the lights is something of an art and requires a lot of practice and absolute knowledge of how your machine reacts.

From the time your brain says "go" to the time your hand begins to let out the clutch is a finite piece of a second. Likewise, the time it takes for the driveline to absorb the shock of the torque, then take up the slack in the chain, load up the transmission and start the rear wheel to turn just far enough to expose the rear staging light is also a measurable period of a second.

Reaction Time

Each rider's elapsed time starts when the bike moves from the starting line, not when the green light comes on.

Using a four-tenths Street Tree for example, the reaction time is measured from the instant the last amber light goes off and must be greater than .4 seconds (.5 seconds in some classes, such as Sportsman or Handicap). The reaction time for typical riders is between .4 and .52 seconds.

Let's assume the interval between the amber lights is four-tenths of a second, so there's a whole .400 of a second between the time the bottom amber dies and the green comes on. Should the bike un-stage the rear staging lights before this time is up, the red will come on instead of the green. I'm repeating myself for a reason—an important reason you will hear numerous times throughout this book. Most races are won in this split second.

Reaction times are recorded and displayed on the scoreboard and shown on your time slip. A perfect start would show a .400 reaction time. This means that the rear staging light broke exactly as the green came on. Any time below .400—say .397—means you moved before the green light had a chance to come on and you get a red light instead.

When you first start racing, you will see more than your share of green lights before your bike starts to move. This is normal, as most novice racers are more afraid of red-lighting than being slow off the line. A reaction time of .680 isn't uncommon for new racers. That additional .280 second seems awfully short, but after you've been racing for a bit, it will seem like enough time to send out for a pizza—especially when the other guy cuts a .420 and is nothing but noise in front of you.

Cutting consistently fast reaction times, .410 to .415, seems like a major effort, and it is. Time and many runs will help, though. The trick is to feel the timing of the lights, develop a rhythm, and learn to leave on the count in your head, not what's happening around you.

One suggestion I would make is to go to a few races and watch how all the different starters function after the bike stages. Each starter has a different way of operating. One will wait a second after staging to mash the button, another will give it a second-and-a-half count; the third might hit the button just as the last lights stage.

I learned to anticipate the lights by keeping a count in my head as though listening to a musical score. This comes from having a family of musicians and me so tone deaf that I was relegated to serving drinks at family get-togethers. I tried by force of personality to do what came naturally to my brothers and sister. I tried to keep track of the music by counting to myself as I listened to them sing. Didn't work, but it did develop a sense of timing that served me well on the drag strip.

The lights would sequence: Amber . . . Amber . . . Amber . . . Green, with the spaces being the .4-second interval.

I'd count: Bam . . . Bam . . . Bam . . Gone, with the shorter interval being when I dropped the clutch and tried to screw the throttle off the bars, so that the bike's first movement coincided with the "-ne" of "Gone." After a bit of trial and error I found that this system worked well for me. I'm not saying it will work for you, though. You'll have to come up with your own method of departing the line. There is no one right way; whatever works for you is fine. I have a friend who shouts: "Potato, potato, potato, potato" as loud as he can scream in the helmet. He says this forces extra oxygen into his lungs and keeps his count so he leaves on the second syllable of the last "potato." Whatever works.

Starting off, your reaction times will be all over the board, but you will improve. Now that I spectate more than participate, I find myself paying a lot more attention to things I used to just take for granted. In one race, I watched twelve Pro Stock machines (where the required reaction time was .500 seconds) run the first heat of qualification; the highest reaction time of the group

NHRA timing lights at the starting line are covered by the white box. This keeps bits and chunks from smacking the delicate equipment.

was .510. I kept track of various competitors and saw their individual reaction times didn't vary by more than .003–.005. Think on this for a bit. Just how long is .003 seconds? A blink takes .020 second—almost seven times longer than these racers standard variation. Now you see why I hammer on reaction times. When the difference between winning and going home is one-seventh of a blink . . .

Timing: How Do They Do That?

Timers at a drag race record two different events: top speed and elapsed time (ET). Rolling the front wheel out of the rear staging lights starts the ET timer. Crossing a beam at the end of the quarter stops the timer. The finish light and a beam set 66 feet before the finish determine top speed. There used to be another beam 66 feet after the finish line and speed was computed from this one and the one before the finish, but that arrangement has been discontinued for a few good reasons. One, it gives the very fast cars a little extra time to shut down; at 300 mph, that means a lot. Two, If you backed out of the throttle as soon as you crossed the line, you could come up with a set of numbers like: ET = 10.47; Speed 89 mph, when your real speed at the finish line was closer to 145 mph. This looked bad and served no useful purpose, so the new physical arrangement of timing lights has become standard.

Top Bike approaches staging lights.

Middle Front tire of bike breaks first staging light beam. Pre-Staged lights come on

Bottom Front tire of bike breaks first and second staging light beams and bike is ready to race. Pre-Staged and Staged lights are all on.

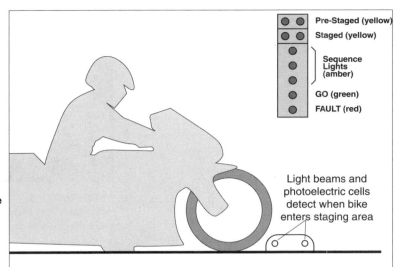

Light beams and photoelectric cells detect when bike enters staging area

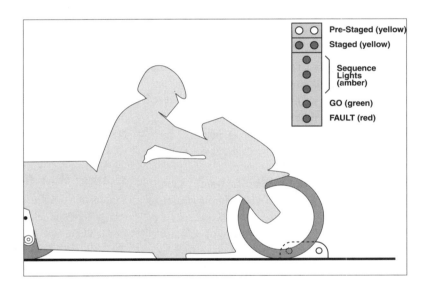

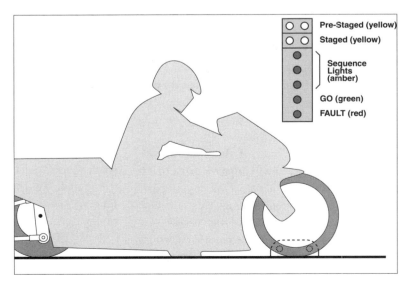

Star Performance – George and Jackie Bryce . . .

George and Jackie are examples of successful business operators whose only product is drag race motorcycles. Right now, their team includes two big winners for 2000: Angelle Seeling Savoie, NHRA Pro Stock Champion, and Fred Collis, AMA/Prostar #1. For the year 2000, Winston Drag Racing has joined them as the major sponsor for Angelle's Pro Stock bike.

I recently spent some time at their business, Star Performance Parts, where I talked with George about his beginnings and drag racing in general.

Author: Okay, now that you have me all comfortable in your office, out of the Georgia heat and humidity [this is taking place in July], why don't you tell me about how you got started drag racing motorcycles.

George Bryce: In 1975 we were just drag racing motorcycles locally. We started doing pretty good, so people began bringing bikes over to us for work. I was working in the air conditioning field at the time and the bikes were a sideline. I was racing on Saturday night for a hobby.

A: Then?

GB: I got more successful until one day I had so many motorcycles to work on in the little garage at home that I was working all night. I couldn't get up and go to work any more doing construction, so I went to work for Miller's Kawasaki in Darlington, South Carolina. The hard part is that I was working for Bryce Mechanical Contractors—my father—when I quit.

I became so busy at the shop just doing regular Kawasaki work that I had no time to work on the race bikes, so I had to quit there, pack up all my belongings and move down here where I had a friend in Americus, Georgia. I rented a shop in 1979 to be involved with a lot of local street racing activity here, unorganized racin' with the city's consent. One hundred motorcycles would show up, with one

thousand people watching and riding on a Sunday afternoon. They kept my front doors open.

Then I went from street racing to National where I won my first race on a Kawasaki. I also owned a Harley Super Glide back in '75–'76 that had been bored and stroked. It went 11.0 with no wheelie bar.

A: How did you and Jackie end up forming Star Performance?

GB: I met Jackie when she was a parts manager for a Harley-Davidson shop where I bought a trade-in Kawasaki. But then, so many people wanted us to work on their stuff because of how good we were doing with ours that we ended up having to start a business just to handle the side work.

After we got married in 1980, Jackie got a teaching job in Americus and that's what kept food on the table while we built the business. When she got out of school for the day, she'd come by and do the UPS and bookwork. One year later, she had to quit her job and work here full time.

(continued)

George Bryce, owner of Star performance Parts, watches Angelle Savoie make a qualifying run at Brainerd, Wisconsin.

23

. . . Star Performance – George and Jackie Bryce

A: From where came the name Star Performance Parts?

GB: The movie Star Wars was real popular when we started. I'm a doodler, I can draw, and I started drawing Star Wars stuff and motorcycle stuff, it just grew from that. By 1985, we had 15 employees and were distributors of all the major component lines.

A: Tell me a bit about your connection with Frank Hawley's Drag Racing School.

GB: I went to his school in 1985 to drive Funnycars as a reward for winning the Funnybike Championship. Frank and I got to be friends— he was a big fan of real fast motorcycles. We decided we needed a motorcycle school; however, I had problems with the idea of someone who had never driven a seven-second bike bouncing off walls and getting crossed up. He explained the step-by-step procedure he used with his cars—how people couldn't get in trouble, the risks were low. We put a deal together in 1992 and started in Gainesville, Florida. I built two motorcycles and three engines. We now do ten classes a year, six students per class.

The school bikes go 0 to 60 in one second, 0 to 100 mph in two seconds. They're 1325cc Suzukis, built from 1100cc engines.

A: While we're talking "fast," what size bike does Angelle Savoie run—your Pro Stock rider who just won the national title for 2000?

GB: She runs a two-valve Suzuki, and it's 92 ci— 1508cc— the limit in NHRA Pro Stock for two-valves. Four valve engines can be 1294cc for roller bearing, air-cooled motors. The late model water-cooled engines like the new Hayabusa can run 1430cc.

A: What is Fred Collis running?

GB: He runs a 1600 Suzuki. He runs AMA/Prostar and they have no displacement limit as long as the stock crank is used.

A: Why Suzuki two-valve?

GB: This engine is the Small Block Chev of the motorcycle world. More R&D, money and time has been put into it than any other. There's more parts and technology available for that engine.

Before every run, the Star crew goes over Angelle's and Fred Collis' bikes. Even before Star had major sponsors, this is the way George Bryce ran the racing effort.

We have two racing teams that were supported by our mail order business until Winston came along in 2000 with their support. Jackie runs Fred, and I oversee Angelle.

A: What makes a Pro Stock bike?

GB: It has to have a 70-inch wheelbase maximum, can't sit lower than 2 inches off the ground, runs on gasoline and has the displacement limits I mentioned. The bike and rider have to be 600 lbs minimum, and the rear tire can be no wider than ten inches.

A: Where are you going from here?

GB: Well, Fred is leaving the team to finish college and Angelle is looking toward her next championship with us in 2001. As for engines and development, I've a set of V-twin cases back in the clean room that could show up on a Pro Stock effort soon.

Star Performance Parts (800-841-7827; www. starracing.com) ■

CHAPTER 2

What's It Like Out There

The nice lady at the gate has taken your entry fee, handed you a ticket, strapped an armband around your right wrist and pointed in the general direction of the pits. Now what? First of all, she probably should have sold you a whole bunch of tickets 'cause you're sure bringing a lot of butterflies with you.

So here you are—first time at a drag race as a participant, not a spectator. You've brought your slightly-modified street bike, a Suzuki GSXR 750 with a few engine mods and sticky tires. Take a drive around before you park the truck. Either all the classes will be marked out with signs, making it easy to figure out where to park, or you'll have to look around to find some bikes similar to yours.

Park the truck so that when the bike's unloaded it will sit on the leeward side out of the wind and dust. Unload and set up the benches, tables, toolboxes, fuel cans, and all the other bits and pieces before taking the bike out. Most racers use some sort of flooring to help keep the area clean. I prefer interlocking rubber mats. A rug will work, but don't use a sheet. It will wad itself around the front tire as soon as you try to move the bike.

If you really want some comfort, use an awning. There will still be enough light to work, but the sun won't beat down so mercilessly. Take this time to check that everything

you'll need is actually here. It's more than easy to forget something like an air tank or small toolbox. I use a checklist and check off everything as it's loaded back at the shop. That way it all shows up.

What's in There? Tool Box Contents

This may sound basic to some of you, but I have to admit, when I went to my first drag race as a participant, I didn't have the foggiest notion of what to take for tools. I had the tool kit that came with my 1974 Kawasaki 750cc three-cylinder, two-stroke and that was all.

I've come up with a fairly concise list of tools over the years—just what is needed and no more. Some things—like welding torches, grinders, and frame jacks—are left out because I've never

Think he's wondering what to have for dinner? The world changes as you line up to run—your perspective narrows.

Some of the Basics You Will Need at Every Race

- Cubic money
- Tool boxes (see below)
- Gas cans
- Air tank
- Spare parts (the one you leave on the bench will be the one that breaks first)
- A good selection of nuts and bolts
- Generator
- Power tools
- Oil and drain bucket
- Wire and electrical connectors*
- Bike stands (both ends)
- Milk crate full of rags, solvent, spray lube, hand cleaner, etc.
- Awning
- Flooring
- Spare bike (have your mechanic ride his to the race)
- Cooler, well stocked
- Water
- Chairs
- Drop light
- Electric fan (hot days)
- Food (this avoids the foot-long tubes of indigestion at the stands)
- Spare bike battery
- Two spare master links and a piece of chain
- Chain cutter
- Tent and camping gear—Winnebego if you have one.

* I once watched a bike fry all its wiring right at the starting line, because of a bad switch. This racer's day was over for want of ten feet of #14 wire.

You will think of many other items I've missed, but this should be enough to get you through a weekend of racing.

In the Tool Box

- A set of good screwdrivers, Phillips and straight blade. Throw the worn ones away before you start rounding off screw heads, or slipping and gouging paint.
- A full set of Allen wrenches 5/64 to 3/8 inch
- A set of Torx tools T-10 to T-50
- Open- and box-end wrenches, 5/16 to 1-1/4 inch
- Pliers and side-cutters with plastic-covered handles
- A set of pry-bars: 12-, 24-, and 36-inch.
- A 3/8-inch-drive socket set, 1/4- to 1-inch minimum, with extensions from 1-1/2 to 6 inches; a 3/8-inch-drive universal comes in handy too
- Two 3/8-inch-drive ratchet handles, 8- and 4-inch, and a 12-inch breaker bar
- A 1/2-inch-drive socket set, 5/8 to 1-1/4 inch, ratchet, and breaker bar
- Three adjustable wrenches, 6-, 8-, and 12-inch, preferably with plastic-covered handles
- A ball-peen hammer, a brass hammer and a rubber hammer
- Steel chisels and punches in various sizes
- A brass drift, which can be no more than a piece of round bar stock, 3/8-inch by 12 inches long
- A rechargeable flashlight and charger
- A magnet on a 15-inch wand
- Lock wire and safety pliers
- Universal gear puller
- Snap-ring pliers
- Piston-ring compressor
- Oil-filter wrench

Some specialty tools you will find handy, but not necessary, include: an inductive timing light, a cylinder compression gauge, a valve-spring compressor, a nylon valve-guide cleaning brush, an engine stand, a volt-ohm-amp meter (I use a Fluke 78), Corbin-clamp pliers, and an air wrench with impact sockets, both standard and Allen.

A good source for tools is Sears or your local Snap-On dealer. Buy good tools and they will last you a lifetime. Buy cheap tools and you will be buying them all your life.

Check the floor. These are interlocking tiles set up on the asphalt. This Japanese team had real-time communication with their shop—in Japan!

needed them at the track, and if I ever did, someone else was ready to do what I wanted for a nominal charge.

Setting Up

Now it's time to unload the bike and set it up on the stands. Have someone who is familiar with the bike go over it and check *every* nut and bolt. Check the safety wired items like drain plugs and axle nuts. Check all fluids. Here's another good place for a checklist. I know it sounds redundant to go over everything again, and it's boring. After all, how could three different people forget to add oil to the engine when the bike was back at the shop. *What are these three extra quarts of oil doing in the box? Thought we only brought a half-case.*

I saw one bike fired up in the pits with zero oil in the tank. Makes some interesting noises after a very short while. Believe me when I say you need to check everything at least three times. When things start happening at a racetrack, logic sometimes gets left behind. I recently saw a bike run up to the water pit with a T-handle wrench happily spinning on a clutch bolt. Then one of the crew tried to kick it off. Everything turned into a Mongolian Square Dance at that point, but the bike was shut off before the wrench head managed to rip off more than a yard of his pants.

After you've gone over the bike, it's not a bad idea to fire up the engine and let it warm a bit. This only goes for stock, or close to stock, bikes. Pro Stock, Top Fuel, Pro Fuel and others had better be right from the start as their only warm up is just before the water box.

Now get a schedule. See what class is running just before yours. When it's called, start to suit up and get the bike ready to wheel over to the pit lanes. Check that the number plate agrees with the number assigned to you. Take a minute and clean your visor. Think about exactly what you're going to do from the time the bike rolls out from under the awning. Drink a bit of water, or get rid of a bit of water, whatever works for you.

When your class is called, line up at the proper lane. Be early; sometimes you will be staged shortly after lining up.

Your Class is Called

The announcer gives the first call for your class. If you have a crew, let them wheel the bike to the pit lanes. Get your gear and walk over to the burnout area. Watch a few bikes ahead of you as they fire up, burn out, then stage. Try to find the best part of the racing lanes. Where is the best rubber laid down? Check both lanes, as you don't know which one you'll draw. If possible, go out to the starting line and walk across both lanes. How my shoes stick to the asphalt will tell me where I want to stage.

I prefer not being the first bike off the line in my class. That way I can watch similar bikes run and get a feel for the track.

When there are only three bikes ahead of you, get into your helmet, pull on your gloves and climb aboard the bike. Nothing should be going through your mind except how to make the run. If you find yourself thinking about anything other than racing, you're not ready to race.

Burnout

Let's say you're positioned in the right lane. Remember from your stroll across the lanes where you want to be after heating the tire. The bike in front of you rolls into the water box. Stay a bit to the side of him unless you think your bike needs a bath. After he rolls up to the starting lights, the starter will motion you forward into the burnout area. This used to be called the "bleach box" when ordinary bleach was used to help liven things up a bit, however plain water is used these days. A slight depression in the track holds enough water to get your rear tire wet so it can spin easily and heat up.

Left The rider can't see behind the bike, so someone has to guide him back on the same strip of rubber he just painted on the track. Walking across the track after a Top Fuel run, your feet stick to the rubber while it's still warm.

Right He's making a solo run. The light's green, the front wheel's up and the rear tire is loaded up—a perfect start.

This burnout isn't just done for show. It's important to get the rubber in the rear tire warmed up so it will bite harder. To perform this maneuver, put the bike in first gear and drive around the water. Go to neutral and back into the water to where your rear tire just sloshes. Shift into second or third. Rock the bike a bit if it won't shift easily. Watch the bike ahead of you on the line. When he leaves it's time to warm your tire.

Hold the front brake with two fingers. Put both feet down to hold you straight up. Wind the engine past the point where you know the rear wheel will break loose. (It's nice to practice this a few times before having to do it for real. Killing the engine in the burnout box is a sure way to get everybody to look at you.)

Don't exactly drop the clutch, just let it out fast enough to make the rear tire break loose. Watch the tach and listen to the engine. Stay in the powerband—9,000 rpm and up for the GSX'er—and spin the rear wheel. Soon a wisp of tire smoke will appear, followed by a heavier cloud of burning Goodyear. Because the tire isn't deep into the water, just at the edge, the spinning tire will actually smoke off the water and start to bite the asphalt as it heats. A rider can actually feel the tire start to dig in. This is when it's time to come out of the box. Start to roll the throttle off and release the front brake slowly. The bike will want to come out hard, but keep it down by backing all the way off the throttle. Stop. In with the clutch and work back to first gear. Hop the bike a bit to make sure everything's engaged and the tire's dry.

It's important to have the rear tire absolutely dry when you stage as you don't want it to spin

hard at the starting line. If water left on the inner fender drips on the tire, it could cause a lot of unwanted wheel-spinning at the start. You only want the rear tire to spin just enough to keep the revs up so the engine doesn't bog.

Sometimes the bikes in street classes won't use the water box. Why? It's because the stock DOT street tires have grooves and sipes in the tread that will hold water, unlike a non-treaded slick. Sure, the tire will spin in the water like you just became master of about 400 hp, but the water will remain in the tread or on the rear fender where it will cause the tire to go up in smoke at the line. The choice is yours.

The person in charge of staging motions you up to the line. You check the other racer on your left. He's a little slower than you and is just now shifting into first. Wait. He's moving. Maybe he's a little behind the bike today. Maybe that's how you'll get him.

Okay, he's rolling up to the staging lights. Your turn. Bring the revs up. Ease the bike forward while watching the two sets of staging lights on top of the tree. His first set lights a good second after you brake the beam with your front tire and turn on the top two lights on your side. Yup, he's a bit slow. This *will* be fun.

A Ten-Second Run

The bike rolls forward another two inches. Both staging lights turn yellow. Right now the tach shows 7,000 rpm, the throttle's wide open and straining against the limiter, but the only thing you hear is your heartbeat. All staging lights light for you and for him. You watch for the top

Arachnid Racing . . .

Larry McBride, "Spiderman:"

15 national event wins; 14 national event runner-ups; 2 Best Engineered Motorcycle awards; Mechanic of the Year award; AMA/Prostar 1991 National Champion

and

The first man to run a motorcycle under six seconds in a quarter mile: 5.993 @ 243.68 mph at Houston Raceway Park, April 16, 2000.

and

August 1, 2000 lowered the 1/8 mile record to 4.01 at Indianapolis Raceway Park

Larry McBride is currently the quickest man on a motorcycle. He first climbed to the top in 1991 when he went 6.49 seconds—a mark that stood for three years. He was also the 1991 AMA/Prostar champion for that year.

Larry and his brother Steve own and operate Cycle Specialist in Newport News, Virginia, a performance motorcycle machine shop where they prepare Yamaha FJ1200 engines for the Legends race car series, along with building all manner of very fast import and Harley-Davidson engines. He runs a four-cylinder, blown, injected, nitromethane-powered bike.

Larry has been drag racing motorcycles for over 20 years. His nickname, "Spiderman," originated at the 1980 NHRA Nationals when an announcer commented on his trademark riding style of crawling around on the bike to keep it straight. He took the name to heart and now can be seen sporting Spiderman leathers when he runs his Top Fuel bike down the track.

What does it take to make a sub-six-second pass? Well, one obvious answer is money; however, there's lots of money in racing—more is needed than dollars. Talent and ability, experience, sponsors, a good crew—all these are necessary. But the single most important ingredient is the will to win. Without the inner drive to compete and be the best in the fastest class in motorcycle drag racing, Larry could never have blasted his way to the top.

Good equipment is also very important. A Top Fuel bike is one of the most tempermental and potentially dangerous machines on the track. The rider is actually stretched out within six inches of an engine that produces in excess of 1,200 hp. The machines are considered so powerful and so explosive that a chest and groin protector must be worn as a blast shield should something go catastrophically wrong and the engine explode in a sheet of nitro-induced flame.

(continued)

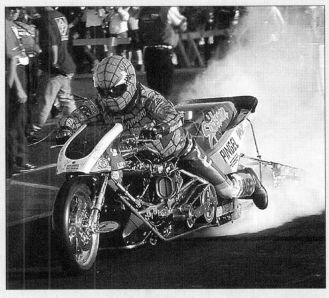

Larry McBride came by the "Spiderman" nickname from his habit of crawling all over the bike during a run. It takes a lot of body English to make a Top Fueler got straight.

Arachnid Racing . . .

Born on January 28, 1958 in Dothan, Alabama, Larry McBride isn't quite your average racer. Most riders tend to be small and wiry, with lots of upper-body muscle. Larry stands a lean 6 feet, 3 inches in a little over 200 lb frame. His height gives him the necessary leverage to control the 17 feet, 4 inch motorcycle at speeds approaching 250 mph. On his bike, a little added weight isn't too important as the engine easily makes enough horsepower to overcome traction and spin the rear slick the entire length of the strip.

The bike is entirely custom made. It carries a supercharged, billet 1500cc Puma motor (similar to a Kawasaki, but entirely custom fabricated—there are no stock motorcycle parts in the engine). The chassis is a 1994 Racevisions, with a total operating weight of 1030 lbs. The motor drives the rear wheel through a B&J two-speed transmission. The all-important multiple-stage clutch comes out of his own shop. An ART clutch had been used in the past, but Larry made his own to suit his particular riding style and engine. The Whipple Charger delivers nitromethane to a Ward Performance Vortex head. All this power is transferred to the 14-inch rear tire by an EK Enuma chain. The engine burns 4 gallons of nitro each run. Track Dynamics inverted forks suspend the front wheel during its very short contact with the track during a run. The body is made from a mixture of aluminum, fiberglass, and carbon fiber panels, with paint and graphics by Terry Pierce and designer Greg Ozubko.

McBride's bike is an incredible piece of rolling sculpture. Get past the graphics and the costumed man on top and some very interesting details become apparent. One striking feature is the four header pipes exiting right behind the seat. Sliding off the back of the bike with the engine at full boost is not an option one wants to contemplate. The right side is dominated by the intricate blower drive, complete with a hand-fabricated belt guard covering the drive, idle and blower pulleys. The drive side of the engine has a similar guard covering the exposed belt drive from the engine pulley to the larger pulley on the transmission. There's a lot of spinning machinery within inches of the rider. All in all, it is quite an imposing vehicle.

Larry McBride can be reached at:
Cycle Specialist
11115 Jefferson Ave
Newport News, VA 23601
757-599-5236
www.larrymcbride.com

Larry McBride suits up for another assault on the quarter-mile.

Left Hole shot! The right lane has launched before the left lane reacted. Check the pre-stage lights on the left lane. The bike's front wheel hasn't moved yet while the right lane is hooked up and moving.

Right The left lane turned a faster time than the right lane, but was last leaving the starting line and last across the finish line. Gotta react fast when the lights count down.

amber start light on your side of the tree. The starter slams the button down.

Amber!

Amber!

Time to leave. If you wait for the green light, you'll be the only one at the starting line. Right hand rolls the throttle. Left releases the clutch. Power hits. All the slack is taken out of the drivetrain. The bike starts to move.

Amber!

Green!

You're-off-no-red-light . . . Go! Go! Go!

First second.

You've pinned the throttle and the clutch is all the way home by the time the green light shows in your peripheral vision. The frame shakes and lurches as the rear Goodyear fights for traction while the front one grabs for air.

Second second.

Fifteen feet out the bike starts to twist sideways as torque tries to steer the rear wheel. Fifty feet gone faster than you can say "fifty feet." First gear about used up. Anticipate the redline and shift to second when the tach needle swings past 13,000 and the shift light momentarily flickers. Still can feel the rear wheel spinning.

Third second.

Second gear is history, time for the next one. Beat the shift light this time. Bike's still trying to walk sideways—think about a little pressure on the bars.

Fifth second.

Into fourth gear. The first five seconds have just been action and reaction—no time to think. Now there's just enough time to look at what's goin' on; actually look at where the bike's headed. Add a little more correction to the bars. There, that pulls the bike closer to the center of the lane. Speed's over 100 now. Wind becomes a factor.

Eighth second.

Through fourth, into fifth gear. All through shifting, now it's time to crawl under the paint and hold on.

Tenth second.

All of a sudden the finish lights appear and flash behind. Race is over. Time to shut it down. Roll off the throttle, sit up, gradually apply the brakes. Look around to see if the other guy made it down the track. Never heard or saw him the entire run. You must have been busy.

Left Go down the return road and pick up your timing slip—were you fast enough? There's always next race.

Right Time 7.687 seconds, speed 170.88 mph. This board lights up after every run. The four yellow lights on top show the right lane won.

Coming Down

There's a half-mile of shutdown track past the finish lights, more than enough to shut down a stocker, but mighty damn short at the end of a Top Fuel run. The race isn't over just because the quarter's done. Now you have to get the bloody bike stopped before the pavement quits. Some tracks, like Sears Point in Sonoma, Calif., have a road race course built around the drag race track and use part of the course as a shut down area. The shut down area at Sears is on an uphill part of the road race course and that slight incline really helps slow the bike. Tracks that don't change in elevation, like Atlanta Dragway, make shutting down a bit harder, but still not much of a problem for bikes running under 150 mph.

The return road can be on the left or right side of the racetrack. It depends on how the pits are laid out. Somewhere along the road is a small shack with a nice course worker who will give you a slip of paper with a lot of numbers on it.

Analyzing Your Run

As you made your trip down the drag strip, a computer was busy recording the key events of your run. The slip given to you at the timing shack looks something like this:

WELCOME TO ATLANTA DRAGWAY ADBA NITRO CLASSIC	
1:31 p.m. 23/July/2000	
Right Lane	Left Lane
Bike # - - - - - - - - - 50	
Class - - - - - - - SMOD	
R/T - - - - - - - - - - .691	
60' - - - - - - - - - 1.348	
330' - - - - - - - - 3.878	
1/8 - - - - - - - - 6.024	
MPH - - - - - - - 113.93	
1000' - - - - - - 7.906	
1/4 - - - - - - - - 9.494	
MPH - - - - - - - 139.76	
left 1st	
Rnd # QAL - - - - 136	

OK, so what happened?

The top part is pretty self-explanatory; date, time, where it happened and which lane you were in.

Below that, things get a little interesting. Bike #? That better be the number on your bike.

Class Super Modified. Your bike has been played with a bit. We'll go into rules a few chapters down the line.

R/T Reaction time. Assuming you were started with a .5-second tree, this is the time it took from the moment the last amber light died until your front tire came out of the rear timing beam.

60' How long it took you to cover 60 feet.

330' Same idea, different distance.

1/8 Time to cover 1/8 of a mile.

MPH How fast at the end of the 1/8.

1000' Time to cover 1000 feet.

1/4 This is what counts. How quick you got there. It is much more important than speed. This is your ET—elapsed time, the time from when your front tire left the rear staging light until you crossed the finish line.

MPH How fast at the end of the quarter.

Lots of information here. By looking at your reaction time (R/T), you can tell how fast you are responding to the lights. The ET timer starts ticking when the front tire of your bike leaves the rear staging beam (the same beams that control the top lights on the tree), not when the green light fires up. The time it takes to move after the amber dies is your reaction time. If your front tire leaves the rear timing beam before the green light comes on, you are disqualified—you "RED LIGHT." In this example, since we are assuming a .5-second tree, your tire must not leave the timing beam in less than .5 seconds after the amber dies.

Looking at the times it took to cover various distances can tell you how the bike is running. Comparing one time slip to another will let you know where changes in riding or motor improvements did the most good.

Reaction Time, Elapsed Time, and Time to the Finish Line

In handicap racing, the E.T. (elapsed time in seconds) clock starts counting when the motorcycle's front tire leaves the rear staging beam, not when the green light comes on. Reaction time is measured from *when the last amber on the tree goes out* (assuming that a Street Tree is used) until the front tire leaves the rear staging beam.

When both contestants get the green light at the same time, it's called "Heads-Up" racing. In Heads-Up racing, the ET clock starts when the green light comes on. Here, the reaction time is measured from *when the green light comes on* until the bike's front tire leaves the rear staging beam. This time can be positive, showing how long it takes the rider to react, or it can be negative, showing the bike left the rear staging lights before the green light came on. If this happens, the rider will be disqualified and the red light will come on.

If two machines can cover the quarter-mile distance in the same length of time (they have equal ET), the rider with the faster reaction time will arrive at the finish line first and take the win. Getting to the finish line first is what racing is all about. One bike might have a higher top speed, but take longer to get there. Or, in Heads-Up racing, one rider might have a quicker reaction time than his competitor, so even if his competitor has a quicker bike, bike number one wins because he got there first.

Let's look at a race started by a five-tenths Street Tree and see how this works.

Bike 1 (you):

Reaction time—.691 (the time from when the last amber died until your front tire left the rear staging light); ET—9.494 (the time from when your front tire left the rear staging light until you crossed the finish line); Time from last amber = 10.185 (the time from when the last amber died until you crossed the finish line)

Bike 2:

Reaction time .991; ET—9.394; Time from last amber = 10.385

End result—you win!

In the following chapters, I'll show you what it's going to take to get you on a bike at a drag strip. You might want to grab a yellow marker to highlight the interesting parts.

Funnybike Mike: High Speed Laughs . . .

What exactly is a Funnybike, anyway? According to the AMA/Prostar rulebook, the Funnybike classification is reserved for "single-engine, alcohol- and gasoline-burning, four-cylinder motorcycles in addition to single- or double-engine nitro burning, high-gear-only, Harley-Davidson motorcycles."

There are nine classes of Funnybike starting with FB/AB (Funnybike/Alcohol Blown, and ending with FB/VN (Funnybike/ V-twin Nitro. Tires are limited to a maximum of 14-inch width and engines have to resemble their stock counterpart. All bikes must be equipped with a lower-engine ballistic diaper to catch all the expensive parts should the engine blow. (Japanese-type four-cylinder engines blow downward; V-twins blow upward—your choice!)

John Davis (J.D.) is the announcer for the California Fun Bike Drags, and for the past 13 years has had the same duties with the American Drag Bike Association (ADBA). He owns Funnybike #773. His son, Mike, rides it. The bike normally runs in the mid-sevens and close to 200 mph. So far, the bike's best run has been a 7.03 at 192 mph, this with a 72-inch wheelbase frame holding a relatively narrow 10-inch-wide rear tire. The engine pushes hard enough to spin the tire all the way down the track. They employ a two-stage nitrous system, and can actually take power out of the bike if needed to let the tire catch up with the track. The electronic Schnitz box will let a rider program the nitrous to suit conditions. Launch rpm and other parameters can also be set to the rider's needs.

J.D. usually sets up the nitrous oxide to a 50% hit when the bike first leaves the line, then sets a timer to bring the flow to 100% at around the 2- to 2.5-second mark. The timer starts as soon as the clutch lever is released. The Schnitz box is set up to retard timing as the percentage of nitrous oxide increases. Two separate timing changes can be made. Most important is to have the timing retard toward the end of the run when the turbo is at full boost, in case the mixture goes lean from fuel starvation. Other factors can also cause a high-end lean condition: state of tune, track air temperature, track traction, air density, and surges in fuel flow. Pulling some of the advance out prevents the onset of deadly detonation.

Mike runs the turbocharged engine right to 10,000 rpm at the end of the quarter. Recently, there was a problem with the turbo's waste gate not opening properly. Actually, it didn't open at all, and boost built unchecked until the metal parts couldn't take any more and let go. The impeller literally blew chunks into the engine and the piston domes sagged from the pressure. The aluminum pistons blew up like nickel balloons.

When the engine let go, the bike caught on fire and the fiberglass panels and electrical wiring started to burn. When the turbo blew apart, it blew the carb off the manifold, so all the fuel/air mixture happily contributed to roasting the bike (and a little bit of the rider). Mike managed to pull the ripcord and that shut off the fuel pumps and ignition, which let the fire die by itself. His new bike will feature a five-pound Halon system—he wants no more 180-mph fires.

The engine of choice for Funnybikes is the two-valve Kawasaki air-cooled four-cylinder as found on KZ-900 and KZ-1000 bikes. Displacement can be as much as 1500cc; however, most Funnybike engines are between 1395cc and 1428cc. Any larger and the output gets too violent to get the power to the ground. The number one Funnybike rider in the world, Gary Clark, actually reduced the engine displacement to take some of the horsepower out of it and then went faster.

(continued)

Mike Davis lights up the tire. Funnybikes can run alcohol, gasoline with nitrous oxide, injected nitromethane, turbo alcohol, or gas injected turbo, but no blown nitro. Two engines, two-strokes, V-twins and four-cylinder engines are all allowed. It's a spectacular class, second only to Top Fuel for excitement.

Cranks are welded so the journals can't shift under power. Normally the journals are press-fit; however, lots of horses will cause the crank to undo. Hence the welding. The rods can't be removed. The biggest danger to the engine is detonation. If the engine backfires or detonates the charge, there is enough cylinder pressure created to break the welds. Then the crank blows up, usually leaving only the head as a useful part (if you are lucky.)

Mike's bike runs an Orient Express automatic four-speed transmission, moving the power from the Kawasaki engine to the 10-inch tire. The transmission is shifted by air from an on-board bottle. Shifting is automatic in that the clutch isn't used and the ignition isn't killed while the shift is made. Just hit the button and the gears change.

Riding a Funnybike with an automatic four-speed transmission is quite a challenge. The transmission is set up so that rolling off the throttle causes the shifter to index back and bend the shift forks. Then, if the throttle is re-opened, the transmission tries to shift into two gears at once—bye-bye transmission. Only when the trans shifts up into fourth can the throttle be rolled off and on.

This creates a bit of a problem for the rider if the bike begins to get out of shape. The rider is conditioned not to roll off, in order to save the transmission, so the tendency is to hold the throttle wide open and ride it out. This makes for some pretty "funny" runs, as normally a rider will only roll off if the bike gets so badly out of shape that it actually crosses into the other lane, or takes a run at the wall. J.D. said, "When things go wrong, everything is happening so fast that rolling off is automatic. Then the damaged trans has to be opened and the shift forks replaced. This can be done in less than one hour if needed."

"Making a pass on the bike is really interesting, because on these larger and more powerful motorcycles you have to physically ride the bike. If you don't ride it, it's going to ride you, and it will go in the direction it's inclined to go. If that big ol' wrinkle-wall Goodyear drag slick on the back should spin and move the rear of the bike to the left, the motorcycle is going to go to the right, toward the

This is what you and your bike should look like. Mike Davis models his Funnybike.

guardrail, and you physically have to make it come back."

"As soon as the bike launches, the front tire's up in the air and ceases to be a factor. You can't steer with the front tire, so you have to drop your shoulder and let your body weight lever the bike over (this is at the slower speeds). At higher speeds, you literally drop your shoulder to the left or right and let the air resistance steer the bike. It's like putting your hand outside a car window at high speed and feeling the air pressure force it back—the air pressure will pull the bike to one side or the other. That's why you see riders crawl all over their bikes as they go down track. Spiderman got his name for that. He's all over the bike like a spider, but it's more like a lizard hanging on a branch in a rainstorm. You're using your body to make the bike tug the way you want it to go."

"You're making decisions and movements like that at 200 mph. And then, once you make the pass and go through the lights, the pass is over, the throttle off, but now you have to go from 200 mph to zero. The ride isn't over yet."

"If the back tire starts bouncing, which they do quite a bit, then you've effectively lost the rear brake, because you've got to lift off the rear brake to stop the bouncing. Calm the bike down so you can get back on the brake. Another thing that happens is the back tire bounces off the ground while your hand is pulling the brake lever and the rear wheel stops turning—the tire's up in the air. So now when the tire touches down it's not turning any more, but the bike's still at 190 mph. The reaction as the tire hits the ground is . . . violent."

(continued)

"That's how Johnny Mancuso got thrown off at the Top Fuel World Championships in Australia a while back in 2000 (that was a multi-race championship). The bike was a bucking bronco and it just pitched him off. Part of the problem was the shutdown area was quite short and he had to get back on the brakes—had to. (Note: John wasn't hurt in the get-off."

"Jack Romine, at Sturgis year before last, crashed on the 1/8-mile track. He went through the traps at about 150 mph, and I was talking to him after the event. He said, 'ya know, J.D., I've been doing this for about 18 years. I always thought it would be difficult to step off a bike.' He said it was no problem at all. It was time to go. He was going to go into the guardrail—over the guardrail—so he decided to do it without the motorcycle. He just stepped off."

J.D. went on to talk about tires and the power it takes to turn a wide one.

"The limit on tire size, even in top fuel, is 14 inches for any bike out there. A 14-inch tire is HUGE! HUGE! The difference between a 12-inch and a 14-inch drag slick looks like about 2 feet in width. It's mind boggling. The tire and the super heavy duty beadlock rim are much more massive and have much more rotating weight. The beadlock is mandatory on 12-inch and wider tires. It adds a total of around fifty pounds to the bike, but you really want one when the horsepower gets up to what we're playing with. A 1000-hp drag bike can easily spin a 14-inch tire down the entire length of the strip. Keeping the tire right at the point of going up in smoke and not letting it get behind the power takes a lot of practice."

Mike Davis started out racing drag bikes when he was 15. He started in the Brackets, went into Super Gas, then Top Gas, and is now in his second season of Funnybike. He has beaten the world's fastest Funnybike, Team Kawasaki, at Phoenix last year.

November 2000 saw Davis down at Los Angeles County Raceway at Palmdale, Calif. for the final race of the season. He had a minuscule five-point lead over the second place bike for the championship and had to beat him at that race.

There were a few problems to overcome before hitting the track, though. As explained above, at the previous race, the wastegate on the turbo had stuck shut and the boost climbed over 54 lbs with ugly consequences. So the three or four days (and nights) before the November meeting were rather busy.

I met up with the Davis team the morning of Eliminations. Pressures were running high, so I decided to stay out of the way and shoot photos while the bike went through final setup. First run off the trailer was a 7.47. His opponents were right around 7.44 to 7.45, meaning he wasn't too far off the pace.

J.D. took some of the power out of the bike, because the engine had been missing on the run, and he thought the motor was going lean at the top. He backed down one full turn on the wastegate (reducing maximum boost pressure) and went one size smaller on the second stage nitrous injector. The second run showed he had pulled too much out of the motor—7.67.

On the third run, and the championship, the motor was back where it belonged, Everyone was primed. Mike suited up and they wheeled the bike up to staging. It fired clean. The motor sounded crisp through the burnout. Then it was time for the final run to decide the championship.

Mike rolled up and pre-staged. His competitor followed. Mike rolled six inches forward and the second staging light came on.

The amber!

The gr . . . !

Red light!

He had redlighted!

At the end of the 2000 season, Mike's plan was to run for the championship in 2001 and then take a long, hard look at where to go from there.   ∎

CHAPTER 3

Building a Rider

Before you can build a bike, go racing, and win a few trophies or money, you need to build yourself into a drag racer. It's all well and good to have the slickest racer with a jillion horsepower—that just takes money. But, if you can't drive it, what good is it? If you've been to a few races, you have a general idea of what it takes to herd a bike down a quarter-mile race track. Point it, wind it up, and drop the clutch. Shift when necessary and keep the rubber side on the ground. Sounds easy!

Well, not exactly. Next time you're in the pits, take a really good look at a pro racer as he or she works through the final 30 minutes before a race. A little pre-occupied, wouldn't you say? Some racers look totally oblivious to their surroundings, lost in their own world. The time for signing autographs is over. They're running the race right then.

Riders—good riders that is—usually have a lot of upper body strength. Women don't show it as much as men, but don't get into a handshake contest with Angelle Savoie. It takes a lot of oomph to move a bike around when making a run. Get a Top Fuel motorcycle or Funnybike going 220 mph and see how much strength it takes just to stay on the bike.

Training and conditioning are all-important. Any motorcycle rider can aim a bike down an empty strip of asphalt and run it through the gears. It's even fairly easy to put a burnout in front of that run. Now take something with a bit of horsepower—300 or so—out to a track, get up against another bike and see just how much harder the whole procedure becomes.

A lot of races are won by the rider, not the machine. Many times I've seen a racer with better and faster reflexes beat another person on a faster bike. Drag races are won by reactions, not long-term thinking. If you have to think about what happens next, it's way too late.

Cathy Silva wanted to race, so she sat down with experts and asked them what she had to do to learn to race a drag bike. Not what kind of bike and how much horsepower, but how to make *herself a racer . . . (see next page)*

. . . And here's where Cathy ended up: on a 1982 Suzuki GS1100. Her best times are in the 10.08- to 10.14-second bracket. The bike is 1260cc, mildly-modified, turning a slick through an undercut transmission.

Get Sleep, Not Drunk

What you eat and drink matters a lot. Most of the racers I know stick to ice tea and light meals until the competition is over. I had to learn this the hard way, of course.

Back in the days before the drag strip at Fremont, Calif. had been turned into one more Silicon Valley engineering complex, I ran a series of Kawasaki drag bikes. We usually ran Wednesday grudge races for fun and Saturday Eliminations for money. One Friday night before a summer race we had the bike ready and loaded and all the necessary bits and pieces packed to go. It is not necessarily a good thing to have all the crew and hangers-on together in the garage with nothing to do.

A large quantity of beer and hours of telling lies later, I stumbled off to bed. I wasn't worried a bit about going racing the next morning—partially because it was already the next morning, and partially because I could feel no pain.

I made a total fool of myself at the races. I killed the engine on the first run, and when I finally got it started and made the run, was slower than my grandmother on her little red tricycle. I couldn't have driven a nail with a sledgehammer, to say nothing of driving a drag racing motorcycle. I should have packed it up there and then, but I kept at it long enough to be laid away in the first round of eliminations. I was back on the trailer by 10 a.m.

Now, it's a good steak and salad, washed down with iced tea, and at least eight hours of sleep the night before any type of competition. I save the partying for after the race, after the bike's been cleaned and put away and there's nothing left to do but explain why I just didn't leave the line quite fast enough.

It's very early in the morning and everybody's lined up for tech. Usually the track opens at seven and runs start at eight.

What's a Lady Like You Doing in a Fast Place Like This?

Connie and Marc Cohen are a happily married couple who enjoy doing domestic chores like mixing nitromethane for their Top Fuel Harley, or getting Connie's Pro Stock Harley lined up for another 8.3-second, 157 mph pass down the quarter-mile. Truly this couple believes in the adage "The family that races together, stays together."

Connie is unusual in that what she considers fun would terrorize most other women. In 2000, Connie took the family Fuel Harley to the AHDRA Pro Stock/Top Fuel races in Orlando, Florida, where she managed to put on the show of the day. No, she didn't win first place, nor set a new track record. What she did was lose the fueler in a massive get-off just past the 60-foot mark when the tire stood up and shook her loose. She rolled and bounced all the way to the 1,000-foot line where she stood up and walked away. What made it doubly nasty was that she was leading at the time.

Connie and Marc run CC Rider Racing, of Bristol, Conn. (www.ccriderracing.cc), where the bikes are built and campaigned. Her Pro Stock Harley runs a Delkron-cased 160 ci V-twin, breathing through four Lectron carbs and driving a four-speed transmission with a Primo primary belt drive. A chain takes the thrust to a 15-inch Performance Machine wheel that holds a big Mickey Thompson slick. Her chrome-yellow bike and black and yellow leathers make her quite visible on the track and off.

Connie's first year in Pro Stock—1996—earned her a sixth-place finish in National AHDRA racing. In 1998, she moved up to fourth; in 1999, she held #5 plate in AHDRA; and in 2000 she moved back into fourth. Back in 1998 she became the first woman racer in NHRA Pro Stock to run a National event. She has run in three sanctions: NHRA, AHDRA, and ADBA.

Connie Cohen stands next to her NHRA Pro Stock bike. She races in NHRA, AHDRA and ADBA—not quite your average homemaker.

Connie makes a pass on her Top Fuel Harley. As of June 2002, her personal best was 7.34 and 188 mph.

**You will spend a lot of
time within yourself—
thinking, planning,
hoping.**

Run Your Own Race

Yes, you are racing against a clock and a competitor in the other lane, but the real race is with
yourself. When running bracket races, you have
to turn consistent times right down to, but not under the bracket time. The temptation is to run
harder if the other guy starts to pull you, but this
can lead to running below your time and disqual-
ification. Just because you get there first doesn't
mean you win.

Concentrate on being consistent. This means
your bike has to be totally reliable so you can be
sure it will perform the same, run after run. Then
you have to learn how to be consistent yourself.
One way that helps me make an even pass down
the strip is to visualize the run before I get to the
line.

If you watch a pro rider, you'll see what's
called the "thousand-yard stare" as he waits in
line to stage. He's not thinking about the night
before, or what's for lunch; he's running the race
in his mind, over and over. When he levers a leg
over the seat and lights the engine, he will just be
making one more run in his mind, this time for
real.

When I first started going fast a quarter-mile
at a time, I would concentrate so hard that I
couldn't hear my crew talking to me. Last minute
directions were a waste of time as I was long
gone inside my head. One time that really stands
out was a money race at the old Fremont, Calif.
drag strip. I was buttoned up tight, looking
down-track through the face shield of my new
Bell full-coverage helmet. The V-twin below me
was doing its best to suck all the alcohol out of
the tank. The bike in front of me left the burnout
box and I was motioned up. My mind had been
on the coming race and I wasn't quite up with the
bike mentally as yet and either missed the signal,
or just dialed it out. There was a pounding in my
ears that was increasing in tempo as I sat there. I
had been half listening to it for a while and I
wondered where it was originating. It took me
about two seconds to realize that what I was
hearing was my own heart beating! Over the
noise of the racers in front of me, over my own
engine (I had to look at the tach to make sure the
engine was running), over all outside influences,
I was listening to my heart spin up as the time to
run approached. If you think this be fiction, just
wait.

My brother was racing at Sears Point Raceway, Sonoma, Calif. a few years back, running
his first or second drag race on my Harley. When
I picked him up at the other end, he had an interesting story to tell. Somewhere between third
and fourth, he happened to glance up in the sky
and saw a biplane that since the morning had
been towing a banner around the track. He said
that once his eyes locked on to the plane, he
watched it fly for a bit. Now remember, there
were a few things going on around him while he
was skywatching. He said that he was just wondering what it would be like to fly a plane like
that. We had a serious talk about his drag racing
after that, and he gave it up for something
safer—road racing. His mind wasn't on the bike
and what it was doing, so he wasn't 100% into
the pass and it showed; he went .27 seconds
slower than ever before.

Racing Schools—Speed Limit? None!
Frank Hawley's Drag Racing School . . .

So you want to go racing—preferably in a money class—but you really haven't done much other than run enough street classes on your 750 to know you have a long way to go before you are competitive in a pro class. Now what? Well, think about this. Why not spend some money to go to a school where you can learn to ride a real drag bike, properly set up and maintained, and all you have to do is learn to ride from people who do it for a living? Plus, you don't have to work on your own bike. You only have to learn how to race. Let the pros take care of the mechanical end while you handle the racer end.

Frank Hawley has been in the business of turning out drag racers for more than 14 years. In that time he has seen more than 11,000 students make a pass down the strip at Pomona. The majority of participants have been car racers, running in the Super classes: Super Comp Dragster, Super Comp Firebird, Top Alcohol Dragster, and Top Alcohol Funny Car. However, there is one class available for bikers that will provide enough adrenaline-filled passes for the stout of character and that's Pro Stock Motorcycle.

When it's track time, you strap on a 250 hp Pro Stock Suzuki that bears much more than a passing resemblance to Angelle Savoie's very own Pro Stock Suzuki. It's no coincidence that the bikes have a similar appearance because hers and the school bikes are built in the same shop, owned by George Bryce, a former Pro Stock motorcycle champion himself.

Bryce is the owner of the Winston Pro Stock Motorcycle Team with Angelle the current NHRA champion and Fred Collis laying down winning times in the 7.28 range, to ensure that everybody else gets a trailer ride real soon in AMA/Prostar. Not only does George build the engines but is the man standing in front of you when you put 250 hp to the ground in a smoky burnout.

There's a bit of classroom time needed, but a lot more time is spent in leathers with sweaty hands.

The bikes are built on a Kosman chassis with wide 15 × 10 rear tires and Suzuki GSXR bodies. Engines are the reliable four-valve Suzuki four-cylinder, equipped with an on-board Racepack computer.

The school pulls no punches by running a detuned bike or limiting the rpm. Drop the hammer and the engine spins to 9,000 rpm. Shift up through fifth and seven seconds later, you're through the lights with a 170+ mph pass. If you ever wanted to know what a .44 Magnum bullet feels like when shot from a long-barreled hand cannon, here is your chance.

The first few passes feel like you're sitting on your bike watching someone else pull the world past your eyes, but soon enough it all comes together and you'll start catching up to the bike and anticipating what it will do next. As with other types of racing schools, you will start out slow and work up to speed.

(continued)

All track sessions are taped, and in the classroom you will have a chance to see exactly how you are progressing (or not progressing, as was true for an author who shall remain nameless). Classes are small and George Bryce takes the time to show each student what he or she personally needs to do to run cleaner and faster. Each student advances at their own ability level, and each student gets the same number of runs.

Do well in school, cut a fast ET, and you can qualify for your NHRA Pro Stock license—you'll be racing for points the next weekend. Or, you can just enjoy the drag bike experience, with no intention to ever go Pro racing.

Anyone can sign up. Matter of fact, zero racing experience is needed to run a drag bike 170 mph! Take a class and fly! Cost is reasonable considering what's provided. A weekend course runs $1,950, everything included. However, I highly

George Bryce instructs a student. He owns Star Performance, builds the school bikes, and when not doing those jobs, hauls around a bike for a lady named Angelle Savoie who took his Pro Stock bike to NHRA #1 in 2000 and again in 2001.

recommend that you bring your own leathers and helmet—they fit you. Nothing is more uncomfortable than trying to race while wearing something too small or too large.

What do you need to attend? Mostly, the will to do well. Angelle Savoie went through the class many times. Initially, she fought hard to attend and then later learned how to race to win in Pro Stock. Bryce said she had more "want" than any other rider who had ever attended the school. She went so far as to send him a letter saying in part:

"One day, whether it is in this lifetime or the next, I will see you on the starting line."

Think you have that much drive?

Frank Hawley's Drag
  Racing School
PO Box 484
La Verne, CA 91750
888-901-7223   ■

Training and Conditioning

You wouldn't think that sitting on a hard seat for less than 10 seconds could tire a person out, would you. Well, stir in a 100-degree day and the kind of humidity that makes mint juleps taste so good in Atlanta, throw in the pressure of eliminations, the fact that the motor just isn't quite right and you only have 30 minutes to figure it out, plus your closest competition has his bike buttoned up and is teaching his crew chief how to play Canasta. Your stress levels build all day long. By the time the last run of the day comes at 7 p.m., you are more than ready for a long rest.

Drag racing is a fast sport. The contests are measured in seconds instead of hours, so long-term endurance isn't quite as important as fast muscle reaction and instant coordination. You must be able to react within fractions of a second that aren't quite as important as they would be in a half-hour road race. The type of exercise you pursue I'll leave up to you, but it should involve something that trains eye-hand coordination and will help you react without conscious thought. Volleyball, tennis, basketball—games that involve coordination and fast reaction—will do more for you than simply lifting weights and building upper body strength.

Should you be the anxious or nervous type, breathing exercises and workouts that help build lung power can help alleviate hyperventilation at the starting line, and will improve your reaction times. I've found that when my only major exercise is lifting liquid-filled 12 oz. containers, my reaction times deteriorate rapidly. The better condition I'm in, the better my times out of the hole.

The Training—Drag Racing School

The first picture in this chapter shows Cathy Silva getting suited up to make a pass on her Suzuki GS1100. She started racing with only the knowledge that she wanted to be a racer and little else. She did have one thing going for her though: she knew what she didn't know about drag racing a motorcycle. She had ridden the street for years and her husband had drag raced a number of seasons, so she knew a bit about how to control a bike at speed, even though she had never been on a track. She also knew a lot of people who had been drag racing for years, and she wasn't afraid to ask them for help. She told me that everyone she talked to took the time to show her exactly what to do and corrected her when she did it wrong.

When you start racing, there's a whole world of knowledge you have to assimilate in a short time. No one hits the track knowing exactly what to do and how to react. Let's face it: you may be the fastest rider in Sioux City, Iowa or the terror of Flatbush Avenue, but running the street bears little resemblance to racing at a sanctioned track. Should you not believe me, go find a drag race, enter and run, then write me care of Whitehorse Press and let me know how you felt when the light turned green.

There's no substitute for training. The only way you're going to learn drag racing is to do it, of course, but you also need to learn from the pros, just like you have to learn how to build an engine to race; you have to learn how to build yourself as a racer. How? Go watch a few races, talk to the competitors, talk to people running similar bikes. Or, you can take the express route to becoming a drag racer and go to a drag racing school.

Even pros like Jim McClure, who has been watching the green light for more than 30 years, needs to be in good condition to race. Here, his pit crew hook him up to his Top Fuel Harley.

Mind Games

When the pressure is intense, psychology is important. I was running 7.90 Brackets and had a competitor who had a whole lot more go than he needed to run a 7.91 ET. He had to get out of the motor by the 1000-foot mark or chance turning 7.8–7.83 as he had done all through practice. On the other hand, I was doing everything except paddling with my feet to run 7.95–7.98. I knew if he ran true, he was going to drive by me and wait, so I figured I was going to have to do something constructive if I wanted to beat him.

I cut a pretty good time off the line—.510 if memory serves—and had him by the distance between two sheets of plastic wrap. I knew he was waiting for my motor to run out of puff and then would pull by me just enough to win. Well, I couldn't have that, so as I neared the 1000-foot mark where he would start to pull me, I abruptly sat up a bit and leaned forward. He must have figured I was backing down to stay in the bracket, and without thinking he lifted just enough that when he saw I actually hadn't slowed at all, he couldn't gain back the lost distance. I ran a 7.956 to his 7.958. We crossed the finish line less than three inches apart.

My buddy J.D. who runs a Funnybike told me a few things about getting inside the other guy's head. J.D. would hook a switch to his Funnybike's tail light, so if he felt the other racer pull-

Full leathers, armor padding, Kevlar gloves and quality boots, with a full-face Snell 95-approved helmet make up a good racer's gear.

ing up on him—out horsepowering him—he'd hit the switch. The other dude would think J.D. was running too fast and trying to slow down, so he would lift a bit and J.D. would take the win.

Of course, there are endless games to be played in the pits, too.

"Oh, I'm just running tune and test. This is my mild motor."

"Naw, I'm sandbaggin' a bunch. Had to back out of it waaaay before the lights or would have run at least .3 under."

"I don't think the motor will hold up. It's pretty old. Think I'll just run to finish."

Most competitors are good friends or at least nodding acquaintances, but that doesn't preclude

mischief like firing your motor long after he did, then taking a little extra time in the burnout box before rolling up to the line. Delaying like this can make him get good and steamed (bike and rider sitting on the line getting hot while you take a few seconds longer to do your burnout), and blow the run. Or, show up on the starting line, light just the first staging light, then drag out the next six inches while the other lane builds a good case of anxiety. All's fair in love and drag racing.

Dressing the Part

Motorcycle drag racing is a spectacular sport, but it isn't an inherently dangerous one. There's a much higher chance of breaking body parts or grinding up some skin while racing mountain bikes. That stated, you must remember that these machines run on two wheels with the rider in the breeze. Should the worst transpire and you get spit onto the asphalt, you need to be protected from the elements by proper apparel.

Riding Suits

This means leather—real high quality leather such as the garments made by Vanson Leathers (508-677-6773; www. vansonleathers.com) or Bates Leathers (562-426-8668; see their web site at www.batesleathers.com). You can buy their leathers off-the-shelf or custom fitted. Either company will make you whatever design you want. If you want to include graphics and logos, they are scanned and then cut precisely to your specs.

When your bike is tech'd, your racing gear will be examined to make sure it's safe. My advice? Buy the best leather money can buy. You may never, ever need them, but if you do . . .

Vanson Leathers offers a wide range of rugged racing suits, including custom designs to meet the wildest imagination. *Courtesy of Vanson Leathers*

Joe Rocket's Highside one-piece leather racing suit is made from 1.4mm cowhide and has Speedmaster body armor and a spine cushion for protection. It has stretch panels in the crotch, back of legs, lower back, and knees. Colors run the gamut from gun metal gray to red, with many different styles available. *Joe Rocket*

This Speedmaster leather suit from Joe Rocket is made from thicker cowhide than the Highside suit. It uses 1.7mm drum-dyed leather and has more reinforcements than the Highside. It comes with ceramic knee sliders, body armor, race-style speed hump, and carbon fiber reinforcements on the shoulders. *Joe Rocket*

To help you size and specify your leathers, Vanson will send you a free drag race suit kit. Both companies have on-line ordering. One or the other or both can usually be found trackside at the larger events.

One other manufacturer whose gear is normally seen on road racers, but is beginning to show up at the drags is Joe Rocket (www.joerocket.com, 800-635-6103). Their leather racing products are designed in Windsor, Ontario and have graced the backs of road racers such as Nicky Hayden (Honda) and brother Tommy Hayden (Kawasaki) and Larry Pegram (Superbike). Feedback from the riders I spoke with at a number of races was that Joe Rocket products work well and hold up extremely well to any unplanned contact with the track.

Body Armor

All racing suits can be fitted with body armor, either their own or specialized protective devices from another manufacturer, such as Bohn (888-922-9269; www.actionstation.com).

Falling off a bike at speed isn't something you'd choose to do for fun, but with proper protective gear, your chances of surviving without serious injury are pretty good. Falling off without body armor in the leathers—well, let's just pass on that. Bohn has had enough written testimonials about their products that I didn't think it

Bohn makes armor for all types of competition. It has been notable by its absence in drag racing, but is making inroads. *Bohn*

necessary to give their carbon/Kevlar spine protector an asphalt test. I don't need that experience to know that body armor is a good thing.

Their Pro Racer spine protector comes in two lengths: long and short. It protects your spine, shoulder blades, kidneys and ribs. This is one $190 product that you hope you'll never need, but if you do, it will be a cheap price indeed if it keeps you from breaking your spine.

A Strong Knee'd

Whenever I'm racing, or burnin' the canyons near my house in Nevada, I feel like my knees are hanging out at least ten feet and made of Christmas ornaments, so I opt for full-sized knee pads in my suit—not just the hero pucks that most of us grind down with a file so we look the hero part. I tried to move a curb with my knee once and I don't need to ever hurt like that again. It only takes one of those deep, sick-to-your-stomach pains to cure riding with no knee protection. (It was 20 years ago and I still walk sideways like a crab.)

My Aching Feet

Moving on down the body, we find feet. These extremities need to come in out of the wind, too. Lately I've been wearing boots from Motonation (858-513-6280; www.motonation.com), the SIDI Strada. I don't like the extremely colorful racing boots normally used in dirt racing; I much prefer something subtle but strong.

The Strada has two particularly strong points that appeal to me. There is a steel shank in the arch area that will keep the boot from folding if it gets trapped under the bike. There's also a tall, internally padded, shin protector for those times when your tibia just wants to bang off a footpeg, or tap some immovable object. All this for $200 retail is a good deal.

Many different companies produce boots. Whatever brand you choose, look for high quality construction; don't skimp on price. Any good boot will be built from high grade leather with ankle support, toe protection, Kevlar armor, and a high quality lining (pig skin for instance). I paid $300 for a set of Kushitani Power Max boots; most of the good boots are around the same price. Check boots made by Alpinstar,

Good foot protection is essential. Tennis shoes don't offer a whole lot of ankle support and that's what usually breaks when your bike lands on your foot. Plus, leather grinds better against asphalt than canvas. The SIDI Strada is an inexpensive boot that offers good protection and support. *Motonation*

Good boots are a must. Great boots, like these Kushitani Powermax boots, are even better. They are reinforced at the shin, heel, and especially at the outside of the toes, but they are still flexible enough to give good feedback when operating a shifter or brake pedal. *Kushitani*

Any one of Shoei's helmets—XSPII, Xtec, or RF800— pass Snell M95 and are accepted by all sanctioning groups. There are enough different colors, graphics and replica options for anybody. *Shoei*

Buy good gloves for racing. These Kushitani GPR gloves are reinforced at all the necessary places and will slide down the asphalt without grinding away. The last two fingers are heavily padded and the gloves are pre-curved to fit a hand on the throttle. *Kushitani*

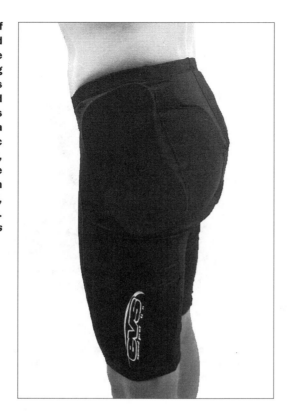

AGV, Firstgear, Hein Gericke, and Dainese—all available from Motorcycle Boots directory (info@accessoryinternational. com). Joe Rocket offers a less expensive Rhino boot ($149.95).

A Head of the Game

Okay, that's enough poor plays on words, but I'd like to talk about helmets for a bit. Modern helmets can take a tremendous impact, spread the energy around the liner and pads, and let you walk away from a bad fall with nothing more than having your chimes rung. Any helmet that passes the current Snell ratings will be legal for racing, but some helmets are better than others for fit, area of protection and comfort.

Shoei has been around long enough to be familiar to everyone in motorcycling. Their current offerings, the X-SPII and the X-tec both pass Snell 95 standards, both come in many different styles, and both provide full-face protection. Their only differences are in the weight—51.0 oz for the X-SPII and 54.0 oz for the X-tec—and outer shell construction and graphics.

The X-SPII is a multi-fiber composite, while the X-tec is a single-fiber layup. Either helmet will do an outstanding job of helping to prevent your brains from scrambling should the worst happen.

Hand Protection

Gloves are mandatory for all classes of drag racing. Usually leather gloves are specified, but there are some newer types of gloves on the market that work better than simple cowhide. Many manufacturers make racing gloves for strip and dirt, but the people I'm most familiar with—and who are somewhat new to the racing market—are Kushitani (www.kushitani.com). Although their suits, gloves, and boots are better known for road racing, their equipment is also well suited to drag racing.

Kushitani's GPR2 gloves have a memory form for the fingers that fits the bars better than conventional gloves. Plus—and this is a big plus—they have Kevlar padding on the back of the last two fingers (the first to meet the asphalt). Expect a price around $225. Vanson Leathers (www.vansonleathers.com) are best known for their racing suits, but they also have a good selection of gloves made from cowhide and deerskin.

Your local bike shop should have a good selection of racing gloves, but make sure they are more than decorative. Cheap gloves can look somewhat similar to the good ones, so look for real Kevlar reinforcement, double stitched seams, foam inner linings, and extra protection for knuckles and the back of your hands.

Underneath it All

Okay, gentlemen, here's where *you* get to wear Spandex. I've talked with a jillion long-distance road riders, AMA road racers, and drag racers. Their general preference is . . . bicycle shorts! These Lycra or Spandex shorts don't wrinkle, ride up, or trap sweat. Granted, you're only on the bike for a few seconds, but you are in the leather suit a lot longer.

For your upper body, any good T-shirt that will wick moisture and look good on the winners' stand works great. I would suggest one of the sport shirts that wick water away from the skin, except that there are no sponsor's names on them.

Running Your Street Bike

Now come the hard choices: Which bike are you going to race and what modifications will you make to it? Will you take your street bike, pull down the front end, throw a pipe and jet kit at it, add struts, and race; or will you build a drag bike from scratch? If you want to run your street bike, whatever its brand and size (I've actually watched a bagger touring bike do wheelies off the line), starting off is easy. Most sanctioning groups have a class for street-legal machines. Start by getting a rule book. Check the list of organizations at the back of this book for addresses and phone numbers. To set up your street bike for an occasional run is fairly easy. However, your street bike will never be a top competitor even in a stock street category. All street classes strive to create equal bikes, but some bikes are more "equal" than others.

After you get a rule book and see what modifications you can make, take a moment to run some numbers and see exactly how much money you really have available to spend. This sport is a hungry one and it feeds on hundred-dollar bills.

For the first few races, I advise you to leave the engine stock. You will have enough to do just racing the bike without worrying about keeping it running. You can buy more horsepower later.

Running Your Street Bike

Most of us start off drag racing by taking whatever we're riding on the street and making a few changes, mostly to follow the rules of the sanctioning body, then painting some numbers in a visible place and going racing. This works for a while as you learn the ways and means of drag racing; however, it isn't the best way to spend a

Suzuki GSXRs are very popular at the drags. Check the large exhaust pipe in front of the rider's left knee—it's turbo time! This bike runs 8.80 @165 mph; not quite your average street scooter, is it?

Anything can run—fringed saddlebags and all. The rear wheel's spinnin' and the fringe is flyin'. This racer runs a modified Buell, also.

Here's another inexpensive way to get on the track. Buy an older Kawasaki KZ 1000, bolt on some parts, lower the bike, go race—it's really that simple.

Here's what a minimum budget and an older Kawasaki ex-police bike can do. There's a total of $3,500 in this bike.

season racing. Usually what happens is you begin to make modifications within your class rules so you can be a little more competitive. Pretty soon you reach a point where you either have to keep the bike on the street— and by that time it has become pretty uncomfortable—or you have to take it off the street completely and dedicate it to racing.

If you can profit from another person's mistakes, let me offer this: If you are bitten by the racing bug, and you know you are going to become seriously involved in drag racing, then make a plan of attack before you take a wrench to your bike. Know exactly what you want to build and what kind of finances are involved before you lift a wrench. Many projects end up sitting in a corner of the garage, half-finished and collecting rust. Sometimes this is due to lack of interest, sometimes lack of money. Be sure you can build your racer with the resources at your command. Go ahead and run your street bike with a few modifications for three or four races, but don't turn it into a slow compromise bike or a fast uncomfortable bike. Build a bike specifically for a class and make it a dedicated racer.

Street Bike Racing

If I were going to start out with a fairly fast street bike at the drags, I'd want something like a Kawasaki ZRX or Suzuki Bandit to race in the Streetbike Shootout class in AMA/Prostar racing. Right now these bikes offer the most bang for the buck and they are winning their brackets. First I'll outline the bikes, then we'll look briefly at the rules.

Streetbike Shootout Pro Street Kawasaki

This is a bike that takes the worry out of being close. It wouldn't be the fastest street bike ever to hit the strip, but it would be reliable and run you down the track in the nines all day long. It would be a perfect bike to race during your first season while you learn. See the chart on the next page.

If you want to run competitively in the AMA/Prostar Street Shootout Series, be prepared to spend some money. Right now, turning a 7.97 at 179 mph is what it takes to run with the big dogs. For racing at that level, something with a lot more horsepower is needed. For that job let's build a Suzuki. Here's how I would do it:

Streetbike Shootout Suzuki—A Basically Stock Bike Powered by *Money*

All bikes in this class must be street-legal with functioning headlight, taillight, horn and turn signals. Frame and swingarm may only be stretched to a maximum wheelbase of 68 inches. No wheelie bars allowed. See the chart on the next page for details about this bike.

Costs?

The Pro Street Kawasaki can be built for under $5,000, plus the bike. The Streetbike Shootout Suzuki is another story. It isn't really a street bike, it's just sorta, kinda street-legal and has an electric system. Going with everything I've listed in the chart, expect to have $15,000 to $20,000 into the bike (including the bike) before it turns a wheel under its own power. I wouldn't start with a 100% stock new Bandit, because so much of it is going to end up on the shelf. Look for a one-year-old bike with less than 5,000 miles on it. This would help with initial outgo also. As for chassis work, I'd have a *good* frame shop do the cutting and hacking on the frame. I don't advise trying to cut down your own frame unless your day job includes Porta-Powers, heli-arc machines, and frame jigs. The motor is another item I'd let a pro builder like Muzzy or Star Performance build until I learned enough to do it myself.

You could build a Streetbike Shootout bike without all the pro equipment. You could also go out and cut 8.30s all day long with it. You could also be the first one on the trailer, too. The streetbike classes are getting to be so competitive that some racers are bringing a dyno to the track for tune-ups between runs and data acquisition and storage between passes down the track. (More about dynos later.)

On the track, plan to spend $25,000–30,000 to run one season, counting the transporter, tools, spares, fuel, *ad infinitum.* Each run will squeeze a minimum of $500 out of the ol' Mastercard. Don't believe me? Think about this. There's fuel, tires, oil, nitrous, spare parts (You do replace chains and stuff before they break, don't you?), entry fees, motel rooms, meals, crew expenses, etc. before you even pay the entry fee. Five hundred might be low.

Streetbike Shootout Rules

The Streetbike Shootout class was organized to get some of the street racers off the highways and on to the racetrack. The class is for stock-appearing motorcycles with unlimited engine modifications and any approved fuel except nitromethane. Turbos, blowers, and nitrous are all okay. If you run nitrous, the bottle must be clamped within the frame rails (no hose clamps). The maximum allowed wheelbase is 68 inches. A V-twin has no weight restrictions, but all other engine types must weigh at least 635 pounds with the rider on board.

Right now, the Streetbike Shootout is only six races during the season, but this type of class is becoming more popular and similar classes exist in all the other sanctioning bodies, and use similar rules. The six races that Prostar runs are held at Prostar National events. Get a rulebook online through Dragbike.com. Streetbike contenders will amass points toward the championship at every event, and to determine the quickest streetbikes in the world.

Streetbike Shootout Kawasaki

Bike	Kawasaki ZRX1100 or 1200, depending on whether it's new or used
Engine modifications	13:1 pistons, 1198cc kit for the 1100 engine, five-angle valve job, stiffer valve springs, stock cam, nitrous oxide system with 5-pound bottle, Mikuni RS40 Flatside carbs, remove air box, Kerker or similar exhaust system. Modify radiator fan for 100% operation.
Trans/shifter	Magnafluxed gears and shaft, procut and heat treated gears, heavy duty bearings, shift drum mod. Air shifter using the same tank as the nitrous oxide system.
Chassis mods	Rear: lengthened and bridged swingarm, struts, or Ohlin shocks Front: stiffer springs, tie-down straps, steering damper
Wheels	Front: 3.5-inch stock Rear: 6.5-inch RC Components with 190 Mickey Thompson MCR2 Street/Racing slick
Other modifications	Cut down seat, mechanical cam chain tensioner, kill switch, Tsubaki chain

Streetbike Shootout Suzuki

Bike	Suzuki 1200 Bandit
Engine	1500cc Flow Tec or Star Performance 375–400 hp. Progressive NOS nitrous system, Force exhaust system, Lectron carbs/intake manifold
Trans/shifter	Fast by Gast gears, electric-over-air shifter
Chassis	37 degrees of rake on a stretched frame, extended swingarm used as air tank reservoir, stock fork with heavy springs, suspension lowered to 2-inch ground clearance, Mickey Thompson MCR2 semi-slick rear tire, Metzler front, custom rear shock
Other modifications	Much altered bodywork, custom stepped seat

Rules for Streetbike Shootout

Approval. All bikes must be street-legal with a VIN number and license. They must run motorcycle engines only, with self-starters onboard. Each race will be run with a 32-bike qualified field and a .400 second Pro tree.

Road Run. Now, here's where this particular Prostar class gets interesting. All competitors must complete a 10-mile road run on Saturday morning to prove street-worthiness. The course is laid out by AMA officials and closely monitored. At the immediate completion of the road run, each rider must kill the engine and immediately restart it. Any bike that cannot be restarted within 30 seconds is disqualified. Any rider who passes or is passed by any of the pace vehicles, kills the engine prematurely, is stopped for safety reasons, or pulls off the course for any reason is disqualified.

Lights. The bike must have an operating headlight and taillight, and both must be on at all times. If a rider is unable to ride the road course, a substitute rider may be used. All engine configurations must be the same for the road run and race. Engines are subject to being sealed— from the frame, to cases, to block—after the road run. From then on, the only work allowed is limited to head gasket and up.

Appearance. All the main body parts, tail section included, must have stock appearance and shape. This eliminates one-piece bodies or tank shells. Alterations to the gas tank are limited to changing the slope at the rear of the tank. The motorcycle brand name must appear on both sides of the tank. Replacement parts can be used, but must retain the same shape of the replaced parts. All stock body alterations are subject to AMA/Prostar approval. All nitrous bikes must have thumb (butterfly) body fasteners on all aftermarket tail sections to allow removal by hand.

Electrical. The electrical system has to have a working charging system and the motor must be capable of being shut down with a kill switch. The turn signals may be removed. Both the headlight and taillight must be retained in stock position and operate automatically when the ignition switch is turned to the ON position, and must run through the road ride and all qualifying and eliminations. Aftermarket lights may replace the stock lights. Should the system fail, the charging system will be checked and must be repaired by the next round. Throttle-activated nitrous oxide systems are allowed, but not recommended.

Engine. Here's where you get to be creative: the engine may have any internal modification. This is a run-what-you-brung class, so be innovative. There's no engine size limitations, no cam limits, no restraint on the amount of head work allowed. Automatic transmissions and slider clutches are prohibited, but air or electric shifters are okay. The engine must be self-starting by a starter that is bolted to the engine, with no roller or push starts allowed.

Ballistic Restraint. All engines must be equipped with a Prostar-approved lower-engine ballistic restraint device, or the chassis should be equipped with a belly pan with a minimum one-inch rise that will hold at least four quarts of oil. There must be enough clearance under the pan/restraint for a two-inch bar to pass. By the time you read this, the rules may have changed to require all engines to have a diaper to keep oil off the track. All engines must use a flat oil pan with no protrusions and must have a side mounted or recessed drain plug. For instance, Suzuki engines should use a 1052cc oil pan with a recessed drain plug, or have a minimum three-inch ground clearance. The rules don't specify using safety wire on the oil plug, but I highly recommend using it on all filler and drain plugs. Should you oil the track and stop the races, you can count on hearing from the officials. If it happens again, you will be fined a minimum of $75 and can be charged up to $350 per minute of down time.

Frame. The frame has to be a stock OEM type. The VIN must be displayed in the original location. The frame may be reinforced (as long as the structure isn't weakened) by additional tubes or gussets, but none may be removed. All replacement tubes, brackets and gussets must be made of 4130 chrome moly steel on OEM steel frames, or a compatible aluminum alloy on OEM aluminum frames. All welding must be done by heli-arc in a professional manner. Accessory brackets such as radiator mounts, shock reservoir mounts, seat tabs, helmet locks, etc. may be removed or altered as long as they aren't part of the structural members. The steering head rake must not be less than stock degrees or more than 40 degrees maximum rake. The frame may be polished. Aftermarket suspension is allowed, but no struts (rigid frames that replace the shocks) or wheelie bars are permitted.

Minimum seat height. With rider and fuel onboard, measured from the lowest compressed point to ground, is 20 inches. The front suspension cannot be tied down with restraining straps. Actually, most classes now prohibit restraining straps of any sort. Think about what would happen if one broke while you were somewhere up in fourth gear about 1,000 feet down the track.

Tires. Must be DOT approved; no slicks are allowed. All cast wheels must use a 180, or greater, section width tire. Any wheels wider than 6-1/4 inches must run beadlocks. It's highly recommended to run beadlocks on *all* rear tires. They add a bit of weight, but will keep the tire on the bead should it go flat. You cannot switch tire type or size after the road run. All tire changes must be approved by the technical inspectors.

Verification. After each round, the bike must pass a weight check, tire check, and wheelbase check.

Hot Rod Cruiser Class Rules

Should your choice of motorcycle be of the V-twin configuration, there's a whole world of racing available to you. American Drag Bike Association (ADBA; www.Dragbike.com) runs everything from Top Fuel—where you have to wear a Kevlar vest just to get on one of the things—to Street Class for your "daily" street-ridden V-twin. AMA/Prostar runs a Hot Rod Cruiser class that's specifically for V-twins. Rather than try to cover rules for all the different sanctioning bodies, let's discuss the AMA/Prostar Hot Rod Cruiser class. The ADBA's Street Class is fairly similar.

The AMA/Prostar starting tree will be set to a .500 delay and will count down three amber lights before the green. Racing can be either a dial-in—where the bikes are handicapped by starting delays—or a total heads-up, no-breakout eliminator. Whoever is first across the finish line wins.

Some of the V-twin rules are shown in the table on the following page. Where they are the same as Streetbike Shootout, I have not included them.

Hot Rod Cruiser motorcycles are four-stroke V-twin production cruiser machines manufactured for street use. No sport bikes like Buell or Ducati are allowed. All bikes must be approved for the class by the sanctioning bodies. AMA/Prostar limits racers to 1998 or newer production models produced by Excelsior-Henderson, Harley-Davidson, Honda, Kawasaki, Moto Guzzi, Suzuki, Victory or Yamaha 1100cc to 1800cc V-twin engines. (I expect this will be updated if the rumored "Monster" cruisers of 1800+ cc are ever built.)

(See table on the following page.)

That's about it for the big street classes, but there are other ways to go.

Perhaps a smaller-displacement class is more to your liking. One of the more popular size classes for street motorcycles is 600cc displacement. Modern technology has enabled a 600cc engine to put out more than 100 hp and drive a stock, totally unmodified bike over 125 mph with ease. The AMA recognizes this and has

In racing, it seems like a lot of time racing is spent waiting. Your class is called, you line up, you wait. It's a good time to look over the other guy's equipment—might learn a thing or two in the process.

Not everyone has a massive, air-conditioned, fully-equipped transporter, but that doesn't stop this guy from enjoying the race as much as the pros. U-haul has transported more than a few racers.

formed a specific 600SS class for AMA/Prostar drag racing.

The bikes are relatively inexpensive, just about bullet-proof, and easy to run. Allowable modifications are few. Here is a short summary of the rules.

Rules for Hot Rod Cruiser Class

Minumum weight.

Single overhead cam (SOHC) or dual overhead cam (DOHC), 750 pounds

Pushrod engines, 650 pounds

Body. Must have originally been produced as a V-twin cruiser. The stock fuel tank and side covers are mandatory. Fenders may be replaced with cosmetic duplicates visually resembling the original parts in design and style for model year as determined by VIN. Any updating of bodywork is only allowed using parts available within the same model type. Fairings and windscreens are permitted; lower air dams are allowed. The brand name must appear on both sides of the motorcycle. OEM headlights and tail lights must be used, but may be mixed between models. Turn signals and mirrors may be removed.

Hydraulic brakes. Required front and rear. Minimum size for rotors is seven inches diameter by .187 inches thick for OEM or approved aftermarket parts.

Fuel injection. Permitted if OEM. Any aftermarket fuel management systems must plug in-line with the bike's ECU and stock wiring harness. The aftermarket systems must be generally available commercial parts with a retail price of less than $1,000. Electronic or mechanical enrichening devices must remain installed, but may be deactivated. Fuel and vent lines may be replaced, and aftermarket fuel filters may be used. Aftermarket carburetors or throttle bodies may be used, so long as there's only one carb or throttle body per cylinder. Multi dual-throat carbs or throttle bodies not permitted. A snap-back throttle must be used.

Slider clutches. Prohibited. No air clutch, proportioning valves, or hydraulics permitted. The cable-operated clutch may be converted to a manually-activated hydraulic type. Any type of mechanical lock-up is permitted.

Handlebars. Must remain in the stock position, but the break pedal and shift lever may be rear set. Footpegs must be at least 15 inches in front of the rear axle centerline.

Computers and data recorders. Not allowed, with the exception of an exhaust gas temperature meter. Any aftermarket ignition is allowed. Replacement ignition systems must be available to the public. No belt-drive magnetos allowed.

Engine. Must be an 1100cc to 1800cc 4-stroke V-twin production engine specifically designed for motorcycle use. Engine displacement can only be increased by overbore; no stroke changing allowed. The stock stroke length must be maintained. None of the fun stuff—nitrous, turbos, or superchargers—are permitted. The engine manufacture will determine the make of bike.

Engine (continued)

Engine type or configuration with relationship to the crank and stroke, cam drive location, number of valves, material and castings of cylinders, cylinder heads and crankcases, and any major element used in the crankshafts or camshafts may not be altered from the existing model except:

- OEM crankshafts can be lightened
- Aftermarket stock-sized rods allowed (no titanium rods)
- OEM cylinder heads required, but may be ported
- Valve locations and angles must remain stock
- Oversized valves permitted
- Aftermarket rocker arms and pushrods permitted
- Cylinder castings must be OEM; sleeving, re-plating or re-coating is okay
- Cams may be reground or replaced; drive must be OEM

Transmissions. Must be OEM; must be shifted from gear to gear manually, or by electric or air shifter. All rpm or computer-shifted gearboxes are prohibited. Final drive must remain the same as OEM. No push starts, external starters, or rollers permitted. The bikes must be ridden from the end of the track back to tech inspection.

Frames. Stock OEM frames must be used with VIN in original location. The frame may be strengthened as in Streetbike Shootout. Steering head angle must be between stock and 38 degrees rake. Swingarms or struts may not be welded to the frame, and a maximum of three struts per side are allowed. Minimum compressed seat height with rider aboard is 18 inches. All frame welding must be heli-arc, done in a professional manner.

Wheelbase. Cannot be altered, but wheelie bars may be used. The maximum length from the center of the rear axle to the center of wheelie bar axle cannot exceed the length of center of front axle to center of rear axle.

Fuels. You can't play much with the gasoline, either. It must have a dielectric constant within 1/10 of 1 point of spec fuel. No propylene oxide allowed. All bikes must have a method of providing a fuel sample from the fuel line system between the carburetor and fuel pump or petcock. VP C-12 is the spec fuel for the class and the only permitted fuel. It may be purchased at each event. Sometimes there's a two-mile ride, similar to Streetbike Shootout, prior to a qualifying or elimination run, so allow enough fuel for the event.

Cooling. No cool cans, ice, Freon, or other artificial fuel cooling or heating systems are permitted. No circulating systems not part of the OEM fuel system are permitted.

Seat. May be replaced by a custom model with a step to prevent the rider from sliding off the end. The seat, tail section and rear fender may be incorporated in one unit.

Tires. Must be approved by tech. The front tire must be race- or V-rated; the rear must be a DOT motorcycle street tire only; no slicks. The front wheel must be one inch or more in width. but no wheel made of carbon fiber or composite materials may be used at either end.

AMA/Prostar 600 SS Class Rules

The 600 Super Sport class is a heads-up, no-breakout eliminator designed for OEM 600cc motorcycles with limited modifications. Rules for the 600SS class are shown in the chart.

The series is intended for newer bikes; however, all 1994 and older bikes will be allowed to run if they were competing in the previous season. Most manufacturers' contingency money will be based on 1997 or newer motorcycles. If you are thinking about the class but have no bike, my advice is to buy a new one. The 600cc class is so hot that a three-year-old Suzuki might as well have wooden wheels and a horse to pull it. Technology has changed so much that you're better off with a new bike than trying to make an older, seemingly cheaper bike competitive. It's entirely possible to spend more money trying to make an older bike run up front than running the newest and best.

In 2001 the fastest 600 Supersport bikes were running in the nines at 140+ mph. Look up Team Green's Kawasakis to see how the class should be run. Ricky Gadson set a whole bunch of new records riding for Team Kawasaki, and has cut a .406 reaction time while running under the pressures of last round qualifications. This is .006 seconds from a red light! Reaction time wins races!

There are more than a few 200+ hp, slammed (dropped and lowered), stretched-swingarm bikes with operating headlights and tail lights, running as "street bikes." Actually, about the only parts on those bikes that haven't been modified *are* the lights! The best times in the 2001 Streetbike Shootout class were 7.750 at 191.50 mph, compared with 7.875 seconds and 184.35 mph in 2000 (two different bikes), and 8.413 ET in 1998. These winning bikes aren't anything you will find running on the street every day.

Don't let these numbers dissuade you, though. There's enough racing at the local level to keep you off the streets all year. Racing is great fun and can be enjoyed any way you wish; however, running for a class win is serious work and will eat up your spare time and disposable income right quick

Rules for 600 SS Class

Approval. 600 Super Sport motorcycles are 4-stroke production machines that have been homologated with the AMA, and sold for street use.

Item removal. Parts such as lights, reflectors, mirrors, instruments and related brackets and cables, radiator fan and wiring, passenger footrest and brackets, and some other non-essential parts can be removed. Safety wiring is not required.

Aftermarket parts. Some items such as handlebars, controls, instruments, oil and filter, sprockets and chain, and exhaust (street legal) may be changed.

Bodywork. Some bodywork may be replaced so long as the replacement is a duplicate. Plastic or fiberglass must be used—no carbon fiber.

Brakes. Rotors may be drilled, brake pads and lines may be changed.

Clutch. Plates and springs may be changed.

Carburetors and Intake. Jets and needles may be replaced. Some work on CV carbs permitted. Fuel lines and filters may be changed. No air flow modifications, including heat shields, are permitted.

Engine. For the most part, the engine must remain stock. The rule book spells out in great detail what can and can't be modified or removed. The idea is to make competition as close as possible, with equal horsepower across the board.

Frames and forks. As close to factory as possible. No wheelie bars. The swingarm must be stock and not lengthened. A fork brace may be used. A steering damper *may* be added. (My advice: put one on. I'd tell the story, but just believe me, a #1 tank slapper will scare the purple hell out of you.)

Fuel. Pump gas specification is VP C-12 sold at the track.

Sound. The exhaust system can't exceed 105 dB at 20 inches. There are some excellent aftermarket pipes and cans available that are quiet and make very good power, although the stock systems are getting harder to beat.

Tires. OEM size, DOT rating.

Wheels. Stock (you can polish them, but cannot remove any metal).

Minimum weight. 560 pounds, with rider.

Another Plug for School

A young friend of mine told me that he was about to pour some serious money into his street Suzuki GSXR 750 because it had reached the point where he was faster than his bike—or at least he thought so. After a fairly heated discussion about his ability ("I'm real quick, the bike's just slow.") and after he spoke with a couple of pro racers, he decided to attend one of the schools. Not that he needed it, you know, but just that we had hammered him so much that it was the easiest way to get us off his case.

In school, he found that he had picked up some bad habits along the way, and the first session's critique came as quite a surprise to him. I won't say he was humbled, but he had his eyes opened to his style of riding. In particular, he had a slight, but very noticeable hesitation just before he dropped the clutch off the line. When the last amber lit, he would turn and look down the track before releasing the clutch. Not much, but it was hurting his reaction time. He shaved almost a full tenth of a second from his ET just by improving his clutch release and not looking down the track until he actually was moving.

Did he win his next race? Well, no, but he did shave .17 off his best time. How much would he have had to spend to do that with horsepower? It would probably take 25 to 30 horsepower to make that improvement in ET. How much would it cost to coax another 25–30 hp out of a stock GSXR 750? ∎

Your nice, basic, stock Sportster. Why, then, the wheelie bars? Because it went 10.80 in Super Stock, that's why.

ADBA Eliminator class is extremely popular with street Harleys. Eliminator #9 is fairly serious. That's an air shifter bottle in front of his frame downtubes.

Sometimes what passes for stock is very interesting. Yup, the lens is painted on a piece of lightweight fiberglass.

Building a Chassis

In the previous chapter, I covered street bikes. Here, I want to talk about pure race bikes. The best way to build an out-and-out drag racer is not to start with a street bike and try to modify it for drag racing, but to build a racer from chalk marks on the floor. Start from the chassis and build a complete racer. This chapter will focus on the chassis and tires, since the choice of those two elements defines so strongly what kind of bike it will be. In later chapters, I'll cover engines, induction systems, drive components, and so on.

Before you start chopping up tubing to build a drag bike, you need to study the racing classes and decide which one you want to compete in, and what kind of bike you need in order to be competitive. First of all, there are many restrictions that apply to competition class bikes, whether Top Fuel or Pro Stock. When I started, the rules were pretty simple. If it had two wheels in tandem and one rider, it was a motorcycle. (No, no wooden wheels allowed.) The first bike across the finish line was the winner. Now AMA/Prostar has 14 classes that take 68 pages of rules to describe. Of course, back when a hot time was 15.5 and you were lucky to break 100 mph, little control was needed. Now Top Fuel bikes play in the five-second bracket and speeds above 230 are the norm, so rules had to be made for safety alone, if for no other reason.

In Chapter 18, I've included an outline of drag racing classes, to give you an idea of how they are generally structured. But that chapter is necessarily just an overview. Before you cut the first piece of metal or spend any money on goodies, get the complete rulebook from the sanctioning body you want to race with, and study the rules carefully.

Probably the single most important component of a drag racing motorcycle is the chassis. In this context, *chassis* means the frame, wheels, front suspension, and brakes. The *frame* is the collection of tubes that everything bolts on to, or fits in.

Frames

What you need to build a frame is part experience, part talent, and part black magic. If you have little or no frame experience, you will be far better off contacting someone like Koenig Engineering (515-244-1410) and letting them supply you with a proven frame. Another good source

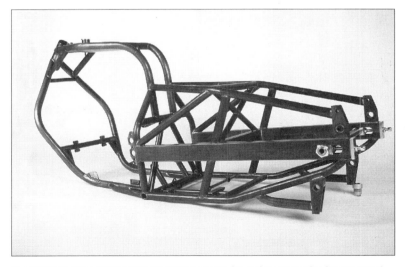

A complete Trac Dynamics T4 frame ready for paint; note the heavy steel rectangular tube running from the rear axle up through the frame. This helps distribute loads through the entire frame, not just the rear section.

This is a main frame jig. It can be adapted to numerous frames, and ensures the frame will be straight.

Good build quality is important when fabricating frames. This downtube is mounted in a jig while being welded to the frame tubes.

Trac Dynamic's new T4 frame incorporates a rectangular steel fuel tank as a support member. The high quality of the welds is apparent in this photo.

for everything from drag race swingarms to wheelie bars to full chassis is Trac Dynamics (www.tracdynamics.com; 661-295-1956). Both builders have many years of experience building drag bikes. If you're serious about building a race bike, contact them. Racers such as Matt Hines (NHRA Pro Stock champion), Paul Gast (AMA pro Stock champion), Shawn Gann and Gary Tonglet Jr. are running the new Trac Dynamics T4 frame, and winning.

If you want to build a frame yourself, you will need a good working knowledge of steel tubing, a heli-arc welder—MIG or TIG—some fairly specialized tools such as a drill press, lathe, mandrel tube bender, cutting/welding torch, clamps, frame jig, grinder, and very accurate measuring devices such as dial indicators. You will also need a good shop area with lots of light.

The rules specify that all frames must be constructed of 4130 chrome moly. Minimum diameter for the main tubes is one inch with .058 minimum wall thickness. If a single-tube backbone type frame is built, the top tube must be two inches diameter. Ground clearance, measured with rider sitting on the bike and four psi in the rear tire, must be at least two inches. Minimum seat height is as required in specific classes, but no lower than 16 inches, compressed seat to ground.

Building a frame, tube by tube, requires that the frame jig be built first. A jig is a series of brackets and clamps set up on a solid stand, usually about waist height, that will hold the frame straight and true as it's welded. The jig must be built to exact dimensions, plus or minus a few thousandths of an inch, for whatever class the bike will run. The wheelbase is set up first, then the main tubes are bent and connected to the steering neck and rear axle plates by tungsten inert gas (TIG) welding.

Next come cross bars, support bars, gusset plates, wheelie bar mounts, brackets for the engine mounts, gas tank and, finally, mounting tabs for bodywork. Take a good look at the photo of the Trac Dynamics T4 frame to see how a finished frame should look. If you have the capabilities needed to turn out a finished product like this, build it. Otherwise, use a professionally-built frame.

Give Trac Dynamics a call and one of these—ready for drivetrain—can be delivered to your door. Trac Dynamics, 661-295-1956, www.tracdynamics.com.

Trac Dynamics uses Glass Werx bodies on their TS and TSX frames. Numerous colors are offered, impregnated in highly-finished gelcoat, so bodywork and painting needs are minimal. They can provide custom colors on demand. *Trac Dynamics*

Wheelie Bars

What exactly are those long bars that stick out behind a drag bike and what do they do? The name *wheelie bar* makes you think that their single purpose is to keep the front wheel within a respectable distance of the track during a run. That is one reason for them, but they do have other functions to perform than controlling the height of the front wheel. When the bike leaves the starting line and the front tire is kissing the sky, the only steering available is through the rear tire and wheelie bars. Picture a triangle with the rear tire at one point and one wheelie bar wheel at each of the other two points. When the rear tire is spinning, it has a tendency to move the bike to one side or another, depending on how the chassis is set up. By rocking the bike from side to side, sliding your weight up and back, over to one side or the other, and shifting the load on the wheelie bars, you can steer the bike until the front end meets Mother Earth again. Adjusting the wheelie bars takes a bit of trial and error to make the bike run straight; this will be covered a little later in the book.

Most aftermarket wheelie bars are made of 4130 chrome moly tubing, but aluminum bars are beginning to appear at the track. They are 35% lighter than chrome moly and have no rivets or bolt holes in the tubing which could lead to fatigue and failure. Both types have top tubes of 7/8-inch

All the weight has transferred onto the wheelie bars and the bike is just lifting the front wheel. His feet will be used to stabilize the bike during the first few seconds.

Wheelie bar roller wheels have sealed bearings and can be spun safely over 100 mph. Picture how fast that is for a 2.5 inch diameter ball.

All Pro Stock bikes must have a catch can for oil overflow. This one mounts back on the wheelie bar, and its breather is vented because under certain conditions air flows backwards into the breather can.

Coat your wheelie bar wheels with white shoe polish before a run, and . . .

. . . after the run, you can see how much the frame was rocking side-to-side.

diameter with counterbored ends. Bottom tubes are 3/4-inch and both use 3/8-inch rod ends at each end. Some Honda, Kawasaki and Suzuki bars are made with 3/4-inch tubing for both top and bottom bars.

The wheelie bars are designed with vertical and top bar cross-bracing to provide adjustment and eliminate side play. Bars mount to street frames by using mounting plates that bolt to the rear foot peg and lower swingarm eyelets—or shock mount, depending upon make and model of bike. All rear shocks must be removed and struts must be installed to convert the rear to rigid. There can be no rear swingarm movement when wheelie bars are installed. Bolt-on wheelie bars are available for bikes that occasionally see street use. They can be installed in less than an hour, unless you own a bike like a Buell that has a single shock under the engine. In that case, a bit more work is necessary to pull the shock and install the single strut and wheelie bars. Rear ride height on any bike can be set by changing the length of the strut(s).

Mickey Thompson offers racing slicks in many sizes. This ET Drag tire is for a Funybike, but all M/T tires are similar in appearance. *Mickey Thompson*

Axle

If you run wheelie bars on a street bike, remember that the rear axle takes a considerable pounding when the wheelie bars slam down on the track. All factory axles are plenty strong when used with mildly hopped-up bikes, but when running nitrous and a turbo on your Suzuki Bandit, a change to a titanium axle will eliminate the possibility of breakage. All Pro bikes should have a titanium rear axle.

Tires

Front Street bike classes have to run whatever stock size tire came as OEM. All other Pro and Modified classes run one size tire: 2.50/2.75–18 on an 18-inch rim.

Rear Mickey Thompson (M/T), Hoosier, and Goodyear make racing slicks for drag racing. Depending on class rules, the slick can be anywhere from seven inches wide to 14 inches wide. All the slicks run the same tread compound. For street comp classes, M/T has a new MCR street tire for bikes that have to run DOT-rated street tires.

Mickey Thompson Drag Tires		
Location	Size	Tread width in inches
Front	2.50/2.75–18	1.7
Rear	26.0 x 7.0–17	6.5
	25.0 x 5.5–18	5.2
	25.0 x 7.0–18	6.6
	26.0 x 10.0–15	9.8
	190/50VR17 MCR2	8.8
	190/50ZR17 MCR	7.4

Mickey Thompson also manufacturers automotive drag slicks in 13-inch to 14-inch widths that are used by Top Fuel and Funnybikes. Tire prices vary and are set by the dealers.

Goodyear Drag Tires		
Location	Size	Tread width in inches
Front: Goodyear Frontrunner	2.50/2.75–18	
Rear: Goodyear Eagle Motorcycle	23.5 x 4.5–18	3.3
	25.0 x 5.5–18	6.1
	25.0 x 7.0–18	6.1
	26.0 x 9.0–15	8.7
	26.0 x 10.0–15	10.0
	28.0 x 10.0–15	10.0
	29.0 x 13.0–15	12.8
Rear, Top Fuel and Funnybike: Goodyear Eagle Dragway Specials	32.0 x 14.0–15	14.4 inches

Goodyear Tread Compounds	
Compound Number	Type
D-9	Soft
D-6	Soft
D-5	Harder
D-3	Harder
D-10	Hardest

Most rear tire sizes can be had in two compounds. Suggested retail prices start at $132.00 for the 23.5 × 4.5–18, and run to $261.00 for the 32.0 × 14.0–15.

Whatever tire you run—Metzler, Goodyear, Mickey Thompson, Dunlop, Avon, Michelin, or others—make sure it's rated for 20% over the speeds you will be traveling. A V rated tire is good to sustained speeds of 150 mph. A Z rating

The front tire on most Pro bikes are a 2.50/2.75–18 Mickey Thompson or Goodyear like this one.

Mickey Thompson's MCR racing rear tire comes in 190 width and either V or Z rated. It's considered a street tire because it has some semblance of tread, but it sticks like contact paper to the track. *Mickey Thompson*

is for 150 mph and up. All H rated tires are good for 130 mph, and that's too low a rating for drag racing.

Wheels

Other than appearance and the ability to hold air, what can we ask of wheels? Almost all classes allow aftermarket wheels—even the street classes. Appearance is pretty much a matter of choice, but there are a few things to look for when building a drag bike from scratch and shopping for wheels and tires. Aluminum wheels cannot be magnafluxed because they aren't magnetic, but they can be X-rayed, and I highly recommend having all wheels on bikes that run 180 mph and faster run through an X-ray machine. Then mount both wheels on the chassis, hook up a dial indicator to measure rim runout and don't run any wheel with more than .002-inch runout at the side of the rim. Check the wheel circumference for out-of-round. This dimension isn't quite as critical as side runout, but .005 inch is the limit.

Next, check the wheel for balance. Make sure it can rotate freely on the axle, then rotate it so that the valve stem hole is on the bottom and release it. The wheel should show no tendency to rotate. Rotate the wheel 90 degrees and check again. Do this every 90 degrees around the wheel. If the wheel wants to rotate when set in any particular spot, it needs to be balanced. This is a job for a wheel manufacturer, so I'd call the company who made the wheel and talk to their tech department. They may just exchange the wheel. Finally, mount and balance the tire, then check it for runout and concentricity (Is it round?). Make sure the tire sits evenly in the rim. Check both sides where the bead meets the rim. The tire should be seated to the same depth on both sides.

Wheels aren't cheap and if they get a small nick or slight dimple, the tendency for some racers is to continue running them. This is not a good idea. None of the wheel manufacturers I know will repair bent wheels, and none of them advise racing with a wheel that's damaged in any way whatsoever. My advice is to inspect your wheels frequently and replace them every two

Precision Metal Fab Racing builds beadlock wheels in 12-inch, 13-inch, and 15-inch widths. These are one-piece machined inners, not welded. They also build a beadlock wheel, size 7 x 17, for Streetbike Shootout. (952-496-0053) *Precision Metal Fab Racing*

Both Kosman and RC Components make front wheels of 1.85 inches width, and rear wheels in widths from six inches to nine inches.

years unless they show any signs of damage, at which time they become mailbox holders.

Wheels for Top Fuel, Pro Stock, Pro Mod and All the Others

Competition wheels for just about all the Pro classes are build by Performance Machine (www.performancemachine.com). People such as Bill Furr (1999 ADBA Champion), Jim McClure (eight AHDRA Championships), Larry McBride (AMA/Prostar Top Fuel Champion), and Rickey Gadson (AMA/Prostar Pro Superbike Champion) run their products. PM's beadlock rear rim comes in widths up to 14 inches. Their Superlite spun aluminum wheels are available in a number of sizes to fit either the front or rear. They have two catalogs available on the web: one for Harley-Davidson, and one for all the imports in metric sizes.

Beadlock Rims

All bikes running a 12-inch or wider rear tire must use a beadlock rim. Beadlocks are *recommended* for 11-inch tires. The purpose of a beadlock rim is to keep the tire from spinning on the wheel, or popping off the bead. The tremendous amount of traction available through a 12-inch to 14-inch tire can cause the wheel to spin so fast inside the tire that the tire bead gives up and

the tire comes off the wheel. Beadlock wheels weigh quite a bit more than a standard eight- to ten-inch wheel, but the added safety factor is well worth the increase in weight over a billet aluminum wheel.

One other product from Performance Machine that is a necessity on drag bikes is their four-piston, and six-piston brake calipers and matching discs. These brakes can haul a Top Fuel bike down from a 230 mph run in less than 1/4 mile without fading or warping. Couple a dual set of disc brakes on the front with a single six-piston disc on the rear, throw in some braided metal brake lines and fresh DOT 4 or 5 brake fluid, and enjoy the best set of stoppers available. Their $112 \times 6RSB$ caliper for 11.5-inch diameter discs will stop the fastest and heaviest drag bikes quickly and safely.

The Schnitz catalog showcases wheels from Kosman and RC Components in various sizes to fit all racing situations. Kosman has a modular front wheel, size 1.85×18 inches, and a modular rear 6×18 inches. They also manufacture a three-spoke billet aluminum rear wheel in 8-inch, 9-inch and 10-inch widths. None have beadlocks, though. RC Components lists ten billet front wheels in 17-inch and 18-inch diameter, six billet rear wheels, and two Top Fuel beadlock wheels in 11-inch and 12-inch widths. They

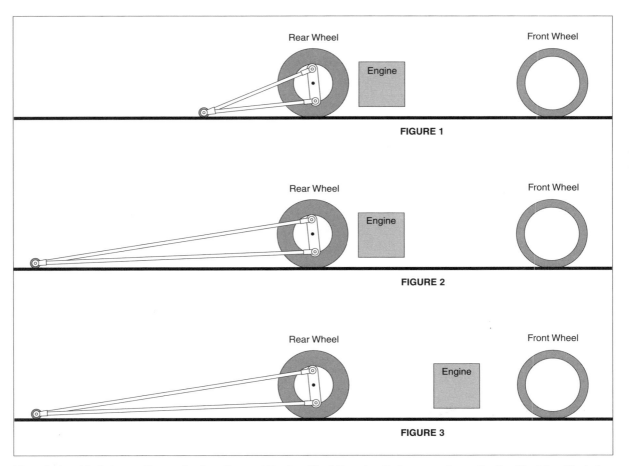

The relationship between the engine location and the length of the wheelie bars can dramatically affect handling of the bike. See text.

manufacture spun aluminum front and rear drag wheels for Sportsman racing that fit Harley-Davidson, Suzuki, Kawasaki and RC Comp pattern. All rear wheels come with a choice of one sprocket.

Motor Placement in the Chassis

Engine placement in a chassis depends on a number of parameters, horsepower being the most important. To picture this, I've made some drawings demonstrating different engine layouts and what happens in each case as power is applied. It would seem that having the engine back close to the rear wheel would be the best layout for putting the most weight on the rear wheel, but this isn't always the case. It *is* true when the bike is standing still, but check the following three scenarios:

Engine close to rear wheel with short wheelie bars (Figure 1)

When you drop the hammer the bike jumps up and tries to pivot around the rear wheel until the wheelie bars hit the ground. This can be so violent that the entire bike tries to pivot around the little wheels on the wheelie bars and it lifts the *rear* wheel off the ground. With no traction, the rear wheel spins up *right now* and when it re-contacts the ground, it hops back up again. This continues until something breaks or you back off the gas. Hopping can throw a bike out of control instantly and spit you off just as fast.

Hitting the wheelie bar hard can also upset the chassis, causing more handling problems. Last, but hardly least, when the front end bangs back on the track, parts can break, frames can bend, etc. The higher the wheelie bar wheels are off the track, the more magnified the problem will be.

Engine in the same place, wheelie bars lengthened (Figure 2)

With this geometry the wheelie bars can take more load, but their leverage is higher. The leverage will lift the rear wheel if the torque is high enough. Remember, the addition of a wheelie bar in essence moves the center of rotation from the rear wheel to the axle of the wheelie bar. If the weight and torque are applied too violently, the wheelie bar longitudinal struts can wrap up like warm spaghetti.

With the engine still this close to the rear tire, only enough torque can be transferred to the rear wheel to overcome inertia and the weight of the engine and part of the frame. After that, all the horsepower is doing is lifting the bike, not driving it forward.

Engine moved way forward, same bars (Figure 3)

With the motor forward in the chassis, more horsepower is required to lift the front end. The idea is to carry the front wheel while riding on the wheelie bars for 1,100 to 1,200 feet. When the engine is located in just the right position, the chassis will drop when you hit the throttle and plant the rear tire, then pull itself up. It's real easy to see a fast bike drop then climb as it leaves the starting line. Watch about halfway between the bottom of the engine and the lower part of the rear tire. The chassis will actually drop down before lifting.

The engine hangs out on a long lever arm, applying leverage on the rear tire as long as the front wheel is in the air. If the front tire hits the track too early, weight transfers to the front wheel and the rear tire can spin, slowing the bike. Most of the hard acceleration is over by the 1/8-mile point so you should try to carry the front wheel up to that point.

Shake, Rattle and Roll

One item guaranteed to grab your attention—if it doesn't just spit you off the bike—is tire shake. The rear slick flexes when power is applied. It actually wrinkles at the contact patch (where the rubber meets the asphalt) and that's where the name "wrinkle wall" originated. Then, as rotational speed builds, the tire grows taller, getting

The rear disc does 25% of the stopping. If the tire starts to hop, the brake has to be released, and then it does zero braking. Sometimes this can get interesting toward the end of the track.

There's no way to mount a parachute on a drag bike, so the front brakes have to do most of the stopping with a skinny, 2.50 x 18 tire. This brake on Angelle's bike is a single-piston Grimeca.

narrower in the process. So you start out with a tire with a wide footprint off the line and a narrow, taller profile at the other end.

This accomplishes a couple of things. First, it lets the rolling resistance decrease as the contact patch shrinks. Next, as the circumference grows, the overall effective gear ratio changes, allowing the bike to run faster for the same rear wheel rpm.

To do this, rear tire sidewalls must have a fair amount of flex built into them. Should things go wrong and the tire start to wind up and bounce—

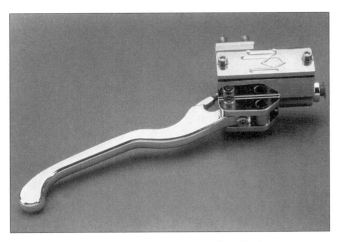

For the final custom touch to your drag bike, Performance Machine has master brake cylinders and levers with different bore sizes to operate single or double disc front brakes. *Performance Machine*

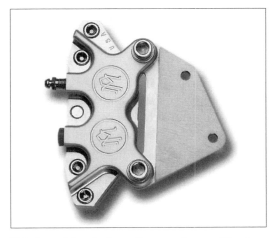

This four-piston brake caliper can be used front or rear. It will stop the world's quickest bike; however, Performance Machine also makes a six-piston differential-bore caliper which is intended for today's heavy Top Fuel bikes. *Performance Machine*

This massive bearing support offsets the drive sprocket to clear the slick. The aluminum side plates take the load off the weaker transmission case.

say due to changing track surface traction, uneven horsepower application, poor weight transfer, or other reasons—the rear tire will hop up and down, or actually set up a rapid wave motion in the sidewalls between the tread and bead called "tire shake."

Once the tire starts to dance, there is no choice but to back off the power and wait for the shake to subside. On some bikes with automatic transmissions, this can result in bent shift forks. Knowing this, a rider's tendency is to hang on, keep the throttle pinned, and ride it out. Some-

times tire shake can become so violent that it's impossible to stay on the bike, tossing the rider off to let him slide humbly down the track. Also, severe shake can send the bike in a direction you may not want to go. A bike can swerve instantly and those concrete walls are very unforgiving.

Check inflated tires carefully before mounting them to the bike. When the wheel is on the bike, run a piece of string around one edge of the tread. Then mark the string and wrap it around the other side. If it won't fit, or is loose, the tire is not symmetrical and can't be used. An uneven circumference—one side of the tire larger than the other—can cause a bike to pull badly no matter how much you hang off. A loose bead can cause a wheel to spin inside a tire, loosing all air pressure and taking you on Mr. Toad's Wild Ride.

Riding a Big Tire

A lot of newer riders have a very difficult time trying to get big-tire bikes to pull in a straight line when the throttle's wide open and the speed builds. I've watched more than one bike head for the centerline while the rider is leaning off the opposite side so far that sparks are flying. Shutting off the power does nothing—it's still on its way to the cones. What's the problem?

Good brakes are very important. Performance Machine's front or rear rotors can be ordered in many different styles and diameters from 8.5-inch rear to 13-inch front. *Performance Machine*

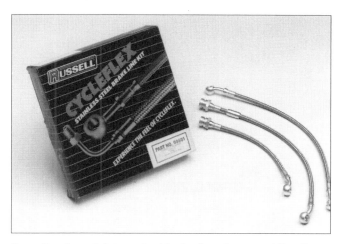

Russell makes stainless steel brake lines for every bike. If your bike doesn't have them, get a set. *Russell*

Picture the rear slick standing upright. The contact patch is the full width of the tire. This is the way the tire works the best, has the most traction, and goes the straightest.

Now lean the tire to the right. What happens? As you lean the bike to the right, the contact patch moves to the right edge of the tire, causing the tire to drive the bike to the left. Reverse steer. In other words, when you lean to the right, the bike wants to go to the left.

So, if you want to turn to the left, lean to the right until the slick's contact patch shifts far enough to drive the rear of the bike in the opposite direction. This takes a bit of getting used to, as you can imagine.

Once the bike is fairly stabilized, but still on the wheelie bar, and your feet are on the pegs, you will actually steer the bike through those pegs. When you want to go left, you put pressure on the right footpeg, loading the right side of the tire. This tips the chassis slightly to the right, loading the right side of the tire, and driving the bike to the left. At the same time, you lean your upper body to the left so the bike doesn't tip too far.

This raises the issue of footpeg location. If you mount the pegs too high on the frame, you won't have much leverage and not much will happen when you load the peg. The best place to mount the pegs is down low on the frame. This

A Top Fuel bike can run up to a 15-inch-wide tire. Their engines produce enough power to burn the tire the entire length of the track. Of course, that's the slow way to race; the racer who keeps the wheelspin down to a manageable level usually wins.

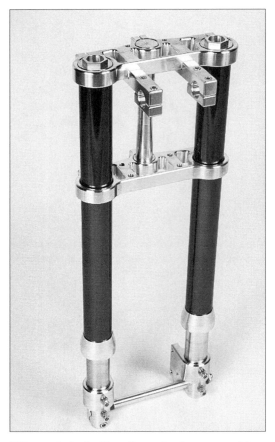

ICS race forks for Trac Dynamics frames provide much-needed stability at high speed. They are made in lengths from 25 inches to 28 inches to fit various frames. They're the best; use them when you build your Pro Stock or other drag bike. Retail price is around $1,865.

This swingarm is bridged for additional strength. The brake caliper locating arm uses Heim joints to set length and allow for pivoting.

will offer the maximum leverage when you want to tilt the bike.

In summary, it's best to ride a big-tire bike under full power and on the wheelie bar, with the chassis as upright as possible. When corrections are necessary, use the foot pegs to move around.

If you want to experience just how hard big-tire bikes are to ride slowly, ask someone to let you ride their bike back to the pits while it's being towed. These aren't so much motorcycles as unicycles. A rider would actually be better off if he had never ridden a bike before. That way there'd be no bad habits to unlearn.

For those of you contemplating a shift from a street bike to some monster with a lot of Goodyear on the ground, I wholeheartedly recom-

mend a day or two at a drag racing school where instructors can show you the techniques of riding a big tire bike under low-pressure conditions.

The Other End of the Chassis

After all the smoke and thunder at the starting line, the finish line would seem to be pretty tame. Not so. This is where the ride gets very interesting. Remember, the ride isn't over until the wheels stop turning. After shutting off power, the front end will return to the ground, and steering geometry and fork construction will become very important.

If your class requires stock forks, then they will have to be modified for drag racing. Normally, a strap is used to tie the forks down to help lower the front end and limit its travel. Sometimes the forks can be slid up in the triple clamps, sometimes the tubes can be cut shorter. Total slider travel should be no more than two inches. Further, the suspension can be given high damping by using 30-weight or heavier fork oil. Air pressure can be set to 15 psi. The idea is to make the forks as stiff and heavily damped as possible, while still providing some suspension travel.

The reason for tying down the forks is to allow them to reach their extension more quickly,

This turbo Suzuki Hayabusa needs all the swingarm it can get. The stock engine is good for 150–160 hp; with a turbo and nitrous oxide, over 330 is on tap. He rides it on the street, too. Must be interesting!

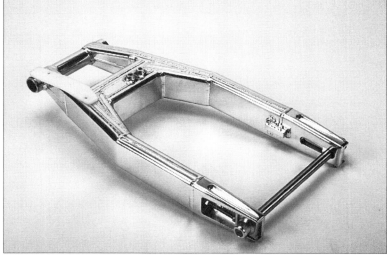

To lengthen the wheelbase on a street bike, a longer swingarm is used. This Trac Dynamics "Alumi-trac" swingarm comes up to eight inches longer than stock. It includes front pivot bearings, chrome moly rear axle, aluminum slider blocks, and all necessary hardware. Expect to pay $1,300 retail.

to control weight transfer, and to provide the quickest front-to-rear weight transfer when the light turns green.

If the class allows aftermarket forks, purchase the best racing forks money can buy. Do not—repeat, do not—go cheap on the front end. Until someone figures out how to keep a parachute from winding up in the rear wheel, the front brake is going to do a great deal of the stopping, and you surely don't want any flex, sag, or bending.

Most chassis companies like Koenig will provide a complete chassis kit, right down to the forks and wheels. This is the best and least expensive (I didn't say cheap) way to go.

When building your own or modifying a stock frame, the front fork rake can be altered to lengthen the bike and get it a bit lower. Steering head rake on most street bikes is somewhere in the range of 25 to 28 degrees. This can be stretched up an additional three to four degrees, but two factors will determine total rake: class rules may specify a certain wheelbase, and you might want to put the extra stretch in the back by using a longer swingarm.

Stretching the Rails

The purpose for adding a longer, wider swingarm to a chassis is to achieve a better weight transfer, mount a wider tire, and lengthen the overall wheelbase, which helps the bike run straight. A less obvious use for a long swingarm is as a hidden air tank for the air shifter. It makes a cleaner, lighter installation.

Most swingarms are from 8 to 12 inches longer than stock. One thing to beware of is the larger torsion forces that a longer swinger will apply to the chassis mounts. Usually the stock mounting points are strong enough to take a mildly-oversized swingarm without any problems, but longer and wider arms will require that bracing be welded to the frame at the attachment points.

Lately, I've seen some street bikes running around with long swingarms hung off the back and enormous tires between the arms. Be advised that long swingarms have only one use and that's for bikes used strictly for drag racing. A long swingarm on the street, especially in some of the current 1300cc, 170–190 hp bikes, can easily lead to trouble. When subjected to high side loads, a long swingarm can easily put more load on swingarm bearings than the manufac-

Shared Workspace

With two street bikes, one drag bike and a road racing car at home, I had to slide sideways down the wall to open the garage door. My girlfriend said she hadn't seen the washer and drier in weeks. So, she avowed, if I didn't want to start washing my clothes in the bathtub, I'd better damn well empty the toys out of the garage.

I had four other friends who were in the same situation. Over a few adult beverages we decided to look for some workspace where we could all work and have enough room to move around. Counting up the cars, motorcycles, partial airplanes, and machine tools, we decided that 3,000 square feet would be about right.

In almost any city there's an industrial area where divided warehouse space can be rented or leased by the year. San Jose is full of older concrete-walled buildings with sheetrock interior walls and some sort of office in the front. Sizes vary, but the smallest interior division is around 1,000 square feet and the largest can run up to 25,000 square feet.

We located a building divided into 3,000 sq. ft. office/warehouse cubes and signed a one-year lease. Before we moved in, we painted the walls, washed the concrete floor with muriatic acid, then laid down two coats of semi-gloss urethane paint. Next came the most important part: the stereo. That got mounted with the speakers pointed into the work area.

Our space had a roll-up door with a conventional door next to it in the back of the warehouse, and a regular steel-cased front door with a sliding window along side. The front 250 sq. ft. was office space with a mezzanine above. That's where all the light stuff—body panels, fiberglass parts, boxes, that sort of thing—got hid. I mounted a good set of speakers on each side of the mezzanine, right against the rail, facing the open floor space. The tuner went into the office.

We hung lights everywhere. The building had a 20 ft. roof, so we hung the lights 10 feet off the concrete. I ran a half-inch copper air line around the perimeter walls and installed air quick-disconnects every 10 feet. We also installed 110-volt electrical outlets on the same spacing. We hid a 5-hp compressor in the back next to a parts washer.

Some of the larger equipment like the milling machine, heli-arc welder, and lathe ran on 220 volts, so they had to be wired up. The mill, a monster Bridgeport we picked up at a going-out-of business sale, took three-phase current, so we installed a converter to change single-phase into the needed three-phase voltage.

Along with these toys, we had a drill press, sheet metal brake, tube bender, large cutting/welding torch, and portable car hoist. All this came from five garages. It sure made the wives happy. One of us was a Snap-On dealer, so we had lots of red roll-arounds.

Not all this is needed to build a racing bike, but it sure made life easier. Two buildings over was a machine shop and across the street a plating shop. There was even Eric's Deli nearby.

This shared workspace was an ideal setup, giving me access to equipment, expertise, and the companionship of good friends. ■

turer ever designed the frame and bearings to take over a long period of time. A long bike will track much straighter in a straight line, but it will require more steering effort to cause it to turn. Throw a fatter tire into the mix and high-speed handling can become very "interesting," to say the least.

Companies such as Adams Performance (704-663-1905) or Alumi-Trac (661-295-1956; www. Tracdynamics.com) provide braced, extended swingarms in lengths ranging from stock to 12 inches over stock. Check your class rules before picking a size for your bike.

Workshop

To get any useful work done on a project as complex as a drag racing bike, you need a good workshop—a warm, clean, dry, well-lighted place—with enough room for the motorcycle, the machines and tools you'll need, storage for parts and supplies, and you. A lot of fast bikes have come out of one-car garages. Maybe that's all you can afford and that could work just fine in your situation. At the other extreme are professional shops where building two-wheel rockets is the main focus of a money-making business. See the sidebar on Star Performance Parts in Chapter 1 for an example of a successful drag racing business. Companies such as Star can afford to have the best possible equipment and space to turn out winning bikes.

Another possibility is to share workspace with friends who have similar interests. If you can find a compatible group, you may be able to assemble more equipment and facilities than any of you alone could afford, making it a win-win for all parties involved. I was fortunate enough to find such a group and enjoyed a great partnership with them. (See sidebar in this chapter for that story.)

Kids, don't try this at home. If you want a professional and safe bike, go to the pros with the right equipment. This is the type of shop necessary to turn out quality frames.

Larry McBrides's shop, Cycle Specialist, is typical of what it takes to build and run a Top Fuel bike. He's the man to call if speed's your need.

Setting Up a New Bike to Go Straight

(Written by Puppet Jim DiTullio, Race Visions. Reprinted by permission from StripBike.com.)

The first thing we have to do in designing a bike is to design the chassis. We need to figure wheelbase, seat height, engine placement, steering head angle, wheelie bar length and more. The easy way would be to make one that handles well and runs straight, then make a bunch more of them. It also would be a good way to make a lot of money. The problem is that a chassis is very horsepower sensitive—engine placement depends on the amount of horsepower available. There is no "one size fits all."

I build a chassis with aluminum axle blocks in the rear so that the rear wheel can be adjusted rearward up to six inches as available horsepower increases. If the engine is moved forward one inch, not much changes in the handling department. If you move the rear wheel back one inch, you are effectively moving all the weight, including the rider, forward one inch, and this will make a difference in how the chassis handles. One inch doesn't sound like much, but small adjustments can make a big difference in the way the bike tracks. Of course, if you plan to build a bike that runs in a restricted wheelbase class like Pro Stock, this won't work. The chassis has to be right on the numbers the first time.

When a chassis is working right, and you hit the throttle, the rear of the bike will drop and plant the tire, then pull itself up. The wheelie bars have to be set high enough in relationship to the rear of the frame so they don't hit before the tire is planted. To adjust the bars, the bike needs to be set on a flat surface. Place a level through the rear wheel and across the swingarm and another across the wheelie bar's axle. Adjust the bar via the rod ends at the frame connecting points until both are parallel. (See diagram.) This is a starting point. Make some runs and check the handling. First, though, make sure your

(continued)

Both axles must be parallel in all dimensions.
Use adjustable rod ends for alignment.

R = adjustable rod ends

R R

Axle

Wheelie
Bar
Axle

Wheelie Bar
Wheels

Rear Wheel

R R

TOP VIEW

Rear Wheel

Both axles must be parallel.
Use level for alignment.

R
R

SIDE VIEW

rear tire is either brand new, or in excellent condition. If you aren't running a beadlock rim, ensure that the tire has enough air pressure—12 to 14 psi—to keep it from collapsing or the rim from spinning in the tire.

Getting a new bike that runs eight seconds or faster to go straight can be a problem. Every bike has its own personality, so to speak, and it's your job to figure it out. My bikes are built with the axle all the way to the rear (of the frame) so if you measure from the inside of the chain adjuster to the axle block, this measurement should be exactly the same on both sides to start with (I measure with dial calipers). The bike should be balanced so that it stands alone with the front wheel pointing straight ahead. If it's not, you can move the rear tire side-to-side a bit. The most offset I've ever seen with no ill effects is 3/8 inch. Next are the wheelie bars. Put a level (magnetic works best) on the rear rotor then shim the frame rails until the rotor is perpendicular to the ground. Next, put the level on the wheelie bar axle and adjust the axle until it's parallel to the ground.

Now that the wheel is straight in the chassis, the bike balanced, and the wheelie bar straight and level, it's time to make a test at the strip. The single most important point is to be sure the bike is lined up perfectly straight in relationship to the track. Sometimes it's hard to tell when a new bike is lined up correctly. It's a good idea to have one of your crew stand in front of the bike to aid in getting it straight, at least for the first few passes.

You must be sure you are sitting in the middle of the seat—at its balance point; not too much weight on one side or the other. Try lifting your feet and if the bike balances, you're okay. If not, slide around until the bike sits level. Sometimes in a real lowboy chassis there's a hump on one side for chain clearance that can push you off center. Do three or four sixty-foot runs to get a feel for the bike as it leaves the line. Then do some 330-foot runs and gradually work your way down the track from there.

If the bike is pulling one way or another, now is the time to adjust the chassis to make it go straight. There are three different areas to check. If the bike wants to veer right or left, try moving over on the seat a little bit in the same direction. If the bike wants to go to the right, by moving to the right the tire will load on the right and straighten out the bike. This is opposite to how you ride a bike through a corner and you have to mentally think out what you are doing for the first few runs. Try to remember: "Veers right, shift right."

If that doesn't work and the bike still wants to drift to the right, try raising the right wheelie bar a half-turn at the rod end where the bar bolts to the chassis. When the bike leaves the line and the front wheel isn't touching the track, the wheelie bars are actually helping to steer the bike. By lifting the right side wheelie bar wheel a bit, the bike will lean to the right a small amount then track slightly to the left. The same goes when correcting a left drift. Raise the left, go right. *Don't* cock the rear wheel to steer the bike. This will cause major problems at the other end of the track. All adjustments must be made with the rider in the normal riding position.

The next adjustment is for mid-track corrections. The bike will still be on the wheelie bar, but the rear tire is starting to round out and the speed will be in the 150–180 mph range. Now, to adjust for a tendency to pull right, you have to drop the left wheelie bar a half-turn. A change here can affect how the bike leaves the line, so you will have to check that again. If the bike still won't leave straight, try shifting your weight a bit. That's how Larry McBride got the name Spiderman, remember. He crawls all over his Top Fuel bike to make it go straight (sorta straight, anyway). Bear in mind, a high-horsepower drag bike is a real handful. Either you're going to ride it, or it will ride you. Usually if a bike leaves straight, it will be okay at mid-track.

(continued)

The last area of concern is when the front wheel comes back to earth and picks up some of the steering duties. At this point, the rear tire is fully rounded out and your speed is over 180 mph. If the bike tends to go to the right after the front tire bites, and you are sure the problem is with the bike and not your steering (this can happen real fast and can easily be caused by the bars being turned ever so slightly off-center), back up the right chain adjuster .010–.020 inch. Providing the tire is fully rounded out, this causes the rear of the bike to go to the right and leans the bike to the left, which drives the bike left. Be careful and accurate. A small adjustment at the rear wheel will cause a major change in how the bike tracks. The opposite adjustment corrects for a left-turning bike. Cocking the rear tire helps only when both tires are on the ground and you are flat out.

One neat trick to check alignment and tracking is to paint the wheelie bar wheels with white shoe polish. Check them after a run to see if the wheels are running down the track evenly.

There is no substitute for seat time. The worst thing you can do is take a new bike to a national meet and try to set it up there. It's best to go to a local track on a test-and-tune day when there is no pressure and set the bike up at your own pace. Go to the national meets when you and your bike are ready.

The biggest problem in getting a bike to run straight is chassis flex, which is usually caused by leaving out some tubes to save a few pounds. *The chassis/frame is not the place to save weight.* This is especially true when engine horsepower climbs over 350. Also, the larger the tire, the higher the applied loads will be when the power hits the track.

Now let's look at a typical frame and see where flex is a problem. Start at the front of the bike with the steering head. On a drag bike there is virtually no load applied to the steering head, especially when the front wheel is off the ground. On a fuel bike, or any other bike that carries the front wheel way down the track, you could cut the backbone off the frame at the seat and front motor mounts and still make a pretty good run until you had to set the front end down. Some side loads are encountered during braking, but these are light compared to the loads that run linearly down the frame during acceleration or braking. Any type of strong backbone frame will make for a good, stable racer that will run straight.

The trend in Pro Mod, Funnybike, and other classes is to a lowboy chassis with double downtubes outside the exhaust headers, similar to a Koenig Lowboy chassis. The idea is to get the rider down as low as possible in the bike for better weight transfer and lower wind resistance. A longer chassis is good too. The farther forward the engine can be legally mounted, the more torque can be applied to the rear wheel before the front wheel lifts.

Most of the loads that concern chassis developers are created by the twisting force of the chain pulling on one side of the axle plate as power is applied. The more the power, the bigger the tire, the worse the twisting force. The rear sprocket is offset from the chassis centerline to clear the rear tire. Loads at the sprocket try to twist the axle around the wheel's centerline, causing the rear of the chassis to try to turn into the sprocket.

Involved testing has seen the rear pulled over as much as .200 inch. Proper bracing can reduce this—sometimes down to .010 to .020 inch—but there is always some flex. When you watch a bike from the rear as it goes down the strip and see it wiggling from side to side, the torque around the rear axle is responsible for most of the movement. The rear of the chassis is being torqued over toward the sprocket, then springing back again as loads change, only to do it over and over throughout the run.

Note: If you are experiencing severe movement of the chassis on the track and none of the suggestions above seem to work, strip the body off the bike and carefully inspect all the frame for paint crazing or cracking. That would be a good indication of severe frame flex. ∎

CHAPTER 6

Building an Engine

No matter what type of bike you race—V-Twin, Suzuki, Kawasaki, Triumph or any other—the engine and its peripherals are the major consideration of most riders. When building any kind of engine, one needs to strike a suitable balance between power and reliability, but drag racing motors are usually built with emphasis on power. The elusive chase for more horsepower goes on forever.

This chapter won't be a blow-by-blow description of building engines. My objective is to give you an overview of the most important considerations involved in building an engine to reach your goals. To do that, I'm going to walk you through building an engine by using Kawasaki cases as a starting point, but everything here will also apply to Suzuki, Yamaha and, to a certain extent, Honda.

Block, Cases, and Heads

An engine is little more than an air pump; the more air (and fuel) it pumps, the more power it makes. Therefore, the place to put your money is in the head, because its construction ultimately determines air flow and that in turn determines horsepower for a given displacement.

Workhorse Heads

For the four-cylinder racer, there are two main choices for an engine: Suzuki or Kawasaki. Right now in Pro Stock, Funnybike, Top Fuel, and many other classes, these two engines dominate. The interesting thing about these motors is that both are old designs, both have two valves per cylinder, and both are air-cooled. Lately, the Suzuki four-valve head has begun to show up on

Cases are stripped down, cleaned and checked for cracks before being modified and reassembled.

This block is modified with fittings for oil to the head and return. High oil flow is necessary on a high horsepower, air- or water-cooled engine.

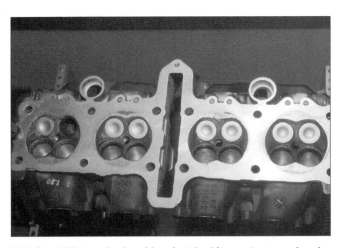

This Suzuki four-valve head has just had its seats ground and is being set up with valves after having been ported and polished. It's going on a street bike.

More and more four-valve heads are showing up on V-twin engines. This Rivera head is set up for dual carburetion, and will produce more power at high revs than a two-valve head. (www.riveraengineering.com) *Rivera Engineering*

some engines, but the two-valve design still predominates in drag racing.

The newer design four-valve heads can be made to flow more air than the older two-valve heads, and in stock condition they make a lot more horsepower. The problem with them lies in two areas: porting and inclined induction angle. The ports are thin-walled and cannot easily be opened up for increased flow. The angle of the intake ports is so close to vertical that a drag racing frame would have to be raised quite high in the area of the intakes to clear the intake horns.

Newer heads may eventually proliferate because the older, air-cooled, heads have a finite life and there are only so many good ones still around; they were designed for bikes built back in the 70s, and early 80s. Today's engines—which will eventually be used on drag racers—are all liquid cooled, and cannot easily be used in today's frames because the radiator and related plumbing won't fit in the available space.

Custom Heads

There is another alternative to the older heads, and that's a custom fabricated design, if one is allowed in your class. Custom heads designed specifically for drag racing are built by a few racing machine shops, such as Ward Performance (763-493-3400; www.wardperformance.com).

The heads made by Ward are cast of 356-T6 aluminum and machined to final shape on a CNC mill. They accept 46mm intake and 38mm exhaust valves, allowing a flow of 160 cfm. No further porting or finishing is required. As cast, the ports can support up to 300 hp. Pro Stock heads are available fully CNC ported. The casting is drilled for dual 10mm spark plugs per cylinder. Retail price starts at $1,499 for the bare head; you have to add the valve train to that.

Modifying Stock Heads

If you're on a tight budget, modifying your stock head is a good way to increase horsepower. I strongly advise you not to modify heads yourself unless you have a machine shop in your garage and ten years of experience.

Here's where the pros can be helpful. Schnitz Racing (800-837-9730; www.mpsmall.com) has built more than a few winners over the past 25 years. Bill Vose, AMA Pro Mod #1 last year, went over 200 mph using their engine parts. So has Keith Lynn on his Schnitz-sponsored Funnybike.

Schnitz Head Modification Packages

Schnitz has a number of four-cylinder, two-valve head-modification packages available that will fit different requirements and wallets. These modifications are for the KZ900 through KZ1100 engines, but are typical for other brands.

PreStage This is a complete head overhaul, with a little extra. It will increase the mid and top range on a street bike.

Includes teardown and cleaning, replace and resize valve guides, competition valve job, boring and blending of throats, heavy duty valve springs, matching carb boots, assembly, surfacing head, bench shimming for valve clearance. This works well with cams up to .360-inch lift.

Cost with Web 118 cams, $825.

Stage I High performance street head. Ports are reshaped, and diameter increased. They are left small for good throttle response and torque. Power is greatly improved at the upper end. Use on street engines 1015cc–1200cc. Use 31–33mm carbs and 4-into-1 exhaust with a 1.5-inch-diameter baffle core. Cams to .360-inch lift.

Includes all of "PreStage" with full street port work.

Cost with Web 118 cams, $1,250.

Stage II Street and strip for 1100cc–1075cc motors. Can be used as an entry level racing head for 903cc–1015cc engines, or as a street head for 1200cc and over engines. Use 31mm carbs for engines larger than 1015cc. Some loss at low end, but not significant. Use a cam with up to .435-inch lift.

Includes all of Stage I, stainless steel valves (37.5 or 38.5mm), underbucket shims, aluminum retainers, additional throat boring, new keepers.

Cost with Web 118 cams, $1,625.

Stage III Sportsman Racing. A good head for 1015cc–1325cc engines. Cam selection must match displacement, compression and intended use. Will take cams up to .485-inch lift.

Includes all of Stage II, additional port work and throat boring, head and cam cover

clearancing for cam, sinking of valves if needed.

Cost with Web cam of choice, $1,800.

Stage IV Semi-Pro racer. Stock seats opened to the limit. A 1015cc–1270cc all-out racing motor, and a good head for 1300cc and up. Requires 12:1 compression, and will take up to .520-inch cams.

Includes all of Stage III, adds pro port work, larger carb boots and Allen bolts to facilitate mounting.

Cost with Web or Cam Motion cams, $2,000.

Stage V Pro racing engines of 1325cc and larger. Oversized seats accept 40mm or 42mm intake and 33mm or 36mm exhaust valves. Some flycutting of the pistons may be necessary. Titanium intake valves should be used.

Includes installation of big valve seats, custom valve machining, additional throat work.

Cost with Web or Cam Motion cams, $2,400.

Schnitz can also perform custom services on your head. Depending on your needs, you can have them do basic machining and grinding, including matching the carbs to the head and machining the exhaust ports to match the header flange. Other individual services available: cutting custom valves out of a blank, boring and blending valve throats, valve guide replacement, port work, machining valve spring retainers, cutting valve keepers, and installing oversized valve seats.

A quality shop with the right equipment is needed to build an engine. That's why I advise you to let the pros do your critical work. They've been doing it right for a long time and have equipment that you'll never have. Most of us can't afford to own these machines tools just to build an engine or two.

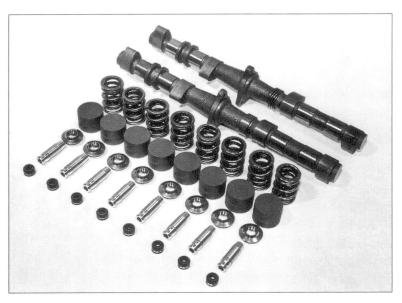

A complete cam kit for a Suzuki or Kawasaki consists of cams, springs, shim buckets, valve keepers, valve guides and Teflon valve seals. You still need valves, shims and gaskets. *Star Performance Parts*

Crane makes many different racing cams for V-twin engines up to 200 ci displacement and running fuel. Cams are also available for Sportster-style cases. *Crane Cams*

Cams

Now it's time to make the valves go up and down. Camshaft selection is one of the more mysterious topics in the racing business. You often hear racers discussing cams with heavy emphasis only on "lift." Very seldom do the words "overlap" or "duration" enter the conversation. Lift is important, but getting the proper overlap and duration are equally important, since all three factors contribute to how, and at what rpm range, your engine makes power.

If all the engine is going to see is quarter-mile runs, it might be acceptable to have a cam with monster .425-inch lift that hardly makes enough power to pull the skin off chocolate pudding below 7,000 rpm, comes on at 8,000 rpm, pulls like Jack-the-Bear up to 10,500 rpm, and then falls on its nose above that. However, if you want to run that bike on the street, you would find it hard to keep the revs up in the power range as you proceed from stoplight to stoplight in rush hour traffic. Some sort of compromise is necessary for day-to-day riding.

How will your riding affect your choice of cams? It's important to choose a cam for what you really *will* be doing instead of what you'd *like* to be doing. Let's take a look at what a cam does and how its various specifications affect engine operation.

First, I'll explain some terms.

Basic Lift The distance a cam lobe rises above the base circle of the camshaft. Valve lift is the total distance a valve lifts off its seat. The greater the lift, the more room there will be under the valve for the mixture to flow. Lobes on high-lift cams have a tendency to hit things as they rotate because the head wasn't designed to accept cams with so much more lift than stock. Usually the cam cover has to be cut, or the head flycut to create more lobe clearance. Lots of lift will give an engine a lumpy idle, and usually puts the power range way too high for street use. Note that valve trains employing rocker arms will usually have a higher valve lift than cam lift, since the rocker arm multiplies the cam lift through unequal-length arms. The valve lift ratio of a stock Harley Evolution engine is 1.6:1, but other valve trains use ratios ranging from 1.6:1 up to 2.2:1. The factors influencing a designer's choice of valve lift ratio are complex, involving considerations of rocker arm geometry, spring pressure, rev limits, component weights, and many others.

Even though they sometimes refer to "cam lift," cam manufacturers always specify lift at the valve (assuming a particular valve train) and usually express it in thousandths of an inch. Valve lift typically ranges from stock, at around .310 inches, to a maximum of around .470 inch for general racing. Cams with more lift are available, especially for V-twin motors and out-and-out drag racing four-cylinder engines, but they are pretty specialized. Some Pro-Stock KZ engines from Star Performance are running cams with .507-inch lift. These engines have to be modified extensively to take advantage of such high lift.

Overlap This is the angle, expressed in *crankshaft* degrees, during which both the intake and exhaust valves are open at the same time. Increasing overlap can have a ram effect on the incoming mixture. As exhaust gasses leave the cylinder, they create a low pressure that will help draw fresh incoming air/fuel mixture into the combustion chamber. At low speeds too much overlap can cause the mixture to spit back out of the carb and cause the engine to run erratically. Again, low speed performance is degraded when overlap is too great.

Duration This is the angle, expressed in *crankshaft* degrees, through which a cam lobe lifts the valve. Duration figures are determined by a lot of factors. The size of intake and exhaust ports, gas velocity, and low-range response all factor into the cam duration profile. Sometimes, to keep inlet velocity up so that fuel droplets won't fall out of the mixture, and to hasten cylinder recovery time, shorter duration cams are used with smaller intake valves and ports.

Long duration cams, when coupled with large valves and intake runners, will only work well at high rpm. Most cam grinders measure cam dura-

Before the cams are installed, all dimensions are checked and recorded. This information and everything else pertaining to the engine will be kept on file as long as the engine is used.

tion between the points at which the lift is .050 inches. This measure won't give total duration, but provides a standard of comparison with other manufacturers.

Ramps, cam timing, cam indexing, lobe centers, base circle, intake/exhaust opening/closing all affect cam design. We'll let the engineers worry about these details. For our purposes, we'll discuss cams in relationship to each other by using just lift and duration.

Thanks to Web Cam for the following information.

Web Cams for Kawasaki and Suzuki Engines			
Web Cam Number	Valve Lift (inches)	Duration @.050 Lift (degrees)	Intended Use
247	.340	234	Turbos, nitrous Funnybike
119	.384	240	Street/turbo
218	.418	242	Street/turbo
118	.365	246	Performance street
110	.395	256	Big bore, mid & top end
109	.425	260	Mid & top end
122/125	.460/.435	262/261	Pro Gas
136/122	.480/.460	266/262	Small Pro stock engines
206/231	.500/.470	275	Large Pro Stock
24	.520	270	Pro Stock, .900 base circle

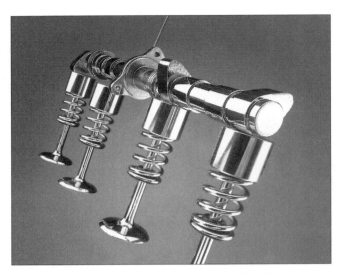

Web Cam make a racing cam for Kawasaki KZ1000 two-valve engines for Funnybike and Top Fuel engines. *Web Cam*

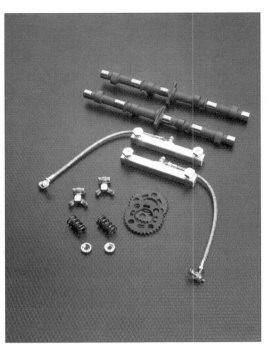

Web also makes Suzuki two-valve cams for the GSX series from 1986 to 1990. *Web Cams*

A Kawasaki or Suzuki Pro Stock cam set runs about $325. Some grinds aren't available as new cams but are built onto your camshafts by welding a hard-face overlay onto the lobes and regrinding to racing specifications. For specific applications contact Web Cam (909-369-5144; www.webcaminc.com).

Valves

Motorcycle racing valves take a lot of pounding. The cam turns at one-half engine speed, so when the engine slides through 12,000 rpm as you cross the finish line, the cams are turning 6,000 rpm. This means the valves are being lifted off their seats six thousand times a minute, or 100 times per second. Heavy valve springs with increased spring tension are slamming the valves back on the seat with enough force to make lead flow. Combustion heat is being transferred from the face of the valve to its seat. Exhaust gasses pass across the face of the exhaust valve that are hot enough to make a turbocharger glow bright red. It takes a very strong valve to live in these conditions.

Stock valves work just fine under stock or semi-modified operating conditions. But when you raise the redline, bump the compression, and change the cam specs, stock valves reach their limitations. I've seen more than one valve that failed and whose face was embedded in the pis-

ton crown. When this happens at high revs, the engine self-destructs so fast that you can't react quickly enough even to save the big pieces. If it takes you one-half second from the time you feel the engine falter, to pulling in the clutch, the valve will have tried to open 50 times. "Try" is the operative word. It's hard to compress a valve face that's impaled in the piston. Usually what happens is the engine comes to a very abrupt halt, while pieces of the piston are blown into the cases, sometimes just in time to lodge between the crank and case. Goodbye case and crank. Plus, all the little pieces get to swim around in the oil where they will eagerly get stuck in the hardest-to-reach oil passages.

If you build an engine for racing, it is prudent to replace the valves. If you are fitting a Vortex or other custom head, you will need new valves. There are two materials to choose when selecting valves: stainless steel or titanium.

Stainless valves work quite well with normally-aspirated engines and do okay when used in a forced-induction system. However, there's stainless steel and there's STAINLESS STEEL. Stainless valves are made from different alloys

Larger valves installed on a two-valve head almost touch. It's critically important to check that they don't touch when the cam rotates.

Polishing the back of a valve will only increase the air flow a tiny bit, but it's all these improvements put together that extract the maximum amount of power. This hand work is one of the reasons a Pro Stock engine can cost over $12,000.

which have different tensile strength and different capacity to withstand and transfer heat. Ferrea (sold through Schnitz) builds stainless and titanium valves to fit just about every racing requirement and every bike. Their basic stainless valve is suitable for all drag racing four-cylinder and V-twin engines. High-end stainless or titanium valves are used on pure drag racing V-twins using turbos or fuel.

Titanium valves work well in situations where light reciprocating mass is needed, such as high-rpm applications, or when an enlarged valve seat is above a thin part of the head. A titanium valve weighs on an average one-third the weight of its stainless counterpart, so less spring pressure is needed and the valve will follow the cam lobe profile easier and close on the seat with less impact. The shape of a titanium valve allows more airflow for a given valve size. For example, a 35mm titanium valve will flow more air than a 35mm super-flow stainless because a titanium valve can be made thinner at the back of the face and therefore presents less restriction to air flow.

Still, on a Pro Stock or other high-power engine—even when using titanium valves—the head will have to come off frequently to check the seats and valves, and a valve replacement or regrind will be necessary every 25 to 30 runs.

When installing larger valves in an existing head, or a new head with larger valves, you need to check clearances before firing the engine. There are many ways to do this. I favor putting a small amount of clay on the piston dome right under the valve; then, using an old head gasket, bolt the new head in place. Torque it properly, install the cams and springs (some builders use light springs to make rotation easier), then turn the crank slowly through one revolution. Remove the head and check the thickness of clay left at the point of closest contact. Always turn the crank in the direction of engine rotation. Should the crank stop rotating as the valve opens, cease and desist. Don't continue until you solve the clearance problem.

I repeat: This book isn't intended as an engine-building guide; my purpose is to describe in general what goes into building a complete drag racing motorcycle. I am covering a lot of areas at an introductory level, but to put an engine together properly, you will need the services of a reputable engine builder.

Cylinders and Pistons

In a reciprocating internal combustion engine, the top of the piston takes the force of the burning air/fuel mixture and transfers it through the connecting rod to the crankshaft. The circular area of the piston, multiplied by the length of stroke, multiplied by the number of cylinders, equals total engine displacement.

Cylinders are bored, then final honed before being assembled. A rough finish on the bore helps hold oil.

The pistons have had a hole drilled in the bottom of the pin boss to aid oil flow. They are checked for balance and concentricity before instalation.

Each head/piston assembly stays together with a sheet showing clearances, bore, compression ratio and other information needed for assembly.

$$(\pi/4) \times (\text{Bore})^2 \times \text{Stroke} \times \text{Number of Cylinders} = \text{Total Engine Displacement}$$

Standard pistons are cast of aluminum and normally have two compression rings above one three-piece oil control ring. Compression rings stop blow-by of the burning air/fuel mixture into the crankcase. When you install compression rings, make sure the end gaps are not in line. Usually the three rings are installed with their gaps 120 degrees apart.

Cast pistons work well in all street applications. They're cheap, they run quieter than forged pistons, and they are strong enough for thousands of miles of service. However, when you ask them to work harder than they were designed to work, problems arise. That is why forged pistons are used in racing motors. Forged pistons are also made from aluminum alloys, but their method of fabrication—the raw shapes being formed under high pressure, as opposed to being poured in a mold—creates a stronger part. Because of their higher thermal expansion coefficient, forged pistons have to be run looser, with more side clearance, than their cast brethren. This makes them run slightly noisier, but in a racing engine, a little extra noise won't be a problem.

If you're building an engine for the first time, my advice is to buy a complete overbore kit from a reputable manufacturer such as Wiseco, or contact Schnitz for a complete power package, where everything is compatible and will fit.

A power package for our Kawasaki two-valve engine includes a Wiseco big block (1197cc–1428cc), Wiseco hi-performance overbore forged piston kit, and big-bore gaskets, all needed to open your 1000cc to 1100cc engine up to class displacement limits.

For a larger investment, Schnitz will build a set of cylinders ready-to-run that have been re-sleeved, set to deck height, O-ringed (optional), and bored and honed to proper piston size. Compression ratios vary, depending on intended usage, from 10.25:1 to 13.5:1 for naturally aspirated engines. If the engine will have forced induction, the compression ratio is set to a low 8:1. This kit retails for $1,200.

Some of these kits will require modifications to the crankcase or require that a specific block be used. Let's say the class you're running allows the engine to be opened up to 1400cc. Wiseco has a Kawasaki kit that will give 1393cc, so we'll go with that. To punch out the engine to that size requires a special Wiseco block, p/n W3715-1, to be used. Larger sleeves will have to be fitted to the block and the crankcase will have to be cleaned up to accept the larger parts. The overbore kit without block runs $600.

Similar kits are available from Schnitz for Suzuki and Honda, blown or unblown, two-valve or four-valve. Prices are comparable to those for the Kawasaki.

RPM and Piston Speed

Have you ever wondered what makes a manufacturer put a redline on their engines? Why can some engines turn so much higher than others? There are a number of factors that determine the limits of engine speed: rotating mass, material strength, bore vs. stroke, general engine design, air flow limitations through the combustion chamber, bearing wear, and piston speed.

Most of those limitations are fairly self-evident. Material strength, for instance. Parts such as rods and valves made of titanium can take a lot more loading than the same parts in aluminum or steel. The thickness of an aluminum engine case and how its reinforcing webbing and internal bracing is structured will have a great influence on the maximum horsepower it can reliably produce.

For example, factory V-twin cases will take an incredible amount of abuse, from traveling 80,000 miles in a police bike, to getting run to redline on a drag strip in mildly modified engines. But V-twin cases have a limit. Exceed it and they will break. That's why most out-and-out racing V-twins are built 100% from aftermarket parts. The only Harley on the bike is the tattoo on the rider's arm. Every other part is specifically designed for competition.

Piston speed is also a rev limiter. The piston has to accelerate from a dead stop until the rod jerks it to a halt just before it impacts the head. Then it's yanked back up to speed, only to have to come to another 180 degree reversal at the bottom of the stroke. In the middle of the stroke, it can be moving at quite a rapid rate.

Wiseco builds a complete big-block piston and cylinder kit for most four-cylinder bikes. I've had excellent service from their parts. *Wiseco*

Until recently, a piston speed of 4500 feet per minute (fpm) has been the upper limit for designers—kind of a rule of thumb. Turn an engine much faster than this and reliability goes down fast. However, more horsepower can always be gained by pumping more air through an engine over a given time. Pumping more air means spinning the crank faster. Faster crank speeds mean faster piston speeds. About the only way to get much above the 4500 fpm limit is to use exotic, high-strength materials in engine construction. Trick stuff equates to more money though, and costs can rapidly go all out of proportion when parts built of unobtanium start showing up inside a motor.

Titanium, beryllium, cobalt, nickel, and exotic steels come with a high price tag. They're harder to refine or smelt, harder to machine or weld, and not as common on earth as iron or aluminum. But, if the only consideration is to win, cost be damned, then they may help. In Formula one car racing, money isn't a problem. One year's racing can easily cost Ferrari or McClaren $50 million. The cars themselves cost in excess of two million dollars per.

F1 engines are limited in displacement, so the builders have to find other ways to make more power. Spinning the engine faster is one way. Today's F1 engines shift at 18,000 rpm, and live while they do it. Let's figure out the average piston speed of this engine, with its stroke of approximately 2.3 inches.

To balance a Harley flywheel, material must be drilled from the heavy side.

To figure *average* piston speed, note that with each revolution of the engine, each piston travels twice the stroke (once up and once down).

Piston speed = 2 × Stroke (inches) × rpm = 2 × 2.3 inches × 18,000 rpm = 82,800 inches per minute = 6,900 feet per minute.

Now let's look at a Suzuki Bandit 1200, with a stroke of 2.323 inches and 12,000 rpm redline.

Piston speed = 2 × 2.323 inches × 12,000 rpm = 55,752 inches per minute = 4,646 feet per minute.

Engine	Stroke (inches)	Maximum rpm	Piston speed (fpm)
Ferarri F1	2.3	18,000	6,900
Suzuki Bandit 1200	2.323	12,000	4,646

Quite a difference in piston speed. The Suzuki is close to the rule of thumb limits that have been around for years. The F1 is running way above what was commonly considered an ultimate limit, without compromising reliability. Better materials make the F1 engine safer to spin at higher rpm. Today's street engines can live reliably at piston speeds that were upper racing limits as recently as 1985. The percentage of Japanese motorcycle engines that have blown up on the street runs in the single digits. Have you ever seen one blow that hadn't been run out of oil or beaten like a bad dog?

Still, when building a racing engine that you want to last more than a few runs, you had better take piston speed—and therefore rpm—into the equation. Of course, factors such as cam design, valve spring pressure, and valve size will also limit an engine, but avoiding excessive piston speed is a good reason for rev limiters.

To achieve the Ferrari's 6,900 fpm speed? Well, all you need to know is that the bits and pieces inside their F1 engines are worth more than their weight in gold. Roger Penske has been in the business of building race cars with what used to be called the "Unfair Advantage" because they never broke and always placed in the top three. He was accused of having parts built from "Unobtanium."

Balancing and Blueprinting

Magic words aren't they. "My engine's been balanced and blueprinted." Obviously this dude must be one fast racer. Balanced and blueprinted indeed, but what does that mean?

Balancing

Balancing is pretty straightforward to understand. Everything that moves in an engine, whether rotating or reciprocating, has weight and mass. In our Kawasaki engine, there are four rods, four pistons and one crankshaft that make up the biggest part of the motivating machinery. Picture the crankshaft as a wheel. If there's more weight on one side, that side will want to rotate to the bottom and stay there. When the wheel starts spinning, the out-of-balance weight will try to pull away from the center of the wheel, causing the whole assembly to vibrate. This can easily be felt at the bars as shaking. If it's allowed to run for a long period of time, it will shake things apart. Depending on rpm and the amount of out-of-balance weight, the crankshaft could chew up a set of bearings in as little as one run.

Crankshafts are balanced by removing weight from the heavy side. This can be done by drilling or milling. Those holes you occasionally see on a crankshaft counterbalance weight are for rotational balance.

The pistons and rods don't rotate, but move up and down a fixed and equal distance. Should one piston/rod assembly be markedly heavier than the others (different brand of piston, for in-

Here's a set of Harley flywheels with the rods mounted and one engine case attached.

This is a typical Big Twin rod set from S&S. They make all parts for a V-twin engine up to and including complete motors. *S&S*

stance), the forces will be uneven, which in extreme cases can make an engine shake like a poodle passing peach pits. Engine life would be minimal.

Blueprinting

Blueprinting is nothing more than making sure all the parts in a race engine meet their specifications exactly. If a piston is supposed to weigh 497 grams, plus or minus .05 grams (these are just example numbers), then all pistons in the engine should be selected to ensure they weigh as close to that specification as possible. Pistons must be weighed individually and their weights recorded. Weight can't be added to a piston, so the only way to balance them is by cutting away material from the heavier pistons until they all weigh the same as the lightest. Same goes for rods; material must be removed until they are identical. Where the rods and pistons are cut is important, as whacking away in the wrong area can seriously weaken the part and cause a catastrophic failure at high revs. Usually, pistons are cut below the wrist pin while rods have material removed at the base of the big end or the top of the small end.

The rest of the moving parts, from valve springs to bearings, are measured, machined, cut and weighed or checked for clearance until they match exactly the design specifications for that engine. This is a time consuming job and adds greatly to the labor cost of building an engine.

The idea is to make all the pistons weigh the same, make the rods weigh the same, and bal-

ance out the rotational weight of the crank to cut down vibration and keep the engine running as smoothly as possible. Smoother engines make more horsepower and run longer. Vibration makes heat. Balanced and blueprinted engines run cooler.

Crankshaft and Rods

For a drag racing engine, balancing isn't quite as important as it would be on a road racing engine. The drag motor runs for such a short time that vibration isn't a big factor. However, if you are building a very nasty engine for the street and have ideas of racing it, one of the strengthening measures used on a crank is to weld it together at the sections where it is pressed together. The rods are installed, the crank indexed, and then the faces welded. This process adds material and the crank will need to be re-balanced afterward.

Early Kawasaki crankshafts with small 15-tooth cam drive center journals aren't as strong as the newer larger ones with 16-tooth drive gears. Suzuki cranks in the older two-valve engines run in roller bearings and are strong enough to build sub-nine-second engines. The stock rods should be polished to eliminate any flash or casting marks where cracks can develop. The rods are the weak spot in a highly-modified earlier split-crank engine that's being built for anything faster than 9.50 seconds.

On solid cranks with two-piece rods, such as those used on most of the newer motors, the crank isn't welded and should be okay right out of the box. One-piece cranks with two-piece rods

So the exhaust pipes can come off in a hurry, a stub is welded to an exhaust flange and the end of the pipe is belled to fit over it.

Even at the track, everything is kept clean, with the small parts in bags.

used in four-valve engines will withstand a large increase of horsepower without any problems.

Top Fuel engines are another kettle of bolts entirely. Most Top Fuel motors use billet cranks that have been cut from one piece of steel. Rods are typically of two-piece design available from aftermarket suppliers. Breakage usually occurs only if something else blows first.

If you are building an engine for anything other than Bracket or street/strip use, my suggestion is to use a set of aftermarket rods such as those made by Carillo. They are machined from 4340 chrome moly steel with bronze bushings and 5/16-inch rod bolts. You might still be able to blow up an engine, but it won't be the rods that let go. They are available through Star Performance for Suzuki GSXR, Kawasaki Ninja, Yamaha FZR and FJ, Harley, and—for a suitable amount of money—can be built for any engine. Expect to pay $1,200 per set.

The Kawasaki KZ900 and KZ1000 engines had a weak area in the crankcase that will let the crank flex when power is increased. Star Performance has a crank support plate that supports the center main bearing cap and reduces flex. The bearing cap will have to be machined for clearance.

While we're looking at cranks and four-cylinder crankcases, here's another item that will extend case life. All cases, not just Kawasaki's, flex under power. This will let the crank twist, and in extreme cases, break the cases. The solution is to use a set of Star Performance's heavy duty chrome moly main bearing studs. These will work on Kawasaki KZ900/1000/1100, Suzuki GS1100, and GSXR1100. They are especially needed on engines with forced induction.

Building a Big Twin Engine

Because so many Harley riders have built engines using some stock parts such as crankpin, flywheel, and cases, only to see it all turn into sparkles when the motor let go, aftermarket parts have become available to replace just about everything inside aftermarket V-twin cases.

The list of aftermarket replacement parts includes: crankcases, cylinders, heads, pistons, flywheels, rods, bearings, cams, pushrods, lifters, oil pumps, breathers, ignition systems, valve covers, nuts and bolts, exhaust headers, and more. Be sure to save space on the bike for a Harley decal, though—it may be the only thing that says H-D on the bike.

The easiest way to build a V-twin bottom end is to contact S&S Cycle Inc. (Box 215, Viola, WI

Use a good assembly lube when putting an engine together. Manley makes a moly grease that works well. *Custom Chrome*

Something I saw for the first time this year is this scavenge pump. Its purpose is to keep a negative pressure in the engine cases. Pistons moving down in their cylinders build crankcase pressure. Removing the pressure by means of an engine-driven scavenge pump lets the pistons move down easier. It's driven off the crank, so the power it takes to drive it must be offset by the gains.

54664; 608-627-1488; www.sscycles.com) and ask for one of their catalogs. They've been in the V-twin speed business since May 1958. If they say something works, believe them.

Most people have heard of S&S through their carburetor products. However, S&S is also well known for everything from flywheels to pistons; they have 3000+ parts for different models of Harley-Davidson.

Building a bigger V-twin engine by increasing the stroke is an efficient method of increasing power. Stock bore and stroke on an Evo motor is 3.5 × 4.25 inches. This is known as an "undersquare" engine—the bore is smaller than the stroke. A "square" engine has equal bore and stroke—4.0 × 4.0 inches for example. "Oversquare" motors have a bigger bore than stroke. Japanese engines are normally oversquare; the Suzuki GSXR1100, for example, is 75.5mm × 60.0mm.

As a general rule, undersquare motors make maximum torque at lower rpm than oversquare motors of the same displacement. The road to horsepower and quicker quarter-mile times on a Harley is through bigger engines with longer strokes. Stroking an engine boosts displacement by increasing the distance the piston travels in the cylinder. Boring increases the diameter of the cylinder so it uses bigger pistons.

Big Twins gain the most horsepower through lengthening the stroke—increasing the distance between the crankpin centerline and flywheel centerline. Twice this distance is the stroke of the engine because the crankpin moves the rod from top-dead-center to bottom-dead-center for the total piston travel.

Move the crankpin centerline away from the flywheel centerline and the distance the piston travels increases. The amount of air/fuel mixture that is packed into the cylinder on the intake stroke increases. This results in a greater leverage on the crankpin, which translates into more torque.

Nothing is free, however. As the stroke increases, piston speed also rises for a given engine speed, with resultant accelerated cylinder wall wear as a possibility. This isn't a concern on engines used strictly for racing, but it can pose problems on a street motor, especially if you don't observe a reasonable redline of 6,200 rpm max.

The best way to use the greater torque of a stroker motor on the street is to shift below 5,500 rpm and let the torque do the work. Running much over this provides little gain and a lot more wear. Racing is a different story. If the motor is still making high horsepower at 7,500 rpm, then it's going to get spun up there. In racing, the idea

Cam chain tension is very important in a racing engine (or any other, for that matter), and a billet tensioner like these from Star Performance do an excellent job, and won't slip. *Star Performance Parts*

Everything needs to be accessible on a racing motor. Here, the pushrod tubes have been omitted and the adjustable pushrods can be removed in seconds. This entire engine is custom made of billet aluminum with cast iron barrels.

is to be first, not to worry about conserving the engine.

Many aftermarket companies will help you build a Big Twin motor: S&S (608-627-1497; www.sscycle. com), Custom Chrome (800-729-3332; www. customchrome.com), and Rivera Engineering (562-907-2600; web site at www.riveraengineering.com). As a matter of fact, there are so many manufacturers of Big Twin and Sportster parts that a book could be devoted to them. (I have written that book; check Whitehorse Press or Classic Motorbooks catalogs for *How to Build Harley-Davidson Horsepower,* ISBN 0-7603-0150-6.)

Costs? A strong 120+ ci engine, running racing gas, could be on the track for $10k–$12k. Here's how it breaks down. A set of S&S cases will run $1,200. A cylinder kit is $975. Rods, $325. Flywheels, $450. Pistons, $125. Cam and full kit, including pushrods and lifters, $475. Then there are bearings, crankpins, bolts and studs, fasteners, gaskets, breather, oil pump, valve covers, bearings, and the labor to open the breather, balance and true the flywheels, lap the bearings, assemble the engine and install it in your frame. I can't do that for much less than $4,000, and unless your uncle owns a Harley shop, neither can you. Don't forget ignition, $700; tach, $175; plus numerous other bits & pieces I've forgotten.

You will still need some sort of induction—say an S&S Super E carb, intake manifold, pipes, and brackets. If you run forced induction, throw another $3,500 to $4,000 into the pot.

The cost for a set of heads will vary quite a bit, depending on how much work you want to do on them and what kind of induction is feeding them. Go for a middle figure of $3,500 for a set that has been flowed, ports matched, bigger valves installed with new springs and keepers, a five-angle valve seat ground in and the cylinders O-ringed to take the higher pressures of a blower (if used).

If my calculator is right, I come up with $15,925 before it even turns over. Add the costs of chassis, body, fuel and oil, tires and incidentals like chains, sprockets, and what all and pretty soon $50,000 disappears into a fuel bike.

This isn't to say you can't add a carb, cam, pistons and pipes to your street bike and go racing. You can, and you will enjoy the experience and have some fond memories—possibly even a trophy or two. However, if you are serious about racing a Big Twin, and can do it cheaper than my prices above, write to me care of Whitehorse Press and let me know how you do it.

CHAPTER 7

Fuels

Different classes allow the use of different fuels. Most of the lower classes allow only gasoline, but it can be your choice of racing gasoline unless there's a specific requirement in the class rules. The fastest classes run alcohol, alcohol/nitromethane mix, or straight nitro with very small amounts of other chemicals added for stability. A beginning racer needs to spend one to two years running gas classes before moving up to fuel classes. There's too much to learn about drag racing alone before trying to "tip the can" with alcohol or nitro. These two fuels operate very differently from gasoline and require a large body of knowledge to use them properly.

Gasoline

The trick to running a modified engine on the street is to keep the compression ratio down to a reasonable value—somewhere between 8.75:1 and 9.5:1 for V-twins; up to 10.1:1 for inline four cylinder engines. Those compression ratios will run on the low-octane pump gas available in this country, without pinging. Californians have it worse than most. We enjoy "oxygenated" fuels full of what has been found to be a nasty chemical, methyl tertiary-butyl ether (MTBE), an oxygenated alcohol additive that is added to Reformulated Gasoline (RFG) and premium grades of unleaded gasoline. The EPA requires MTBE to be added to gasoline in areas where there is severe ozone pollution. When MTBE is added to fuel, it reduces the amount of carbon monoxide emission, a poisonous gas produced through combustion. However, MTBE has seeped into numerous wells, poisoning them. This additive holds some of the pollutants down a bit, but really plays merry hell with driveability and mileage because it is an alcohol derivative with a lower specific BTU/pound ratio than gasoline.

It is mainly V-twin engines that have trouble with high compression ratios; compression ratios on Japanese four-cylinder engines are pretty high to start with, since their combustion chamber design promotes much better burning than does the wedge-shaped combustion chamber found in V-twins. The V-twin combustion chamber has poor flame propagation compared to the hemispherical combustion chambers found in the Japanese engines. If you keep the Harley's compression ratio at or below 10:1, you shouldn't have serious problems, but 9.5:1 is a much better ratio for the street because low-octane fuels can produce engine knock with higher ratios.

The sound of two Top Fuel bikes leaving the line cannot be conveyed in words. Ear plugs are a necessity, not an option.

Racing gas comes in octane ratings up to 115 and can be mixed with pump gas to boost its effective octane rating, or it can be run straight for racing if you need the benefits of a full 115 octane. Higher octane ratings will allow you to use higher compression ratios without destructive detonation. Racing gasoline itself won't boost performance in the slightest; however, it will let the engine deliver its available horsepower without detonation, and that's what you need.

The obvious problem with using racing gas on the street, aside from its $7.50+ per gallon cost, is the need to have a supply handy when it's fill-up time. Short of dragging a tank behind you, this poses a bit of an obstacle. Some additives are advertised to boost your octane rating a few points, but I haven't had much experience with them. Give 'em a try and if they work, throw a bottle or two into your saddlebags for long trips, but stick to racing fuels for racing; don't use any octane enhancers in the racing fuel.

I buy racing gasoline in 10- and 55-gallon drums. During the racing season it gets used fast enough to keep from stagnating, so because there is a price break on 55 gallons over smaller amounts, I buy the larger drums. Gasoline weighs six pounds per gallon and the 55-gallon drum itself weighs 15 pounds, making a total of 345 pounds. They are too heavy to wheel in and out of my truck, so I will pump what I need into smaller tanks—normally, two five-gallon containers per race event will do. I keep the gas outside in a breezy shed and have a large 15-pound fire extinguisher inside the nearest door. (I think the extinguisher is mostly a "feel-good" idea as it sure won't be in my hands if 55 gallons of 115 octane gas (or any fuel, for that matter) goes up! I've jokingly told people in the shop that if I holler "Fire!," and they say "What?" they'll be talking to themselves.)

I've tried 100LL (low lead) aviation gasoline with mixed results. It works quite well on mild motors, but still won't prevent detonation on high compression engines because an octane rating above 105 is needed for very high (11:1 and up) racing engines. Racing gasoline, such as TRICK 114 or Turbo 118 (both leaded), have specific qualities needed for racing engines. Some are listed below, courtesy of TRICK

Racing Gasolines (800-444-1449; www.trickgas.com).

Racing Gasoline Glossary and Specifications

Octane A numerical measure of the anti-knock properties of fuel. The higher the value, the stronger the resistance to pre-ignition knock. Its numerical value indicates the detonation sensitivity of the fuel and relates directly to the maximum possible compression ratio that may be used with that particular fuel. Octane is measured by two methods: the *research* method and the *motor* method. The research method usually gives a higher octane number, but is tested in a manner that applies to low-rpm, low-load situations. The motor method usually gives a lower numerical rating, but relates to high-rpm and high load applications more commonly associated with racing conditions. The average of the two is commonly called the road octane, anti-knock index, or (R+M)/2. This octane is on the yellow sticker you see on your neighborhood gas pump. Higher octane fuel allows an engine builder to produce maximum power without danger of detonation. Every engine has a different requirement for octane.

Specific Gravity The ratio of the mass of a liquid to an equal mass of distilled water at 60 degrees F. It's a key specification to consider when building an engine. It determines the fuel density and the amount of fuel in the air/fuel mixture. The larger the specific gravity number, the richer the fuel will burn.

Compatibility All fuels used in the same tank must be compatible with each other.

Lead Fuels containing lead must be used off-road only. Leaded fuels will damage catalytic converters and oxygen sensors. Leaded fuels deteriorate quickly when exposed to sunlight.

TRICK Racing Gasolines manufacturers a racing unleaded fuel that is street legal in muscle cars, showroom stock road racing, sport bikes, and light racing applications. It meets California Phase II Reformulated Gasoline regulations. The table to the right shows its specifications.

Alcohol

Alcohol (Methanol, Methyl Alcohol) CH_3OH is a volatile, highly flammable water-clear liquid with a mildly-spirituous odor. Mixes with water or nitromethane in all proportions and almost all proportions with gasoline. A conservative maximum compression ratio is 17:1.

Most of the world's supply of methanol is produced from natural gas feedstocks. However, coal and biomass (corn, etc.) are being explored as sources for methanol, as a way of reducing petroleum imports and conserving fossil fuels. Methanol is a cool-running fuel because large amounts of it must run through the engine (as compared to gasoline), so the cooling properties are greater than gasoline, and the burn rate is very slow—an important consideration for air-cooled engines. Alcohol will pick up a lot of heat when it vaporizes and this helps cool the combustion chamber. Engine detonation with methanol isn't encountered until compression ratios climb to 18:1 or higher.

Alcohol is a great way to make a lot of horsepower. Methanol has been used as a racing fuel for over 70 years, and is still found in some race cars. Its specific energy (BTU/pound) is much lower than gasoline—9,500 vs. 18,400 for gasoline—but because it is mixed with air at a much richer ratio than gas—6 to 1 compared to 14 to 1 for gas—there's a lot more fuel to burn per combustion cycle. In addition, alcohol can support higher compression ratios than gasoline. These two factors are responsible for how higher horsepower is produced with alcohol.

Ignition timing is critical on an alcohol engine. More midrange advance and less advance at the high end are needed. An example would be an initial advance of 15 degrees at 1,200 rpm; 36 degrees at 4,000 rpm, then back down to 34 degrees for 8,000 rpm and up.

Much different carburetion must be used with methanol than with gasoline, since a greater fuel flow is needed at any given engine speed. Doubling the numerical jet sizes of an alcohol carb will get you into the ballpark. Owners of engines running S&S or Mikuni carbs have a wealth of information available to convert their carbs to alcohol. S&S has specific carbs for alcohol, and

Properties of TRICK Racing Gasolines			
	TRICK Unleaded	TRICK 114	Turbo 118
Research Octane	106	114	119
Motor Octane	96	106	109
(R + M) / 2	101	110	114
Specific Gravity	.745	.72	.73
Color	Clear	Blue	Green
Typical Use		Ideal for 95% of motorsports applications. Aids in combustion chamber cooling.	Turbocharged and blown engines. Engines with high cylinder pressures and combustion ratios. Will aid in combustion chamber cooling.

they say in their Special Application Racing Carburetor Supplement:

NOTES: Most S&S special application fuel carburetors have enlarged internal passageways to compensate for the additional volume of fuel required for alcohol or nitromethane operation (approximately 2.5 times more alcohol than gasoline, or 10 times more nitromethane than gasoline flows through the passageways). For this reason gasoline and fuel carburetors are different from one another. This means that gas carbs cannot be modified to use nitromethane or methanol and visa versa, fuel carbs cannot be used for gasoline applications. Super D gasoline carbs may be modified to use alcohol only. If the final goal is to use alcohol, then it is recommended to purchase an alcohol carb rather than a gasoline carb at the start.

Mikuni carbs can be converted to methanol by multiplying the flow number of the main jet by 2.15 for starters (increasing the size of the jet by double plus 15%), then leaning back for proper mixture. The secret to achieving a proper mixture is to read your sparkplugs very carefully. A good electrode will have a faint ring about one cm from the end of the ceramic, and should be light brown in color. Some of Mikuni's jets are classified by fuel flow, some by orifice diameter.

All these fuel and oil lines are plastic. Legal? Yes. Smart? You tell me.

Get their book and follow their guidelines, as other considerations are important when modifying a Mikuni for various fuels: gaskets, float settings, fuel lines, petcock sizes, idle and low-speed mixture adjustments. (See www.mikuni.com/carbtech/tech)

Methanol can be corrosive to metal and rubber parts, so be sure your entire fuel system is compatible with whatever fuel you burn. Also—here's my safety thing again—methanol burns with a colorless flame. Your bike can be on fire and on a hot day, the only way you can tell is by the heat waves standing off it. (I guess the screams of the rider might give it away, too.) If you have an alcohol fire, spray water to cool the fire below its flash point; ABC dry chemical or foam or CO_2 will put it out. A water jet will spread the flame, as alcohol floats on water. Most importantly, use care in handling alcohol and always check fittings, lines, etc. for leaks before firing up an engine. Have a crew member watch the engine for strange heat waves for at least two minutes after shutdown if possible.

Nitromethane

Nitromethane CH_3NO_2 is a flammable water-clear liquid with a mild odor, containing approximately 53% oxygen by weight. Water will mix with nitromethane only up to 2.5% water. The conservative maximum compression ratio is 6.5:1 (10:1 with rich mixtures).

"Nitro" has been around since the Germans used it as fuel in their all-conquering Mercedes-Benz and Auto Union Grand Prix cars of the 1930s. It first began appearing in American racing engines in the 1950s.

Nitro's first purpose wasn't as a racing fuel, but as a paint thinner. Even today, its major use is in the chemical business as a solvent; less than 3% goes to racing. Funny to think of your racer as a Top "Paint Thinner" Bike, isn't it. "Top Fuel" sounds much more aggressive.

Pound for pound, nitro is quite low on the specific energy scale when compared with other fuels, as shown below.

Specific Energy of Various Fuels	
Fuel	Potential Heat Energy per Pound of Fuel
Gasoline	18,400 BTU
Methyl Alcohol (Methanol)	9,500 BTU
Nitromethane	5,000 BTU

BTU = British Thermal Units, the amount of heat needed to raise one pound of water one degree F. It is a measure of the potential work a fuel can do.

With its low specific energy, how then can nitromethane produce such prodigious power output? It's because of the proportions of fuel and air induced into the combustion chamber: The more fuel per pound of air burned in an engine without being too rich, the more BTUs of energy that fuel will release.

First, a cautionary note. There's a common belief that more power, and therefore more performance, can be gained simply by adding more nitro to your fuel tank. In fact, this is one of the quickest ways of running into trouble. The addition of nitro to another fuel—usually alcohol—is not a matter of adding more until enough power is obtained, but rather of controlling accurately the proportion of nitro relative to other components, and preparing the rest of the fuel system to handle the modified fuel mixture.

For instance, here's a chart showing the recommended jet diameter increase for mixtures of nitro and methanol, ranging from straight methanol to straight nitro.

Track temperature is 100 degrees, humidity 50%. When setting up a fuel bike, these—along with air density, altitude, and track conditions—have to be factored into the mix. The right proportions of nitro and alcohol depend on these parameters.

Required Increase of Jet Diameter for Various Mixtures of Nitromethane and Alcohol		
Percent of components in the fuel mixture, by volume		Jet diameter ratio over what is needed for straight methanol
Nitromethane	Alcohol	
0%	100%	1.0
50%	50%	1.5
80%	20%	1.73
90%	10%	1.8
100%	0%	1.87

This chart shows the increase in jet diameter needed to allow the correct amount of fuel to flow as the percentage of nitro in the mixture is increased. These figures are on the rich side as these fuels are relatively insensitive to a slightly rich mixture ratio (compared to gasoline), and the consequences of running weak mixtures with nitro can be much more serious than the problems with gasoline. This is due to the higher power levels and thermal stresses imposed on an engine using nitro. If the mixture is too rich, the throttle response will be mushy and sluggish. If too lean, detonation will result, with the possibility of burning pistons and valves. (An exceedingly rich mixture can cause detonation because of large unburnt globules of fuel in the cylinders,

but performance would be so poor that you would probably shut off the engine before breaking anything.)

The following chart gives the approximate compression ratios recommended for use with nitro/alcohol fuel mixes.

Maximum Compression Ratio for Various Mixtures of Nitromethane and Alcohol		
Percent of components in the fuel mixture, by volume		Compression ratio
Nitromethane	Alcohol	
10%	90%	16:1
18%	82%	15:1
28%	72%	14:1
38%	62%	13:1
46%	54%	12:1
56%	44%	11:1
66%	34%	10:1
75%	25%	9:1
85%	15%	8:1
94%	6%	7:1

These are starting estimates only. Every engine is different.

The amount of air required by gasoline to burn correctly is several times greater than that required by alcohol or nitro. So, the advantage of alcohol or nitro is that the amount of heat liberated per pound of air is greater. Gasoline requires a 14.6:1 air/fuel mixture; methanol's ratio is 5:1, and nitromethane will burn one pound of fuel for every 1.3 pounds of air.

Nitro isn't particularly easy to ignite when used as a fuel. That's why you will see a crewman with a squirt can prime the injectors or carbs when starting a nitro-fueled engine. Gasoline is used to get the fire lit, after which the nitro will ignite properly in the hot chambers. Some additives had been added to nitro in the past to destabilize it, making it easier to ignite, but most of them—in particular, propylene oxide, various amines, aniline oils, and benzene—caused many a blown-up engine because, although they made the nitro light easier, they lowered its effective detonation threshold down from 10:1 to 8:1, which brought on very severe detonation, which in turn caused a lot of engines to blow up when the nitro detonated explosively.

It takes three people to start a fuel bike: one to prime, one to engage the starter, and one to hang on.

When mixed with nitro, most destabilizers will make it much more sensitive to shock; a container of the resulting mixture can explode if dropped. The basic rule when mixing nitro is *don't add anything whose properties and interactions with nitro you are not familiar with.* Oxidizing agents, certain aniline oils, and anything with -hydroxide in its name, can make nitro extremely shock sensitive.

One of the worst additives is hydrazine, for two major reasons. First, some racers still swear that it boosts horsepower tremendously—which it does by acting as an oxygen scavenger. It will go into spontaneous combustion when mixed with an oxidizer, and it reacts in a very unstable, uncontrollable manner. In other words, it can run just fine with the ignition turned off. Hydrazine is a major fuel component for the Titan family of launch vehicles, and is used as a guidance propellant when in the vacuum of space. As far as I know, it and propylene oxide are illegal in all racing organizations. Second, when combined with some common solvents and fuels, hydrazine becomes very poisonous.

After all this, you would think that nitro must be pretty flammable. Well, it isn't. If ignited in an open container, it will burn just like any slightly-flammable cleaning solvent. As a matter of fact, it does make a good parts cleaner, though a bit expensive. Fifty-five-gallon drums of the stuff have been kicked off high platforms with absolutely no effect except a dented can. In its pure form, nitro is very stable. It does have one very noticeable drawback, however, and that is

its exhaust. Nitromethane burning in an internal combustion engine produces large amounts of nitric acid which, if inhaled, will stop your breathing. That's why you see people who get a blast of nitro exhaust spin away violently when their breathing shuts off. Wear a face mask if you must work in situations that expose you to nitromethane exhaust.

Some racers used to use toluene to destabilize nitro because it increases anti-knock capabilities, but I didn't find it in use by any of the drag bike racers I spoke with. Usually the nitro is cut with good old methanol which burns clean enough to make reading spark plugs much easier.

Getting the proper air/fuel mixture with nitro is extremely important. Because it doesn't atomize well, and can form droplets of raw fuel in the combustion chamber, too rich a mixture can cause detonation when individual droplets of fuel ignite. So can operating too lean. Mixtures have to be spot-on with nitro in order to make a clean run down the strip and not bog or spin up the tire. However, it's better to run a bit on the rich side than take a chance of the engine going lean and self-destructing. Computing the proper mixtures depends on many variables: how much horsepower the tire can transmit to the track, track temperature, air density, air temperature, track temperature, humidity, and state of tune of the engine. Learning how to handle all these variables takes time and much experimentation. You must record all the information about every run. Along with the variables listed above, you will need to know ET and speed, spark plug readings, exhaust gas temperature and semi-unrelated items like tire pressure, tire compound, weight of rider and bike, time of day, and others. It's a long learning curve that needs the advice and help of someone who already is running alcohol and nitro.

Two choices exist for mixing nitro with air: carburetion or injection, same as gasoline. When a supercharger is installed, fuel injection provides better atomization of fuel droplets and more precise metering. S&S provides comprehensive information on jetting their fuel carbs; their Super fuel carbs are the choice of V-twin racers. Two sizes are available: Super B with 1-7/8 inch venturi, and Super D with 2-1/4 inch venturi. The proper size for your engine will depend on displacement. Contact S&S for exact carb size and jetting.

It's best to start off two jet sizes larger than what you think is correct. Keep a record of every run, check plugs for a clean, white powder coating on the insulator and don't start with too cold a plug. Use a plug chart to determine the heat range of your plugs. Heat range refers to the relative temperature at the core nose of a spark plug. The words "hot" and "cold" refer to the thermal characteristics of the plug. They are a measurement of the plug's ability to dissipate heat away from the electrode into the engine's cooling system. A hot plug has a much slower rate of heat transfer and is used to avoid fouling. The heat range of a plug doesn't affect the engine's power; rather it allows the plug to function as designed for the duration of operation.

Racing plugs are much colder than those intended for street use. Their color and condition are used to check engine operating conditions and the air/fuel mixture. Some tuners like to see an ever-so-slight bubbling of the porcelain on the center electrode. Just be careful when making tuning changes. Make only one tuning change at a time, then take a reading. Take everything slowly, talk to others in your class who are running similar setups, and don't be afraid to shut it down if something doesn't feel right.

All sanctioning bodies require a blast shield or ballistic blanket between you and a supercharged or fuel engine. All fuel bikes must have a pre-loaded fuel shutoff with a trigger connected by lanyard to the rider, and a method of shutting off fuel while the rider is on the bike. Lower engine ballistic shields are highly recommended—something to stop all the hot parts when they depart the engine at 6,000 fpm.

Tuning for Nitromethane

In addition to rich mixtures, it's highly desirable when running a nitro bike to have a very clean combustion chamber, no carbon deposits or sharp edges that can get white hot and ignite the fuel.

Ignition settings must be advanced over those for methanol due to the slower burning of nitro. The actual advance curve will depend on engine design, but a good starting point would be 40 degrees advance. Spark plugs will have to be checked after each run to determine the maximum percentage of nitro that your specific engine can run. Increase the percentage of nitro in small progressive steps and look for the following signs of mixture limits:

Chipping of plug insulator, similar to weak mixture

Caused by overheating of all the metal parts of the plug, in extreme cases to the external body of the plug. In extreme cases, the plug can get hot enough to ignite the nitro without a spark being present. If this happens, the only way to shut the engine down is to close the throttle and immediately shut off the fuel. A lean mixture can cause the valves to act the same way and ignite the fuel as it passes into the combustion chamber. The solution for this problem is to richen the mixture.

The center insulator is ashen in color with gray streaks—not to be confused with the normal white gray color of a proper mixture

If you see these symptoms and there is no question of the engine having a weak mixture (always err on the rich side), you should reduce the percentage of nitromethane in the fuel mixture. You have reached the limits of what your engine can handle. You must check at all times that your fuel lines and fuel pump capacity (if used) are more than adequate to handle the heavy fuel flow demand. Never let the engine run lean, as damage will definitely result. High nitro power levels can cause intake and exhaust valves to stretch at the neck, so watch valve clearances closely to prevent broken valves.

Nitromethane and methanol are available from VP Racing Fuels (www.vpracingfuels .com). Nitro comes in one-gallon cans, a case of four one-gallon cans, fifteen-gallon pails, thirty-gallon drums or 500-pound drums. Methanol is sold in 5-, 15-, 30-, and 54-gallon containers. Prices change often, so contact VP Racing Fuels for current costs.

Riding the Hot Seat: Fire!

Unfortunately, I've seen more than one bike catch on fire. A couple of times that really stick in my mind involved loose or broken fuel lines. In one case, the fuel (nitro) line on a Top Fuel V-twin was made out of what looked like clear plastic surgical tubing. Through some mischance—loose clamp, ruptured line, melted line, something—the fuel line opened up and proceeded to wash down the engine, the exhaust, and the rider's right leg.

As the bike was going just over 120 mph the fuel lit off. There was enough air to fan the flames quite nicely, but not so much speed that when the rider got that "warm, burning sensation" he couldn't step off the bike. And step off he did—very briskly. When interviewed after playing self-immolation, he said, "I felt the heat, felt the engine go soft, felt a burning sensation, and felt the ground."

He got away with small second-degree burns where his leathers ended and his shoe began, but that was about it. Oh yeah, he got to buy another set of leathers too—ones without burn marks up the right leg.

Fire systems are cheap insurance. A 2.5-pound fire bottle, two spray nozzles and a release button won't add enough weight to be noticed, but just might save you or your bike. The new fire suppressants don't leave a stain and will suppress any type of liquid-fueled fire. One spray nozzle is mounted in front of the engine and the other goes wherever works best. The most important feature of an on-board fire system is that once you hit the button, your participation is over. All you have to do is get stopped and get off the bike. The fire system will run long enough to give you the necessary time.

The other point I want to mention is the fuel lines I saw on the burnt bike. Plastic tubing? Running nitro through plastic tubing? Give me a break! At a minimum, braided steel lines should be used on a Pro bike of any type, especially one that has a lot of spinning machinery flailing around. Street bikes run synthetic rubber fuel hoses that are somewhat resistant to minor burning, plus they are placed in such a way as to be out of the line of fire if something lets go. The plastic lines I saw ran down behind the engine to a fuel pump, then up to mechanical injectors. I could actually see fuel run through the hoses. Brrrrr! ∎

This plastic fuel line feeds nitromethane and alcohol to a Top Fuel V-twin. Plastic rips easily and can be set on fire by burning oil or fuel. You would never get this past an NHRA technical inspector.

Summary

In summation, gasoline is mixed with air at a ratio of 12:1 to 14:1; alcohol at 5:1 to 6:1; and nitromethane at 1:1 to 2:1. Fuel bikes are somewhat exotic and even a bit scary, especially from the vantage point of camera work on the starting line. They're expensive to operate—at least three times the cost of gasoline-powered bikes. However, no other type of racing bike will provide the amount of adrenaline-charged thrills that a Top Fuel drag bike will do as it makes a 200+ mph run—especially at night.

CHAPTER 8

Carburetion

A carburetor is nothing more than a device to mix fuel and air before it goes into the engine. You can start and run an engine with nothing more for carburetion than a spray bottle full of gasoline squirted into the intake manifold. It's possible to make an engine run for a while simply by pumping the sprayer every time the engine starts to die. Engines will run—though not necessarily well—on a wide range of fuel/air mixtures.

Carburetors rely on the vacuum created by the intake stroke of the pistons to pull fuel into the incoming air stream and atomize it, as opposed to fuel injection which uses positive pressure to force fuel into the intake tract.

Carburetion—as compared to mechanical fuel injection—has better low-end response, is cheaper, and is simpler. Compared to electronic fuel injection (EFI), carburetion has no benefits except for cost. More and more manufacturers are turning to EFI for emissions control, cold start ability, economy, and altitude compensation. No auto manufacturers build an engine with carbs anymore, and haven't in years.

Most new motorcycles still use carburetors because they are cheaper and simpler than EFI, and the smog monsters haven't taken a real close look at them yet. And "yet" is the operative word. In a short time, carbs on street motorcycles will be a thing of the past, and we will be damn glad of it.

Drag racing will still use carbs for the foreseeable future, simply because they are cheap, easy to work on, and don't require an engineering degree to tune. Carbs offer a wide range of adjustment simply by changing jets, needles, or slides. They are simple to tune for drag racing because smooth low- and middle-range performance isn't a requirement. Almost the entire run is spent on the main jet with the slide wide open, so all that's really necessary is correct jetting for the top end, and good enough low- and mid-range to idle and drive to the burn-out box.

Usually turbo Funnybikes like this Kawasaki run one S&S carb in front of the turbo. More and more, though, fuel injection is replacing carburetion.

The S&S Super series of carbs can be found feeding just about every type of motor. They work well with alcohol and nitro. S&S

V-Twins

V-twin engines work happily with Mikuni (www.mikuni.com) or S&S (www.sscycle.com) carbs. Harleys come from the factory with a Keihin carb, which can be tuned a bit, but Keihins were designed to meet emissions requirements and have no place on a serious drag racer. Carburetors made by other manufacturers have appeared on drag bikes—Dellorto, SU, Zenith, and Bendix—but they have faded in popularity over the past ten years.

The carburetors of choice for racing V-twins are the Mikuni HSR-42, CCI Accelerator II, or S&S Super G or Super D for all engines up to 110 ci. For bigger engines, you'll need two or more carbs, or fuel injection. S&S makes single-barrel carburetors for gas, alcohol, nitro and turbo applications. Its Super B is the basic carb for modified V-twin engines in all displacements up to 110 ci. It can also be used in front of a turbo as a draw-through carburetor. Two other carbs are available from S&S: the Super E and the Super G. These are the most popular carbs in their lineup, with improved airflow compared to the Super B. The Super E flows 14% more air than the Super B, and the Super G flows 39% more—enough airflow to handle any turbo or supercharged engines up to 170 ci. Both carburetors are almost 1-1/2 inches shorter than the Super B, which means they will fit under a stock

Harley-Davidson five-gallon fuel tank without modification. On a blown race motor, the overall length isn't all that important, but length is critical on street class bikes.

S&S Cycle Carburetors

I'm most familiar with the S&S series of carburetors because they were developed initially for Harley-Davidson engines, and I've been racing and breaking V-twin motors for over 30 years. The S&S Super B, Super E, and Super G are butterfly throttle valve-type carbs with fully adjustable idle mixture screw and changeable mid-range and high-speed jets. The Super B doesn't have an accelerator pump but the Super E and Super G do. None of the three have a conventional choke; instead, they rely on an enrichment lever for cold starts. This means there is no choke plate to restrict air flow. The Super E and Super G have a slightly better throttle response because they have an accelerator pump, and are really the carbs to use for racing.

Setting the jetting on any S&S carb is fairly simple. Main jet size is best determined by testing at the drag strip, because maximum mph and rpm are the best indicators of the actual horsepower the engine is developing. S&S recommends doing all high speed jetting under controlled conditions at a race track.

Dragstrip procedure should go something like this:

1. Warm up the engine enough to begin testing—the oil should be hot, not lukewarm.

2. Make a test run noting engine rpm, and get the trap speed from the timing booth.

3. Increase or richen the main jet size by .004 inch and make a second run, getting the same data at the end.

4. Continue enlarging the main jet until ET and speed deteriorate.

5. Decrease or lean the main jet by .002 inch to get maximum rpm. When making the runs, do not try for the best ET, but for the fastest and most consistent mph.

Remember that when an engine is modified with cams, carbs and higher compression ratio, more fuel will be needed. Be sure to install a larger fuel petcock for the increased fuel flow demand.

Mikuni Carburetors

The Mikuni HSR42/45 series of carburetors are designed primarily for Harley-Davidson and other V-twin engines. They will work on any application using a single carb, such as with turbochargers or superchargers. Like the S&S, they can be tuned for any engine application.

The Mikuni HSR design incorporates an eight-roller-bearing flat throttle slide assembly. The flat throttle slide allows an unobstructed venturi at full throttle to flow more air, and it carburetes more precisely at all throttle settings, as compared to the S&S carbs with their butterfly throttle valves which do obstruct air flow a bit. The roller bearing slide offers smoother control and allows the use of a lighter throttle return spring. The chances of the slide being stuck open under blow-through, or draw-through forced induction is just about zero.

The HSR42 was developed for the Harley-Davidson 1340cc Evolution engine. It works best when other modifications, such as cams, pistons and an exhaust system are employed. The larger HSR45 works best on larger V-twin engines that are highly modified for racing use only, with high compression, a free-flow exhaust and high-lift cams.

The HSR42 has a smaller venturi than the S&S Super carbs, but it flows more air at full throttle to produce more peak power because of the lack of a throttle butterfly interrupting the air flow. Both HSR42 and HSR45 carbs have high leverage float valves that lessen the possibility of the float bowl overfilling or the needle valve sticking. Their adjustable accelerator pumps can be set to provide instant off-throttle response no matter how the engine is configured—forced induction or normally aspirated.

Tuning the HSR series carburetor for racing is slightly different from working on the S&S. Tuning the jet needle requires that you accelerate from 1/2- to 3/4-throttle in top gear. If the engine seems slow to respond when the throttle is whacked open and response seems flat, the mixture is too lean and the needle needs to be raised one notch. On the other hand, if acceleration is crisp, but the engine hesitates or staggers when shut down from 3/4- to 1/2-throttle, the mixture

Mikuni offers their HSR series of 42mm and 45mm smooth bore carburetor kits for V-twin racing engines. The HSR42 is an excellent choice for engine displacements up to 90 ci; the HSR45 will feed larger engines, or work well on a draw-through turbo system. The HSR-42 works extremely well on V-twins and in front of turbos, since it has roller bearings in its slide which prevent the slide from sticking when operating against a high vacuum. *Mikuni*

is too rich and the needle needs to come down one notch.

The main jet operates from 3/4-throttle to wide open, so it's the one that needs the most attention for drag racing. The most effective method for getting the main jet spot-on is to time the bike's acceleration between two points. Here again, the race track is the place for this. Set up two markers, say at five hundred feet and one thousand feet. Hit the first marker at a speed above 50 mph (or use a set rpm if you have no speedometer). Roll the throttle fully open and have a crew member measure the time it takes to cross the one thousand foot marker. This can be done in any gear that has the engine running at its mid-rpm range when the roll-on begins. The jet that gives you the shortest time is the correct jet. This method is simple, but effective.

Effects of Elevation and Temperature

Carburetor tuning in general for maximum engine output depends on the amount of air drawn into the cylinders and whether the air/fuel mixture going into those cylinders is in the right ratio. Since the amount of air drawn into the

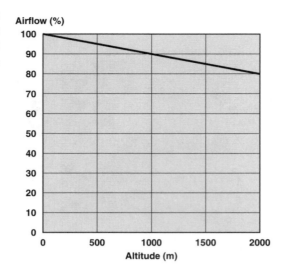

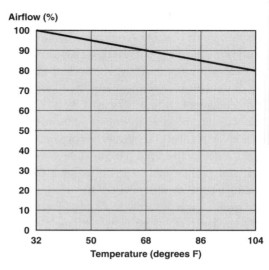

cylinders varies with the temperature, atmospheric pressure, humidity and other factors, the proper mixture ratio is different for every competition situation. It is important, therefore, that the fuel flow be adjusted in accordance with the altitude of the race track and meteorological conditions prevailing on the day of the race.

If the air flow into the induction system can be said to be 100% at sea level and standard conditions of 32 degrees F and 50% relative humidity (%Rh) then the amount of air flow into the cylinders decreases in proportion to a rise in elevation—humidity being constant—as shown at left above. Reduction of the amount of air drawn into the cylinders changes the air/fuel ratio, with the result that power output drops markedly.

The second chart shows the relation between a rise in temperature—with constant humidity—and the decrease in the amount of air drawn into the cylinders, with power dropping as temperature climbs. In the case of a racing engine, where maximum horsepower is needed, it is best to tune the engine by making a matching test of the carburetor operation in accordance with all the conditions at the race track at every event. Electronic fuel injection (EFI) lends itself to precise dyno tuning over the entire rpm range, and can automatically adjust for altitude and other conditions. Chapter nine covers EFI in detail.

Four-Bangers

Back to that hypothetical Kawasaki we've been discussing off an on. It's normally-aspirated— no blowers of any kind—so we will have to come up with some sort of carburetion or injection for it. There are actually only two choices for Kawasaki, Suzuki or Yamaha engines: Mikuni or Lectron carbs. No other carb manufacturers have put the time and effort into building a racing induction system that's as good as these two, and both companies support racing with a large technical department. Mikuni carburetors come in throat sizes from 34mm to 40mm; the size you need will depend on engine displacement. All the Mikuni carbs are Flat Slide designs, with center pull. The older side pull slide isn't as good as the center pull because it can bind when large volumes of air are flowing, and stick open; it is no longer readily available.

Schnitz Racing sells Mikuni Radial Flat Slide carburetor sets, with prices starting at $600 for the 36mm version. (The 34mm carbs aren't a good match for an engine 900cc or above.) Velocity stacks run from a short 15mm to 70mm in length. The 70mm stacks are quite long and might have clearance problems. Racer's net is $42 for a set of four velocity stacks. Pingel offers sets of Mikuni carbs ranging in size from 34mm to 40mm. They are available for different engine setups that require left-, center-, or right-pull throttle linkage. Their "race only" sets work extremely well in the high range, but shouldn't be run on the street due to low- and mid-range operating problems. A large selection of Mikuni pilot and main jets are available to help the tuner set the engine up for different conditions. Get the

Four Lectron Pro Stock carbs feed the motor in Angelle Savoie's Pro Stock bike. The nitrous oxide and gasoline spray nozzles can be seen under the manifold.

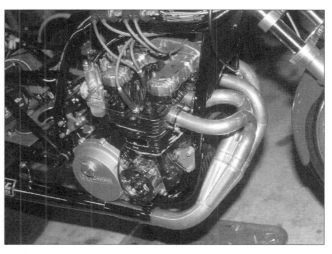

High performance carburetion works best with the proper exhaust. Angelle Savoie's engine has a Star Performance Pro Stock/Spyder pipe. It's available for Suzuki and Kawasaki only.

Mikuni tool kit when you purchase a carb set or extra jets. It makes jetting changes and normal maintenance much easier.

My personal preference for four-cylinder engine carburetion after trying other induction setups is the Lectron Pro carb. Dyno runs show a marked increase in horsepower and air flow at the high end over similar Mikuni carbs when they're installed. The Lectron carburetors use a uniquely designed metering rod to control atom-

ization and fuel flow at the same time. The metering rod controls the amount of fuel entering through the jet; by accelerating the airflow around the rod, it creates a low pressure area on its downstream side that causes more fuel to be lifted into the venturi. The accelerated air flow helps atomize the fuel into a finer vapor than would be the case without the rod's special design. The smaller the fuel droplets, the better and faster the flame will travel in the combustion

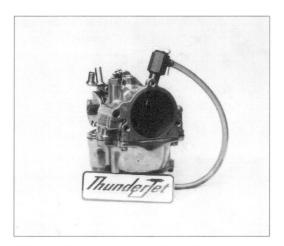

This S&S Super B carburetor has a Thunderjet mounted on the intake side. The Thunderjet can be set up to dump in more fuel when full throttle is reached. *S & S/Thunderjet*

ThunderJets can be mounted singly or in pairs. Placement is up to you. They take about 30 minutes to install, and if you're real good with a drill, can be done while the carb is on the manifold. *Zipper's*

chamber, and the less chance the fuel will have to form droplets where the intake manifold makes turns.

Lectron Pro carbs aren't any more expensive than Mikunis. A set of 40mm Lectron Pro carbs for a Suzuki GS1100/GS1150 costs $650, and comes with quick throttle and cables. If you run a big motor, or a Pro Stock engine, Lectron makes a set of 44mm carbs that flow in excess of 165 cfm. They also have a set of 46mm Monster Trons set up specifically for Pro Stock. These will set you back $1,500, but if you need them and your motor can pull them without bogging, they're the best way to go.

Normally, 40mm carbs are good for engines up to 900cc; 44mm for up to 1150cc (or Pro Stock) and 46mm for larger engines, but these have been showing up on quite a few Pro Stock, 1500cc, Suzuki two-valve engines as of late. All Lectron carb sets come with throttle and cables. Both 44mm and 46mm Lectrons can be purchased with a nitrous adapter plate, and with or without the rubber carb holders that connect the carbs to the intake spouts on the head. You can plug the jet holes with threaded plugs if you aren't running nitrous yet.

Carburetor Tuning Safety

1. Use a push-pull throttle cable assembly on all carburetor installations.

2. Throttle cables must be routed freely without sharp bends between the twist grip and the carburetor.

3. Gasoline is extremely flammable. Do not use it as a cleaning solvent. Make sure your work area is well vented and don't store gas-soaked rags.

4. Never look directly into the throat of a carburetor, lest the backfire monster reaches out and singes thy noggin.

Fuel filters are cheap insurance. Change them once a season on a drag bike; at least every 7500 miles on a performance street bike. *Custom Chrome*

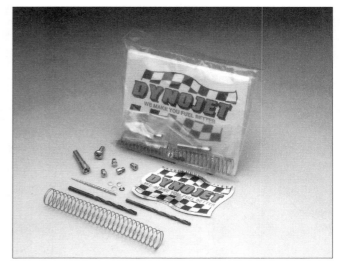

Dynojet makes the Power Commander for fuel injected engines and jet kits for carbureted motors. The kits will definitely wake up a smog-choked motor. *Custom Chrome*

CHAPTER 9

Fuel Injection

Electronic Fuel Injection

More and more motorcycles are coming from the factory with electronic fuel injection (EFI) instead of carburetors to meter fuel to the engine. The reasons behind the switch to EFI are primarily emissions control, driveability and overall power, plus increased fuel mileage. Years ago, all automotive manufacturers dropped carburetors and switched over to EFI for improved emissions control and fuel mileage. About the only place you'll see a four-barrel carburetor today is on a chrome engine powering a hot rod at Graffiti Night. Now, all bike manufacturers either have an EFI engine or are working on one.

So, you might ask, what does this have to do with drag racing your bike? If the bike you ride has EFI and you want to improve its performance, you are going to have to learn to reprogram—or modify the program—in the EFI. Plus, aftermarket EFI systems are beginning to appear, and fairly soon all street bikes will have to go to EFI to meet stricter emissions standards. Look at Harley-Davidson's new 115 hp, liquid-cooled, four-valve, 1130cc, Electronic Fuel Injected V-Rod to see where motorcycle induction is headed. Triumph already uses EFI on its TT600 and others; Kawasaki's Mean Streak 1500cc cruiser has 'Fuel Injection' in big letters on the side covers. Pretty soon, carbureted engines on the street will be a rarity, and once the tuners figure out how to make the EFI systems go fast, there will be a whole lot more laptop computers hooked up to drag bikes.

EFI Operation

A typical electronic fuel injection system consists of the electronic control module (ECM), sensors, fuel injectors, a fuel pump, and related wiring and plumbing. The ECM controls the fuel flow and spark timing through an "open-loop" or "closed-loop" system. An open-loop operating mode is one for which fuel and ignition parameters are pre-programmed into the ECM, ignoring external conditions. An open-loop control mode is used in engines with high-lift cams to aid cold starts and idle, while providing maximum power at wide open throttle. In closed-loop operation, the system relies on input from various sensors

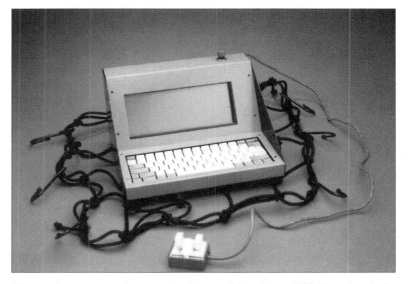

More and more computers are turning up at the drags. With the advent of EFI on engines, the computer will be the only way to change tuning at trackside. *Custom Chrome*

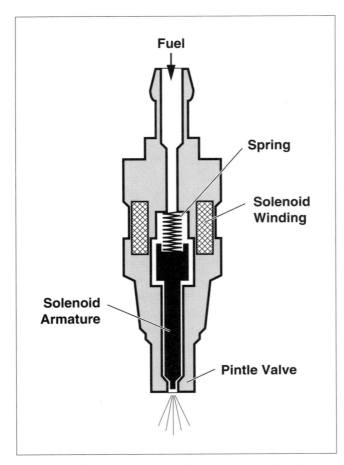

Fuel

Spring

Solenoid Winding

Solenoid Armature

Pintle Valve

In a typical EFI system, each fuel injector is controlled by electric pulses from the ECM. A spring normally holds the pintle valve closed, preventing fuel flow. When the ECM calls for fuel, it energizes the solenoid winding, raising the pintle valve and allowing pressurized fuel to spray into the inlet tract. Typical opening time for a fuel injector may only be a few thousandths of a second.

to measure variables such as ambient air temperature, air pressure, throttle position, engine speed, and so on. From these variables, the ECM can meter the fuel to achieve the most efficient stoichiometric ratio of air to fuel—14.6:1—which results in reduced emissions, improved fuel economy, and power.

Injectors

The only variable that can be changed on a fuel injector is the time when it is open, spraying fuel into the air inlet tract. Each injector (there is normally one injector for each cylinder) is timed to open momentarily during the intake stroke for its cylinder, spraying fuel for a precisely timed duration. It can open earlier, later or longer, but it cannot control the flow rate of fuel leaving the nozzle. An injector is either on or off. An approximate operating time for an injector at idle is 1.5 milliseconds. Wide open throttle requires a longer operating duration—up to 6 milliseconds.

Injectors can be mounted in three places: in the intake plenum just after the throttle butterfly; in the intake manifold just before the head; or as direct injection, into the cylinder itself. The injector nozzle is opened electrically and closed by a spring. Fuel has to be delivered at a fairly high pressure—up to 40 psi—so an electric fuel pump is usually used. The pump can be placed inside the fuel tank or under it. So long as fuel flows freely to its pickup, location of the pump isn't important. Inside a fuel tank seems a strange place for an electric fuel pump; however, all electrical connections are well sealed and the pump's motor is explosion-proof.

The injectors are very simple and reliable. There are no adjustments and no service is required. What can go wrong? The spring can weaken and allow fuel to dribble or the injector orifice can plug if any foreign object makes it through the fuel filters. Be sure to change your fuel filter at least once each season. Aside from injector problems, crud in the filter can starve the engine, causing a lean condition, usually at the worst possible time.

Sensors

Sensors feed information to the electronic control module. There are many different types of sensors for various uses and not every manufacturer uses all of them on their fuel injection systems. Some are:

Oxygen Sensor (O2) This measures the amount of oxygen in the exhaust by either generating a voltage signal or changing electrical resistance. If there's too much oxygen in the exhaust gasses, the air/fuel ratio is too high—say 18:1—and the mixture is too lean. This signal would be processed by the ECM, which would hold the injectors open a bit longer to add more fuel.

Exhaust Temperature Sensor If the exhaust temperature goes above a pre-programmed value (somewhere around 1425 degrees F) the ECM will richen up the mixture. Exhaust gas temperature climbs as the fuel mixture is leaned, until it peaks; leaner still and the temperature begins to drop. Running an engine on the lean side of peak exhaust temperature will burn valves. Running an engine richer than the mixture that produces peak exhaust temperature will provide cooling, by transferring some of the combustion energy to the unburned fuel.

Engine Temperature Sensor (ETS) Cuts back the ignition and/or fuel flow if the engine gets too hot.

Throttle Position Sensor (TPS) This looks at the shaft position of the throttle butterflies by means of a pickup mounted on the throttle body. This sensor allows the ECM to ensure that enough air is flowing to burn the fuel being fed to the engine.

Intake Air Temperature Sensor (IATS) Reads the air temperature as it enters the intake tract before the throttle body. Usually it's mounted in the air cleaner plenum box. Cooler air is denser and can run a richer mixture.

Cam Position Sensor (CPS) Controls ignition and injector timing by reading the rotational position of the camshaft.

Bank Angle Sensor Lean the bike over too far (like flat on the ground) and it will cut off the fuel and sparks.

Operation

The ECM monitors the sensors to determine the conditions of the environment and the engine in order to make decisions about spark timing and fuel delivery. It also analyzes how the engine performs during a ride. Some systems store this information as codes and they can be retrieved by use of a "scanalyzer" or "breakout box" that plugs into an access port on the ECM. Whether the engine is in open- or closed-loop operation, the ECM constantly tunes for optimum performance within smog laws. This is where problems related to poor performance can lie.

Reprogramming

The parameters programmed into the ECM are set to control a number of factors, some of which take precedence over the others. Probably the single most important factor in the ECM's operation is in making the engine conform to smog laws. Because of emphasis on controlling exhaust emissions, the ECM is usually programmed to operate on the lean side of the ideal air/fuel mixture in order to keep pollutants out of the tailpipe. Sometimes this will make the engine run poorly at different power settings. It takes a dyno with a "tailpipe sniffer" to really determine what the engine is doing throughout the entire rpm range, but here are a few symptoms you might recognize.

Lean Idle The engine stumbles and misses below 1,500 rpm.

Midrange Lean During acceleration, the engine goes flat or begins to ping at midrange rpm.

Top End Lean The motor loses power as it approaches redline.

Idle leanness isn't a major problem unless it continues into off-throttle operation. If the engine hesitates when the throttle is opened, it could be due to a severely lean air/fuel mixture. The smog police test at idle and the manufacturers usually have the injection (or carbs, for that matter) leaned out so badly that you could breathe what comes out of the tailpipe.

You can easily feel midrange and top end leanness while riding. While holding the throttle wide open, the acceleration drops off or the engine detonates so badly it sounds like a garbage disposer eating silverware. The first symptom just slows you down; detonation eats pistons. Luckily there are solutions to these problems.

Remapping the ECM

Sometimes the problems that appear on a certain model fuel injected bike—say one built before a given date—have been addressed by the manufacturer and they have provided a new program "map" for your ECM. Usually, upgrades are free and simply require a trip to the dealer where the new program can be overlaid to replace the original. However, some manufacturers will modify the ECM so extensively that its programs can't be retrofitted to the older bike; then, you are just flat out of luck for a dealer solution. The change-over dates for ECM modifications will be keyed to engine serial numbers.

Piggybacking

The ECM has programmed into it a set of instructions to read the position of the throttle butterfly valve as determined by the TPS, the speed and position of the crankshaft via the CPS, the output of the IATS, the motor temperature through the ETS, and the oxygen content of the exhaust gasses through the O_2 sensor. The ECM takes these engine status inputs and applies them against a large store of optimized ignition/fuel instructions (the "map") and provides an output to the injectors (telling them when to open), and output to the ignition module (telling it which spark plug should fire and precisely when).

The ECM can only work within the limits of these pre-programmed instructions. Modifying a stock engine changes all the data coming to the ECM box and can cause the engine to run poorly. For example, when I began to set up my Buell for drag racing, it ran extremely lean. Sometimes the factory will have a next-generation update that isn't general knowledge at the dealer level; a call to a factory service rep may be necessary to learn whether updates are available.

If the factory updates won't cure performance problems with your bike, or if the engine has been modified for increased performance, "piggybacking" another ECM onto the stock unit is the only way to change mixture and spark. Quite a bit of engineering is required to design a black box to change the performance of a fuel injected engine. During the early years of automotive EFI, the aftermarket car guys worked out ways to make changes. For the past 15 years, owners of certain cars have had the ability to replace the EPROM chip in their car's computer for increased performance. GM's chip was probably the easiest to change, while the Ford EEC system required another computer be mounted inline with the factory microprocessor.

Motorcycle ECMs don't have the advantage of a replaceable performance chip; to change the engine parameters, another ECM has to be wired inline with the factory equipment. The new box operates by rewriting or overlaying the factory settings. Any engine modification requiring more fuel than that which the stock ECM is programmed to deliver, will require that the program, or map, be altered to increase fuel flow. If the stock injectors cannot provide enough flow to maintain the proper air/fuel ratio at wide open throttle, then they will have to be replaced with higher flow rate injectors.

Modifying an EFI System for Racing

Electronic fuel injection systems are here to stay, as they offer tremendous flexibility and precise control of fuel flow under widely varying conditions. In the previous sections of this chapter, I've tried to explain how the components work. Here, I want to give you some idea of what's involved with putting a system into service, based upon my recent experience doing just that.

The most popular performance ECM, and the only one I have personally used, is the Dynojet Power Commander III (PCIII). I own a 1999 Buell S3 Thunderbolt that had a few lean operation problems due to the California calibration of its digital fuel injection. Idle operation was poor, but tolerable. The engine hunted and stumbled for the first few minutes of operation due to the very lean incoming mixture during warm-up, and it surged in the 2,500 to 4,000 rpm range during part-throttle operations. On cold days the engine refused to stay running unless I pumped the throttle. This took the engine in and out of open- and closed-loop operation before the Oxygen Sensor was hot enough to start sending a reliable signal. This drove the computer around the bend and it wouldn't operate properly for a while. Then after 30 minutes or more of operation, when everything was good and hot, rapid throttle openings around 3,500 rpm awakened the ping monster that lives in the valve pockets and eats piston tops.

I wanted to run the bike in the American Drag Bike (ADBA; 615-789-3202; web site at www.americandragbike.com) Super Stock Buell Class. When I first became interested in the class, the record was 10.681 and 127.08 mph.

My bike, box stock, ran 11.78 and 109 mph, not anywhere near fast enough to be competitive in the class. My next option was to run their street class for a few races, see how the bike did, then make up my mind about turning the S3 into an all-out drag bike. However, I needed to make the Buell run as fast and as well as it could in totally stock condition before I put it on the track, so a trip to a dyno was in order.

First thing I did was to run a baseline test to see what the engine was putting out in stock form. I used Horsepower Express, (963 Camden Ave, Campbell, CA, 408-866-1683) for all the dyno work, as they are licensed Power Commander reps. Next, I contacted Dynojet Research (800-992-4993; www. powercommander.com) and ordered and installed a Power Commander III, specific to a Buell.

The first, baseline dyno runs showed peak rear wheel horsepower to be 88.5. Dynojet figures a 12 hp loss from motor to rear wheel on the Buell, so engine output was 100.5 hp. The factory advertises 101 hp for the fuel-injected Thunderbolt S-3 engine, so I'd say it was producing at spec.

What was interesting was the lean condition encountered in mid-range, partial-throttle-to-full-throttle roll-ons. This is where a computer and a dyno are invaluable. The computer monitor displays a tachometer and speedometer in the same layout as the Buell, however what the Buell's clocks don't show, but the monitor does, is the air-fuel ratio during all phases of operation. This information is collected by a "sniffer" in the exhaust pipe that is tied into the dyno.

What we saw during part-throttle runs was the mixture going lean when the throttle was held at 40–50% and power was allowed to build. This simulated real world operation and can be recalibrated through the computer after the Power Commander is mounted and wired in place.

Actual installation of the PCIII took less than half an hour. The ECM mounts on Velcro pads supplied with the kit. I located it in the tail section behind the seat. The wiring was very easy, just a matter of pulling plugs at the injectors and putting the ECM in series with the factory's unit. I had to crimp-connect a wire to the green

First the bike gets loaded onto the dyno and strapped down. It's going to run over 110 mph, so it has to be tied down very tightly.

The copper tube connects to a sniffer that measures oxygen content in the exhaust. High content means lean mixture; all the available oxygen isn't being used.

Over 90 mph on the speedometer; force is transferred though a drum, driven by the rear wheel, that turns a water brake. Fans are used to keep the engine temperature stable.

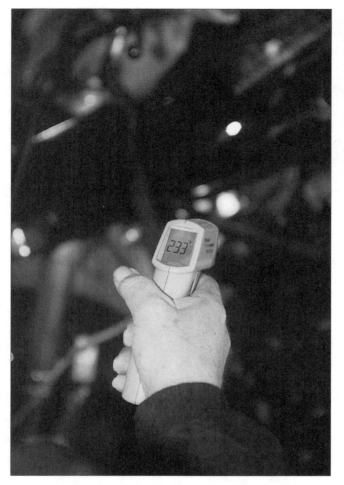

An infrared thermometer measures head temperature at the head/cylinder junction. The engine has to be warm before all the electronics in the fuel injection work properly. At this stage, the Power Commander III is onboard and we're tuning it.

The computer screen shows the road speed, engine rpm and at the bottom, air/fuel ratio. Then we can go into the EFI map and change settings to keep the injectors open longer to richen the mixture if needed.

throttle position sensor wire, and mount a new O₂ sensor in the rear pipe. This sensor has to be changed on the Buell because the factory unit isn't accurate enough to work with the Power Commander.

After installing the PCIII the engine lit right away and idle was its usual lumpy self. Dynojet recommends a run down the freeway at 3,000 rpm or better to let the black boxes re-calibrate, but other than that, nothing special has to be done.

I took the bike out for a 40-mile loop using lightly traveled roads outside the Silicon Valley area so I could play a bit. Right away I noticed a big change in operation. Dynojet had installed a

computer map for my specific engine (stock) which should have put the power Commander in pretty close calibration. The factory has different maps for every bike and just about every power modification—headers, cams, compression, etc.—and the ECM can actually be re-calibrated by the rider fairly easily.

Over the next week, I put about 250 miles on the bike and my initial impressions of stronger mid-range torque were confirmed—I could pull wheelies more easily and in higher gears than ever before. However, I also noticed detonation above 5,000 rpm in the higher gears, indicating a high-end lean condition.

I felt it was time for a hands-on adjustment. The PCIII provides user-adjustable controls to set the mixture in the low-, medium-, and high-speed ranges. First, I set the high range as rich as it would go, but saw no improvement when I took the bike out for another test. Thinking that maybe Dynojet regards 5,000 to 6,000 rpm as mid-range (as it would be for four-cylinder Japanese bikes), I then richened the mid-range to its maximum setting and took the bike out again. Bingo! No more detonation. the bike pulled clean to redline.

I wanted hard performance numbers, though, not just seat-of-the-pants reactions, so it was back to the dyno for more testing.

The first run on the dyno was made with my modified settings, then the PCIII was reset to factory settings and run #2 commenced. These runs established baselines, not peak horsepower. As a matter of fact, all full-throttle runs were done in fourth gear to reduce strain on the engine. We weren't looking for total power output and ratings, just improvement from the baseline.

We made a total of 12 runs, some from part-throttle roll-on at various rpm. Finally, we made a full-throttle run, then compared it to the baseline run. The run with the stock PCIII is TOM.009 and the last, run after the PCIII was re-mapped to provide 13.2 to 14.0 air/fuel ratio over the rpm range from 3,500 rpm to the 6,700 rpm rev limiter cutoff, is TOM.012. The lower chart shows both runs with the new air/fuel settings at the bottom. The stock PCIII (run 009) showed an air/fuel ratio of 14:1 at low rpm, ranging up to 15:1 at high rpm. With the Power Commander remapped for richer fuel delivery, air/fuel ratios ranged from 13.5:1 at low rpm, but got no higher than 14:1 by 6,000 rpm.

What does this mean? Improved torque from 2,500 rpm up to 6,000 rpm and a horsepower boost throughout the entire range. Was all this worth it? One ride was all it took. Highway 17 from San Jose to Santa Cruz was a bit crowded, but not so badly that I couldn't run the bike to redline in third and fourth. Full-bore top gear was out of the question. I tried it once, but all those cars way up ahead of me got too damn close, too damn soon.

Next up was a trip to the racetrack. I picked a Saturday test-and-tune day, so that there would be little pressure on me to win, and I could concentrate on just riding the bike. The bike ran flawlessly, no flat spots, no hesitation, no detonation. Best time of the day was in the morning when the air was cool and dense. My third pass netted an 11.52. The timing didn't record the speed on that run, but the speedometer was pushing past 115 mph as I crossed the line. The bike had gained .26 seconds just from the ECM modifications. I advise anyone who owns a bike with EFI with any driveability problems to find a shop with a Dynojet dyno and have them run your bike. A Power Commander and a dyno tune surely make a difference.

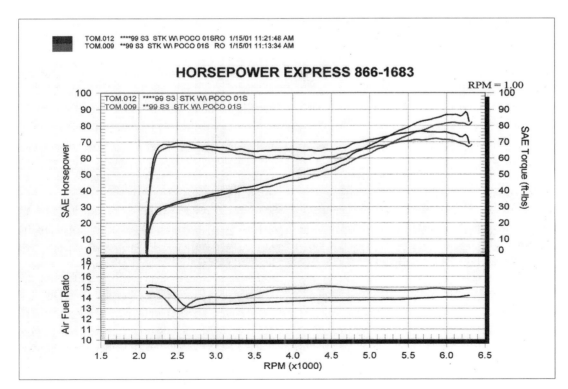

The lower lines on both the horsepower and torque curves are the results of the stock run. The upper lines represent the re-mapped run. The only change was the addition of the Power Commander III. Peak horsepower went from 82 to 87 at the rear wheel, which translates to a peak engine hp of 109 against the stock 101 advertised horsepower. The lower chart shows air/fuel ratio through the testing range.

Diesel vs. Gasoline Engines

A gasoline engine takes in a mixture of fuel and air, compresses it and ignites the mixture with a spark. A diesel engine takes in just air, compresses it, and then injects diesel fuel into the compressed air. The heat of compression lights the fuel.

A diesel engine uses compression ratios in the range of 14:1 to 25:1 to provide the necessary heat to ignite the diesel fuel. Commercial gasoline engines stay right around 8:1 to 12:1 because of detonation limitations. The higher compression ratio of the diesel engine leads to better efficiency and fuel mileage.

Diesel engines use supercharging, turbocharging, or a combination of both to pack more air into the cylinders. The amount of fuel then injected controls the horsepower output. Gasoline engines have to have an exact fuel/air mixture otherwise detonation or lean running problems can occur.

Diesels work on a constant air flow and metered fuel supply system, so a method of injecting with precision was needed. After many different methods and designs of fuel injection were tried (some of which are still with us today), finally, a way of metering the air flow and injecting just enough fuel for the best air/fuel ratio was invented. Supercharging, turbocharging, and fuel injection owe a lot to the diesel, as they were first used to improve performance on the oil burners. ■

Mechanical Injection

Compared to digital fuel injection, mechanical injection is crude. However, in very special circumstances it will do a better job than carburetors. Mechanical injection was initially developed for diesel engines back in the early 1900s.

Gasoline Mechanical Injection

A mechanical fuel injection system consists of a mechanically-driven low pressure pump, a mechanically-driven high pressure pump, a mechanically-driven metering unit, mechanically-driven injectors, and related plumbing. The low pressure fuel pump (1–5 psi) feeds gasoline to an intermediate reservoir, usually about one to two quarts in size. Gasoline in this reservoir is then fed to a high pressure pump (30–100 psi) that delivers fuel to a metering unit which is connected to individual injectors through a mechanical drive system, timed by a cam to bring each injector into the fuel circuit at the proper time.

Most metering units are connected directly to a fuel distributor that pipes the fuel into each injector. The injectors are mounted on the intake manifold in a position to spray precise squirts of fuel directly into the intake port. When an injector feels enough fuel pressure to overcome its preload spring, its nozzle opens. Pressure drops off as the metering unit moves to the next injector in the firing order, and the spring closes the nozzle.

The metering unit is driven by the engine and timed like a distributor. It has a pushrod which is advanced by engine rpm to increase fuel flow volume to each injector as engine speed increases. Excess fuel is bypassed and returned to the fuel tank.

Corvette used a Rochester mechanical fuel injection system on some of its engines back in the late 50s and early 60s. It was an expensive option at a little under $500 in 1958, but due to customer dissatisfaction, it had faded by 1968. Its biggest problem was the lack of knowledge of the people who worked on it. It was a fairly simple device, but not as simple as a good ol' four-barrel Carter carburetor. It needed skilled hands to make it right.

Mechanical injectors can be mounted anywhere on an intake system, from the trombone of the velocity stack to a point directly in the combustion chamber. I've seen mechanical injectors

before the supercharger, after the supercharger, sitting on the stack of a normally-aspirated engine, set up in place of carbs, mounted downstream of throttle bodies and tapped into the head alongside the sparkplug. What works best depends on a whole group of variables that are beyond the scope of this book.

Most mechanical injection systems for motorcycle engines are designed for racing purposes only, and will not provide the wide range of metering needed to run properly in the midrange. The manifolds and injectors are designed for maximum air flow and don't even have a low speed circuit. Idle speeds can be as high as 2,000 rpm.

Hilborn Mechanical Fuel Injection

A typical mechanical injection system for a motorcycle engine, such as the unit made by Hilborn, consists of a high-pressure fuel pump driven off the crank, a metering unit with idle valves and a high-speed circuit, a bypass valve, a modular fuel injector with motorcycle bore sizes from 1-11/16 inch to 1-15/16 inch, and related fuel lines, ram tubes, brackets, and all needed hardware. Prices run around $1,100 for just the

injector module. By the time you purchase the pumps, drives, junction blocks, fuel filter, and everything else, expect to have nearly $3,200 invested.

The mixture is adjusted by changing the size of the restrictor orifice (pill) in the bypass circuit. As the pill orifice size increases, more fuel is bypassed back to the tank and less fuel is sent to the injector nozzles, leaning the mixture. Unlike EFI, mechanical fuel injection systems function with operating rods, bellcranks, and cams that need to be properly adjusted for correct operation. The fuel pressure is checked with the engine above 6,000 rpm and the throttle butterflies wide open.

Mechanical fuel injection systems require some method of building fuel pressure. An electric fuel pump can be used to start the engine initially until mechanical pumps can build fuel pressure; if the system contains only a mechanical pump, the engine will have to be primed to start. The throttle is opened fully during priming, then shut when the engine is turned over. This reduces the possibility of a backfire. If an electric pump is used, it must be piped parallel to the mechanical pump, since it's too small to provide

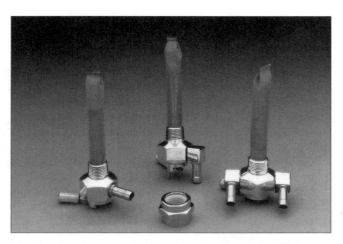

Pingel petcocks are available in single-outlet and multiple-outlet styles. The Power-Flo can be sized to feed up to 90 ounces per minute. Their Guzzler can feed 210 ounces per minute, enough for any Top Fuel bike. *Custom Chrome*

enough fuel flow at high rpm. A separate switch must be used to run the electric pump just long enough to see fuel dribble out the injectors, then it must be shut off.

Adjusting a new fuel injection system usually isn't necessary. The manufacturers have many years of testing and research behind them, and have a good idea about the necessary settings to use. They recommend that you just bolt on the parts, set the desired bypass jet, and go racing.

If you want to learn more about mechanical fuel injection systems, here's a contact and a book to read:

Hilborn Fuel Injection (949-360-0909; www. hilborninjection.com)

Bosch Fuel Injection and Engine Management, ISBN 0837603005

Benefits of Mechanical Fuel Injection

If used strictly for racing, mechanical fuel injection can work quite well. Mechanical injection isn't designed to run under part throttle conditions, so it is inadequate for the street. It hasn't the sophistication of EFI to let it meter the proper fuel over all conditions. Where it shines is from around 4,500 rpm and up with wide open throttle. Mechanical injection works especially well on supercharged engines where the injectors are mounted on the blower inlet.

If you want want good fuel control and smooth running on the street, buy an S&S or Mikuni carb. They will work 200% better than mechanical injection, cost less, and require little maintenance.

Fuel Flow

No fuel injection system in the land will do any good unless fuel can flow at a high enough rate to satisfy fuel demand. The stock petcock on your bike's fuel tank was designed to flow enough fuel for wide open throttle conditions on a stock engine for a short period of time. Add a turbo or nitrous system and fuel demand will at least double; a stock petcock can't handle that. Pingel Enterprise, Inc. (www.pingelonline. com) builds fuel delivery systems that include their Power Flo fuel petcock. They manufacture single-feed and multiple-feed fuel valves with flow rates up to 210 ounces per minute for nitro engines. Their Power Flo single outlet has a flow rate of 85 ounces per minute. An OEM valve flows no more than 30 ounces per minute. Using a stock petcock on a modified engine can starve the engine for fuel, causing the mixture to go lean enough to burn a piston.

CHAPTER 10

Sparks and Electronics

Electronic Ignition

Ignition systems used to have their hands full just getting the plugs to fire at the proper time. Then along came computers and everything changed. Now, a racer needs electronics not only to light the mixture, but also to run the bike, provide shift control, stage various events such as when the nitrous comes on and when the rev limiter changes from "burnout limit" to "race limit." Plus, the ignition has to be capable of providing advance and retard curves over a wide rpm range. Stock systems work well on the street and that's where they should stay. Your street bike can be raced using the stock spark boxes and ignition with good results, but if you are building a drag bike, then a custom ignition is necessary.

Factory ignitions will break down and fail to provide the needed spark when required to work with the high combustion pressures found in racing motors. The stock coils just won't make enough zap to light off the mixture properly. Way back in the dark ages, motorcycle ignitions had points and condensers to tell the sparkplugs when to fire. The best thing I can say about ignition points is that their day is over. There is absolutely no reason to use points in any ignition system.

Electronics rule. Electronic ignition systems are so much more reliable and accurate that they have completely displaced the old points setups. There are many different types of electronic ignition, but they all work the same, so I'll just discuss a typical model: the Dyna 4000 Ignition System.

All solid state ignitions have a sensor mounted near a rotating element of the engine—usually the camshaft. On the rotating element are lobes that trigger the sensor each time they pass by. The sensor pulses are amplified and sent to a "black box" or "microprocessor" or "electronic control unit" (ECU), which in turn generates high voltage pulses to drive the ignition coils and fire the sparkplugs. The ECU controls advance and spark duration and is somewhat self-adjusting in that it can tell when resistance is building up at the plug and increases the voltage to the electrode to compensate.

The ECU can perform other functions beyond simply firing the plugs at the right time. The Dyna 4000 working with the Dyna S Electronic Pickup can:

Dyna makes a complete line of ignition products for drag racing. Clockwise from the top: Dyna 4000 ignition, DRL 2-stage Rev limiter, Dyna Standard Rev Limiter, Dyna S Electronic Ignition, Shift Minder and light, crank magnet for Dyna S. *Star Performance Parts*

A lot of V-Twin fuel bikes are running magnetos to provide enough spark under the infernal conditions found in blown engines. Magnetos generate their own sparks and don't need a battery for operation. *Custom Chrome*

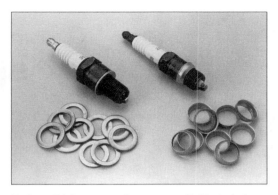

Various thickness washers are available to index the plug so that the electrode doesn't shroud the spark. The electrode should face away from the center of the piston. *Jacobs Electronics*

- Use its "launch limit" switch to operate between 6,500 and 10,250 rpm in 250 rpm increments. This enables the engine to be held on the starting line at a (moderate) set rpm, even with the throttle wide open. When the clutch is released, a micro switch is closed that shifts the redline from the preset staging limit to the operating redline.

- Operate as a rev limiter, adjustable up to 13,500 rpm.

- Self-diagnose ignition problems with an indicator light that can also be used for timing the engine.

The Dyna 4000 system can drive high energy coils (30,000 volts or better) to provide full spark energy to high compression engines up to 17,000 rpm. Dyna 4000 systems are available for Harley, Kawasaki, and Suzuki.

When you install a Dyna system, use Dyna coils, spark plug wires and a new set of plugs for a complete ignition system.

Accel, MSD, Jacobs, and others have similar products. Costs for the ignition, wires, coils, shift counter and a switched clutch lever to make it all work will eat up the better part of $1,100.

Other Electronic Devices

Kill Switch

One other electrical switch you absolutely need is a kill switch. It must be capable of killing at least the engine, but preferably the entire electrical system. Should the worst happen and you and your bike part company, you definitely don't want it chasing you down the track with the engine screaming. I've seen bikes that went down and landed on their right side in such a way as to stick the throttle wide open, just asking for something to break. Needless to say, this can have a detrimental effect on all those expensive moving parts inside the cases. I like the idea of a kill switch that not only kills the ignition, but also turns off the nitrous solenoid, fuel solenoid, and fuel pump.

The kill switch is mounted on your handlebars with a tether running from a pin in the switch to a clip that hooks onto you, preferably at the glove. If the bars and your wrist separate by more than the length of the tether, the tether will tighten and pull the switch pin, killing the electrical circuit(s).

Wiring a kill switch can be a bit tricky, because you want it to kill everything, not just the ignition, as a factory-stock kill switch does. It must kill all the fuel and ignition-related devices. Having a kill switch that disables nitrous and fuel sources also reduces the risk of fire.

Rev Limiter

Normally, a rev limiter is used to keep the engine from exceeding redline by cutting off the ignition as the engine rpm reaches a preset limit. There's another reason to utilize a rev limiter on a drag bike and that's to control the engine rpm at the starting line. A two-stage rev limiter can be set to hold the rpm right at a setting, say 6,000 rpm, with the throttle wide open. This is done to control the engine speed at launch. Listen to a bike rev as the rider awaits for the green light. The engine sounds like it's missing badly with the throttle wide open, but that's the rev limiter cutting the sparks at 6,000 rpm. Once the clutch is released, the rev limiter will switch over to the 'redline limit'. A Dyna DRL-400 Rev Limiter has two ranges: low and high. Low range operates from 3,000 rpm to 10,500 rpm. High range can be set between 10,000 rpm and 13,000 rpm. V-twin limiters operate up to 9,000 rpm.

Line Lock

You are more likely to see a line lock on a drag car instead of a drag bike. Its purpose is to hold hydraulic pressure on the front brake cylinders so the vehicle can't accidentally roll out of the lights and red light. It uses an electric solenoid valve between the master brake cylinder and the front brakes. Bikes really don't need them as both of the rider's feet are firmly planted on the ground at the start, and that serves to hold the bike in place. Either that, or the front brake is held with two fingers, but the latter method is not as common.

Launch Control or Shift Counter

This black box can perform any number of functions. It is a standalone device useful for triggering other devices. The Dyna DSC-1 has a programmable shift kill function that replaces the typical air kill switch. It will kill the ignition briefly while the gears are shifted. The shift counter can activate different devices depending on what gear the transmission is in, such as retard boxes, single or multi-stage nitrous controls, multiple waste gates, and multiple shift minders for different shift points.

Watching the needle swing on the tach will let you know when another gear is due, but setting the shift light just short of redline lets you run without having to watch the tach. Just shift when the light comes on.

Retard Box

A turbo or nitrous bike needs to retard the ignition when the boost or nitrous flow reaches a preset point, in order to stop detonation caused by very high combustion chamber temperatures and pressures. It can also be used on a non-wheelie-bar-equipped bike to take some of the power out of the engine at launch to control wheelies. The Dyna 4000 Retard Box has two different retard stages that can be activated during a run. This gives three available timing settings: the static timing and the two stages of retard.

Datalog Recorder

Data recording computers are used to monitor various sensors over a period of time. They can be set up to check wheel spin, clutch slippage, rpm, exhaust gas temperature, etc.—all against elapsed time. The Dyna Datalog samples data 100 times per second, and can hold 23 seconds of information that can be downloaded and analyzed after a run. The recorder is available with four or eight channels and can be interfaced with a clutch-slip monitor, pressure sensors, thermocouples, oxygen sensors, accelerometers and other sensors.

Just before the bike stages, the crew chief will hit the N₂O and retard switches to energize the electronic modules.

Switches low on the frame are set by the crew chief right before the bike stages. They can control anything from the N₂O solenoids to ignition retard.

The switches and controls on the bars get complicated. There are four switches here that control N₂O, ignition advance, clutch release, and rev limits. The quarter mile gets very busy.

This Competition Systems Racepack has three different output switches and can operate a number of controls, all at different rpm.

Progressive Nitrous Controller

A progressive nitrous controller can be set to bring on or shut off any number of stages at any given time. This gives the racer the ability to set the rate at which the engine will receive the power boost. The rate is adjustable from zero to 10 seconds and zero to 100% flow through up to three stages of nitrous. Some controllers, like the NOS Progressive System come with a "Time to Full Power" knob that will operate as a delay device, holding off switching to other controllers.

All these electronic controls are available through the Schnitz catalog.

CHAPTER 11

Nitrous Oxide

Everyone talks about it. A lot of racers use it. It makes interesting puffs of gas when racers hit the pre-stage button. Just what is it? What is nitrous oxide?

Just a Little Chemistry

Well, first of all, relax a bit; this isn't going to be a chemistry class. Actually, nitrous oxide is pretty simple (its chemical symbol is N_2O). At room temperature it's a gas with a lot of oxygen in it. There are two nitrogen atoms and one oxygen atom in every molecule of N_2O. It's the same stuff dentists use to get you high, except for trace elements of sulfur dioxide (it has the odor of rotten eggs) added at 100 parts per million to keep it in engines instead of noses. (Our friends at the DEA must have decided that racers are crazy enough without chemical help.)

It *will not* burn—no matter what anybody says. It *will* support combustion of any fuel—gasoline for instance. When mixed with gasoline, nitrous oxide (a liquid when under pressure and a gas at normal ambient temperature and pressure) can supply oxygen in much higher quantity than is provided by air in the intake stream. To match the additional oxygen, we can add more gasoline to each intake charge. The combination of more fuel and more oxidizer (the nitrous oxide) lets the engine make more power. The results speak for themselves. The nitrogen in N_2O acts as a buffer, helping to control the combustion process.

When heated above 572 degrees F on the compression stroke, nitrous oxide breaks down and releases its oxygen atoms, which combine with the extra fuel to let it burn completely.

When pressurized liquid N_2O is injected into the intake manifold it turns from a liquid to a gas at –127 degrees F. This reduces the intake charge temperature by 65–75 degrees F. The cooler mixture packs more densely in the combustion chamber, letting the engine make even more power.

Generally, every 10 degrees F reduction in the incoming cylinder charge adds 1% more horsepower. A 75 degree drop will add 7% more power just from the denser air/fuel mixture caused by cooling.

How It's Used

In motorcycle applications, whether street or racing, N_2O and fuel are combined by means of spray nozzles located just upstream of the cylin-

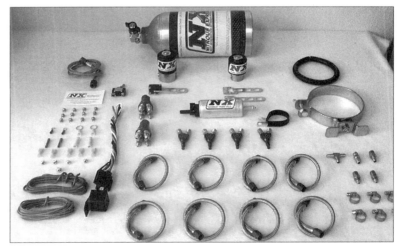

Nitrous Express has a Pro Mod setup for 4-cylinder engines that comes with 100-150-200-250 hp jets. All the necessary mounting hardware is included. *Nitrous Express*

All Nitrous Express motorcycle installations use the same Piranha nozzle to mix fuel and N₂O. This one is feeding a V-twin. *Nitrous Express*

The nitrous oxide bottle must be mounted with the inside siphon tube facing the lowest part of the bottle. There are marks on the bottle to aid alignment.

der inlet port, and mix before entering the combustion chamber. This additional charge of fuel and oxidizer, combined with the normal fuel charge introduced through the induction system, packs up to three times the amount of fuel into the chamber. Result: massive power increases.

A nitrous oxide system consists of:

- A bottle of liquefied N₂O. It can be any size from 2.5 pounds to whatever fits.
- Fuel pump to deliver the extra fuel required when the nitrous system is turned on.
- Braided steel lines to deliver the fuel and N₂O to their nozzles.
- Nozzles placed in the intake stream.
- Solenoids to turn on the N₂O and fuel.
- Wiring and brackets.

That's it! That and a large-flow petcock are all that's necessary to add 10, 20, up to 250 hp with the flick of a switch mounted on the bars or tied into the throttle so that the nitrous system comes on when the throttle is wide open. Electronics are available to control the solenoids so they turn on only in certain gears; kick in after a given number of seconds has elapsed since the clutch lever went home; or fire off in stages.

The average price for a N₂O kit runs between $550 and $750 depending on the number of engine cylinders. There are a lot of extras: gauges, pressure relief valves, two-stage controllers, wide-open-throttle switch, bottle transfer kits (to fill your own from a large bottle), arming switch, gas pressure gauge, and lots of others. What you choose will affect the price considerably.

Bolting on another 35 to 100 hp will affect reliability. The factory nitrous and gasoline jet kits are sized to keep wear to a minimum, but like anything that adds horsepower—turbochargers, superchargers, fuel, or whatever—the rods, pistons, crank, bearings, and power transmission parts will have to take the additional strain. I strongly advise using nitrous on engines with mileage below 5,000; much above that and there's already more wear on parts than you want in a serious racing engine.

Electric solenoids control the flow of N_2O and gasoline. Both are needed because N_2O works by supplying extra oxygen to fuel sprayed into the intake manifold apart from the carb or fuel injection.

This dragbike has the fuel and N_2O distributors mounted to the left of the carbs. There's one fuel line and one N_2O line feeding each cylinder. *Nitrous Express*

How to Control Nitrous Oxide

In drag racing, N_2O is used to provide an instant shot of power at a specific time. A single-stage system can be set to come on in the top two gears only, or it can operate any time the throttle is wide open against its stop (thereby actuating a micro switch). Multi-stage systems can become extremely complicated in operation. Using electronic controls such as those controlling the NOS Progressive Nitrous System (available from Schnitz Racing), a three-stage system can start the flow of nitrous oxide at any level you select, from 10% to 100% of its maximum flow rate, bringing in full flow over an adjustable time period. Nitrous controllers can also be used as a delay device. A delay switch can space out the times that the three stages of nitrous come on. The "time to full power" switch has delay circuits that are adjustable in 10 percent increments up to the total number of seconds from clutch release to full power. A dial-down feature can be set to operate larger nitrous jets in mid-range, but cut them off then turbo or supercharger boost peaks at high rpm.

Another advantage of a controllable three-stage system is the ability to run anywhere from one to three stages of flow at any given time, or in any gear. The launch can be with no N_2O; the shift into second can bring on one stage, third gear can use two or three stages, then top gear can drop off one stage to control lean conditions if you are running a turbo. A single-stage system can be piped to multiple injectors and set to operate with a pulse controller. This way, the flow of N_2O can be regulated through all the injectors by pulsing the solenoid valves. The only drawback to a pulse system is that one solenoid for three injectors may not be able to flow enough N_2O at high rpm.

Using a high-flow or multiple-stage nitrous system requires a fuel pressure regulator between the fuel pump and gasoline solenoid. Most N_2O fuel pumps flow 18 gallons per hour at 4 psi, which can support 200 hp but might be too much for your system. Regulators are adjustable from 0 to 12 psi by a simple screw adjuster on top of the regulator.

How long a 2.5-pound bottle will last depends greatly on the rider. Usually there's enough juice to hold the button down for sixty seconds total. Most manufacturers of N_2O systems recommend no more than 15 seconds at a time.

Nitrous oxide works especially well when used with turbocharging. We'll get into turbos in a bit, but for now, I'll mention that they add power by forcing the fuel charge into the cylinders. This produces heat which can lead to severe detonation. N_2O will cool a pressurized mixture by up to 60 degrees F and the nitrogen will help hold off detonation.

If an engine is being built specifically to race with nitrous, then cams with more exhaust overlap and duration will work the best. On the street, however, 99% of the time the N_2O system isn't being used, so pick cams for general operating conditions. There are specific cams for nitrous which have more aggressive exhaust lobe profiling, but since cam selection depends on bike weight, intended use, and final gearing, stick with the cam recommended for your particular application.

Where N_2O is really fun is in the midranges. It gives a torque hit that feels like kicking in the afterburners on an F-14 Tomcat. I've had the pleasure of riding a Suzuki Bandit 1200 and a Harley Dyna with nitrous systems. Admittedly, the 'Zook gave a better power hit, but they were both punch-it-and-hang-on bikes.

The Harley had what I thought was an interesting switching system. The owner rigged a double-pole-double-throw (DPDT) switch downstream of his left turn signal switch. The way it worked was;

1. Flip the switch over to N_2O operation.
2. Get the bike rolling in third.
3. Pin the throttle.
4. Hit the left turn signal.
5. Wave bye-bye!

The 'Zook was a bit different. It was wired so that the "on" switch operated with wide-open-throttle in any gear. Another manual switch was installed in-line to disable the solenoids so the bike would operate normally. Use a little ingenuity in hiding the bottle and no one will know you are N_2O-propelled. Great Fun!

If you want to learn more about nitrous oxide systems, see Joe Haile's book, *Motorcycle Turbocharging, Supercharging and Nitrous Oxide,* Whitehorse Press, 1997.

CHAPTER 12

Turbocharging and Supercharging

Turbochargers

A turbocharger converts waste heat energy coming out of the engine exhaust into mechanical motion that force-feeds the incoming air/fuel mixture into the engine's combustion chamber. A lot of heat energy is wasted through the exhaust; some of it can be captured to provide a substantial increase of horsepower.

A turbocharger is a rather simple mechanical device. It consists of a single shaft, mounted on a central bearing, with an exhaust impeller at one end and an intake impeller at the other. Each impeller runs inside its own housing, one being fed by the engine's exhaust and the other connected to the intake tract.

Hot exhaust gasses flow from the cylinder head, down the exhaust pipes from each cylinder where they are collected into a single pipe and fed into the exhaust side of the turbocharger, causing the impeller to spin at up to 140,000 rpm. Through a common shaft, the exhaust impeller drives the intake impeller, pressurizing the intake stream and forcing more fuel/air mixture into the cylinders. There is a tremendous amount of heat carried by the exhaust gasses, and it's not uncommon to see the cast iron exhaust case turn a cherry red. It is very important for turbo life to ensure that sufficient oil feed is maintained to the center shaft bearing. Usually the bearing is pressure fed from the engine's oil supply from the positive side of the oil pump, and a piped oil return sends the now-hot oil back to the engine's sump. Some turbo applications on water-cooled engines have a water jacket around the central turbo bearing, which stabilizes temperatures and aids in heat transfer.

I have measured temperature at the exhaust housing of the turbo and found 600 degrees F ninety seconds after shutdown. This is why it's imperative to let the engine run for at least one minute at idle before shutting down. This will let the excess heat in the turbine bearing area dissipate. If the heat isn't allowed to bleed down, oil left in the bearing housing will burn down to a sticky, gummy mess that will stop oil flow and squeak the turbo.

John Baltera got a little carried away when he began looking for more performance from his Yamaha V-Max. There's a supercharger mounted on top of the V-4 engine, and it's driven by the large pulley on the crank. The second pulley in the middle of the engine is for belt tensioning. He says horsepower is "sufficient for whatever needs to be passed." *John Baltera*

A turbocharger consists of an exhaust chamber (on the left), an impeller (center), and an inlet volute (right). *Garrett*

Street bikes can benefit from a turbo, but an intercooler should be used between the turbo and intake manifold to keep inlet temperatures down. This Hayabusa has an aluminum intercooler mounted in front of the radiator.

Controlling Inlet Charge Temperatures

On the inlet side of the turbo the fresh intake charge is compressed by the impeller and forced into the combustion chamber. In the compression process a lot of heat is generated as the molecules are squeezed together. Sometimes, an intercooler is placed in-line between the turbo and intake valve to cool the charge down before it enters the engine. For every 10 degrees F drop in temperature, horsepower increases by one percent. A 70 degree drop will increase horsepower seven percent.

Intercoolers act like radiators, except they cool the incoming air/fuel mixture instead of the engine coolant. There are two types of intercoolers: air-to-air, where the heated incoming mixture is cooled by air passing over it; and air-to-water, where the mixture is cooled by radiator coolant. Either type can lower the incoming charge temperature by 65–85 degrees F. A cooler air/fuel charge will be denser, packing more oxygen and producing more power. As mentioned above, a N_2O kit will also cool the incoming charge, so it makes good sense to use one in conjunction with a turbo installation.

Together, a turbo and a N_2O system will easily add 150 rear-wheel horsepower to a 1200cc–1420cc machine.

Controlling Boost Pressure

Turbocharged engines build power as the throttle is opened, the engine picks up revs, and the flow of exhaust gasses increases in volume and temperature, factors that help spin the exhaust impeller up to speeds at which the intake impeller can begin to build pressure. In a normally aspirated engine, the intake usually runs at a partial vacuum, while a turbocharged engine sees positive intake pressure. A turbocharger is said to be making power when the intake pressure exceeds atmospheric pressure. This means that the turbo boost gauge—which reads from 30 inches of vacuum to 100 psig (pounds per square inch gauge) of boost—will indicate negative pressure (expressed as inches of vacuum) until the turbo spins up fast enough to drive the intake pressure above atmospheric (gauge) pressure. A boost of 5 psi means that intake pressure is 5 psi above the local ambient pressure. An indication on a compound vacuum/pressure gauge of 0 psi is actually measuring ambient atmospheric pressure. This is why you will see pressures sometimes listed as *psig* or *psia,* where psia is pounds per square inch *absolute.* At sea level, the air pressure is 14.7 psia, or 0 psig. In Denver, at an elevation of 5,000 feet above sea level, the air pressure is around 12 psia, but still 0 psig, since "gauge" pressure is always relative to the local, surrounding pressure. I refer to psig in all forced induction readings, even if I just call it psi.

The maximum boost that most drag racing engines can sustain without damage is around 35–38 psi. My friend Funnybike Mike said his boost regulator hung open on one run and the gauge stuck at 54 psig. He said the motor went a little lean at the top, but sure pulled like hell through the lights. Upon opening the engine, everything was found to be straight—surprise! He should have melted or punched a piston with that much pressure.

Turbo pressure is regulated by a waste gate, or exhaust bypass valve, which is controlled by the pressure of the incoming air/fuel mixture. The inlet pressure pushes against a spring-loaded diaphragm which holds the waste gate flapper closed. When the inlet tract exceeds a preset pressure, the diaphragm causes the waste gate to open, allowing exhaust gasses to bleed away from the turbo before they can reach the exhaust turbine. When the inlet pressure drops, the waste gate closes, allowing the exhaust gasses to flow into the impeller again.

Controlling Detonation

The best way to handle detonation is to use a knock sensor with ignition retard that will take some of the advance out of the engine and back down the timing. Most turbo-powered Funnybikes back down on their advance after the second or third stage of nitrous cuts in and the turbo boost has peaked, just to keep detonation to a minimum. Later in this chapter, an interview with Powerdyne Automotive Products (makers of superchargers) explains high boost pressure, detonation, and how to keep your engine from being damaged by detonation. Boost is boost, regardless of whether it's obtained with a turbo or supercharger. Using either one on a race bike

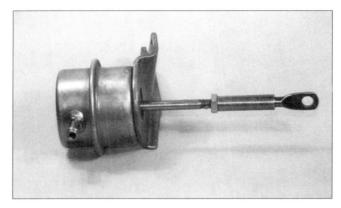

This is a turbocharger wastegate diaphragm. Manifold pressure entering through the fitting on the can pushes against a preload spring set to operate at the required inlet pressure. At that pressure the rod on the right extends and opens a bypass valve that allows some of the exhaust gas to bypass the turbo exhaust inlet. This device creates the "whoosh" sound a turbo makes when it reaches maximum throttle and manifold pressure.

will require some type of detonation control or spark retard. Intercoolers can also help by removing heat from the incoming air. Water injection can be used to cool down combustion chambers, by spraying water under pressure through a spraybar mounted in the inlet tract. Spray operation can be electronically controlled or manually operated.

Turbo Racing Applications

Turbochargers have a lag inherent in their operation that can cause slight driveability problems on the street, but in drag racing lag isn't a problem. The lag is caused by the time it takes the turbocharger to spin up and begin producing effective pressure in the intake tract. To counteract this lag on the starting line, you can open the throttle enough to get the turbo spinning and producing positive pressure. A handy technique is to use a two-stage rev limiter with the first (starting line) rev limit set to about 6,000 rpm. That engine speed will enable the impeller to spin up to a moderate rpm and produce intake pressure. When you launch, the turbo is already spinning fast enough so that it can reach maximum boost very quickly.

Turbo boost can be controlled through the entire run to limit rear wheel torque to what the

Hayabusa Turbo. A pressurized plenum on top of the carbs replaces the stock airbox. The pipe on top is the feed from the turbo. *Mr. Turbo*

track can take without spinning the rear tire. Boost can be kept down below 15 psi through the lower gears, then raised to 25–40 psi for the last three to four seconds of the run by controlling how much exhaust bypasses through the wastegate.

Turbochargers can be set up in either of two configurations on a carbureted engine: blow-through or draw-through.

Blow-Through Configuration

A blow-through installation has the turbo discharge ducted to the intakes of the carbs. This is how most bolt-on kits work. The single biggest drawback with this configuration is sealing the carbs at the throttle shafts and carb-to-intake manifold junction. Newer CV carbs have adequate seals at the throttle shaft; however, you need to be sure that the float bowls are pressurized to the same pressure as the venturi so that fuel can feed and won't be forced out the vent. The best way to avoid these problems is to seal the carbs in a pressure box. An electric fuel pump capable of producing more pressure than boost pressure must be used. Stock throttle linkage and manifolds may be used.

Draw-Through Configuration

A draw-through arrangement places the carburetor in front of the turbo, so the air/fuel mixture is sucked through the turbo inlet, then pressurized and blown into the turbo-to-cylinder head mani-

fold. This system uses only one carb, S&S and Mikuni being the most popular. This system requires all new manifolding and throttle linkage to adapt to the single carb because of its new position on the end of the turbo. A low pressure fuel pump is used in conjunction with a larger petcock and fuel pressure regulator. Some draw-through setups use gravity feed only, but there's a good chance that the fuel feed won't be sufficient and the mixture will go exceedingly lean at the top end.

One disadvantage to a draw-through turbo is that the greater distance between the carb and intake valve can cause fuel puddling or separation in the intake tract. Careful design of the inlet tract can help alleviate this problem; so can thoroughly warming up the engine before making a run. This problem can also cause poor idle and off-idle response, so a draw-through system will perform much better on a drag bike, where idle isn't a concern, than a street bike.

On either type of turbo installation, a pop-off valve should be installed on the pressure side of the intake manifold. It will open and reduce manifold pressure if the wastegate sticks shut or the inlet pressure spikes upon rapidly closing the throttle. Set the pop-off valve to 5 psi above the maximum inlet operating pressure, and be sure to duct its waste gasses away from the bike and rider.

Turbocharging works especially well with EFI, as long as the stock ECM has enough latitude to ensure a proper air/fuel mixture throughout the full rpm range, or it can be reprogrammed to handle the increased inlet flow. Motorcycles with EFI are easy to turbocharge, and the results are impressive. BMW, Buell, Ducati, Harley-Davidson, Yamaha, and others have EFI-equipped bikes on the market, and pretty soon, all motorcycles sold for street use will have to go to EFI to meet emission standards.

Installing a turbo on EFI-equipped bikes is simply a matter of removing the stock inlet tract from air box to intake manifold and bolting on the turbo and related piping and intercooler. A remap of the ECM, or something like a Dynojet Power Commander might be needed, but the whole installation should take a mechanically-inclined person no more than a long afternoon.

With the high quality kits available from more than nine manufacturers, for many models of Honda, Kawasaki, BMW, Suzuki, Harley-Davidson, Ducati, and Yamaha, bugs and start-up problems should be minimal.

Precautions

Turbocharged engines have the potential to develop up to 50% more horsepower than a normally-aspirated engine, while not compromising reliability to a great extent. As mentioned above, a turbo's greatest drawback is heat. On a nine-second run, this isn't too much of a problem, and the turbo's simplicity and ease of installation make it a good choice for improving performance. However, running for longer periods of time will require that the excess heat be removed. Be sure that any pipe or bracket that is in direct contact with the turbo is insulated from the turbo and rider.

I've seen some installations where the turbo on a motorcycle engine was sourced from a wrecked automobile. In a word, don't. Used parts have no place on a drag bike. The auto turbo is sized for a specific type and displacement engine, usually much larger than the bike motor, and operates under conditions very different from a drag bike. All turbos are not the same; some need a water feed for cooling; some need a high flow of oil at 30 to 40 psi for their center bearing—something a stock bike oil pump would have a hard time providing. All bracketry and piping would have to be hand-fabricated—which isn't a real problem, just an added expense for hand labor—but why reinvent the wheel. Most of the companies listed below can manufacture a kit to fit anything on two wheels at a reasonable cost. However, if you've been down the turbo road before, and have the necessary knowledge, tools and equipment, building your own system can save some money.

Turbo Suppliers and Manufacturers

- Mr. Turbo—281-442-7113; www.mrturbo.com
- Hahn Racecraft—630-801-1417; www.turbosystems.com

On this Funnybike, the exhaust is routed through that wrapped pipe up to the turbo. Exhaust gas spins the impeller and exits through the large chrome pipe. Turbo bikes run fairly quietly because the turbo acts as a muffler of sorts.

- American Turbo Systems—941-403-0198; www.americanturbo.com
- Aerocharger—716-345-0055; www.aerocharger.com
- Westech—512-847-8918; www.westech.home.mindspring.com
- Mad Max—203-574-5237

Blowers and Superchargers

The terms "blower" and "supercharger" are used interchangeably in the racing world. For simplicity, I'll use only the latter term here.

A supercharger forces air into the intake by mechanical means. There are numerous types available for motorcycle use. Superchargers and turbochargers accomplish essentially the same thing: pressurizing the intake charge, they force more air/fuel mixture into the combustion chamber. Superchargers use a mechanical drive system to turn two impellers that squeeze the incoming mixture and compress it into the cylinders. The amount of pressure delivered by the supercharger is determined by how fast it turns.

The impellers are driven by pulleys and belts, the mechanical power being taken off the engine side of the clutch or directly from the crankshaft. Boost is relatively constant throughout the engine speed range and does not suffer the delay inherent with turbochargers while they spin the

Larry McBride runs a Whipple Charger on his Top Fuel bike. This cutaway shows how the impellers build up air pressure and force it into the intake manifold. *Whipple*

impeller up to speed. Hit the throttle and the power is there—right now, no delay.

Every good performance increase comes with its own set of restrictions and hazards; various problems can accompany a supercharger installation. In the case of superchargers installed on motorcycles with needle, ball, or roller bearing engines, brinnelling can occur. This happens when very large loads are applied to the bearings while they are rotating at low speed and low oil pressure, as might take place with radial loads developed by driving supercharger pulleys. The net result is spalling—material coming off the bearing—pounding distortion of the bearing, or displacement of metal in the races. None of these problems would be welcomed, and all of them can be avoided, either by using a plain bearing engine with two-piece rods, by keeping the boost down (by proper selection of pulley size) until the revs are up, or by not hammering the throttle wide open until the motor spins up and there's enough oil pressure to support the bearings.

For racing purposes, brinnelling isn't a problem because the engine is revved up without a load on it just before the clutch goes home. Mainly it's something to be aware of on street-driven supercharged engines.

As effective as superchargers are on drag bikes, it's not really practical to spend $4,500–$6,000 to hang one on a 750, so they mostly turn up on Top Fuel bikes and in other classes where supercharging is legal.

An engine has to be built to take the extra stress generated by forced induction; usually this means forged pistons, aftermarket rods and, if not a billet crank, then one that has been indexed properly, welded, and balanced.

A supercharger requires a lot of power to turn, so its drive has to be well planned and engineered for strength as well as safety. A pulley on the clutch or crankshaft has to be supported on both sides to eliminate flex. Locating the supercharger itself is difficult on a street-framed bike since there usually isn't enough room in front of, or behind the engine. The supercharger usually ends up hung off one side of the bike.

Then there's the matter of feeding the thing. You must find room for injectors or carbs on the intake side of the supercharger, and there has to be enough space on the discharge side to build a manifold between the discharge outlet and the intake ports on the head. All this must be taken into account when building a frame for a drag bike. Top Fuel bikes such as Larry McBride's are long enough—at 17 feet or more—to accommodate a blower easily, its idle gear (used for adjusting the belt), and the related manifolds. McBride's chassis has enough room to take all this and still let his lanky body stretch out completely without hanging out past the rear wheel.

If you want to learn more about forced induction systems, see Joe Haile's book, *Motorcycle Turbocharging, Supercharging and Nitrous Oxide,* Whitehorse Press, 1997.

Frequently Asked Questions About Superchargers
from Powerdyne Automotive Products . . .

Q. What exactly does a supercharger do?

A. A supercharger forces additional air and fuel into an engine. This occurs under full throttle or under load, not at normal cruise or most normal driving conditions. A large displacement engine makes more power than a small displacement engine because it can convert larger amounts fuel and air into energy. A supercharger allows a smaller engine, like a 1000cc to 2000cc four-cylinder racing motor, to do the same thing, but only when the power is needed.

Q. What is boost?

A. Boost is the amount of pressure in pounds per square inch (psi) that a supercharger creates. The air that goes into a normally-aspirated engine is drawn in by the vacuum created when the pistons travel downward in the cylinder bore. This air goes into the normally-aspirated engine at atmospheric pressure of 14.7 psi (at sea level). On a blown engine, the boost is the amount of additional pressure the inlet charge has over atmospheric pressure. So, if the supercharger on your motorcycle engine makes ten pounds of boost, that means the inlet charge is atmospheric pressure (14.7 psi) plus the ten pounds of boost for a total of 24.7 psi.

Q. How much boost can you normally run?

A. This depends on what the engine is intended to do. Racing engines can use between ten and twenty pounds of boost for short periods of time, but if the supercharger is on a street engine, six to nine pounds of boost is the limit.

Q. How much compression ratio can be used on a racing engine?

A. This varies from engine to engine. A good rule of thumb is to run nine pounds of boost with a 9:1 engine. Use less boost with a higher compression ratio and more as the ratio drops. You would like to run as much compression ratio and as much boost as possible without the onset of detonation under ideal conditions.

Q. Which is better, high boost and low compression ratio, or low boost and high compression ratio?

A. A low boost/high compression ratio is the best. The combination of supercharger boost coupled with the static compression ratio provides the Effective Compression Ratio (ECR). The math gets complicated when determining ECR; however, as an example, if you are running an 8.75:1 static ratio and six pounds of boost, the ECR will be 12.32:1. Under racing circumstances, an ECR of 15:1 to 17:1 can be run, provided the fuel will support the ratio and the engine components are strong enough to take the strain.

Q. How is the boost changed?

A. On any belt-driven blower, the boost can be changed by changing the sizes of the drive pulley and the driven (supercharger) pulley. Supercharger impeller speed can be raised or lowered depending upon the pulley ratios. A 1:1 ratio means the driven pulley turns once for every revolution of the drive pulley. The driven pulley can be smaller than the drive pulley for an "overerdriven" blower. If the driven pulley has a larger circumference than the drive pulley, the blower will be "underdriven."

Supercharger boost pressure can be moved higher or lower by swapping pulleys around. Without a boost gauge it's impossible to tell exactly what boost the blower is producing. A boost gauge reads either pounds per square inch absolute (psia) or pounds per square inch gauge (psig). Most boost gauges read 0 psi with nothing attached to them, which is psig shortened to psi. If the absolute pressure was taken into consideration, the boost gauge would read 14.7 psi at sea level and whatever boost the supercharger produced would be added to this. Which gauge you use makes no difference as long as you know what you are reading.

(continued)

Q. Doesn't more boost put a higher strain on engine parts?

A. Yes, with qualifications. An engine running under very high boost— 20 to 25 psi—will put a lot of strain on an engine compared to one that is normally aspirated. But—and here's where the technology, work and money enter the picture—supercharged racing engines are built with all rotating components constructed to take a much greater level of stress. This is done by making the parts larger, building them out of better material, or replacing them as often as every run, or all the above.

For instance, some supercharged or turbocharged classes like Funnybike have to run a stock crank, but the crank is balanced, stress relieved, X-rayed for cracks, journals polished and radiused and finally checked and rechecked for end-to-end and rotating trueness. Then, if it will run ten miles (40 runs) before turning into a lawn decoration, it's doing well. Here again, detonation is the biggest problem. As long as detonation is controlled, a supercharged engine should have few problems.

Q. What causes detonation?

A. Too much boost, too much ignition advance, or too much compression ratio, or a combination of the three will cause the fuel to detonate instead of burn evenly. Detonation occurs when the air/fuel charge ignites itself before the piston is in the proper place, or before the spark plug fires. When this happens, ignition takes place while the piston is still rising in the cylinder, which puts a tremendous load on the piston, connecting rod, bearings and crank. The usual result on a mildly-tuned racing engine is broken piston ring lands or, on fuel engines running high blower pressure, the pistons can break, rods shatter, crank bend or break, or the entire engine can disintegrate. This is why retaining straps and ballistic blankets have to be used.

Q. How can detonation be controlled?

A. Some companies who make racing ignitions offer a device called "boost retard." These black boxes allow a certain amount of ignition retard to be added to control detonation. This means the blown engine can come off the line with lots of advance and low blower speed, but shift to less advance as the blower builds boost. Some of these controls have a sensor that can hear engine detonation, and will automatically retard the ignition, which will let the piston travel a bit farther before firing the sparkplug. Some boost retards have a manual knob that will let you back down the advance at the onset of detonation, but a drag race happens so fast and the environment is so loud that either you won't even hear the detonation, or the race will happen so rapidly that the only time you will notice the knob is in the pits.

Q. What will happen if the blower belt breaks? Will the engine blow?

A. The only thing that will happen if the blower belt breaks during a run is that all the horses will go back to the barn. Nothing will happen to the engine's internal parts. On a Top Fuel bike with a large nitro delivery system, the fuel pump could pump a lot of unburned nitro past the injectors if the blower quits and the FI is still delivering fuel at high engine rpm. This scenario can lead to an explosion. Watch the condition of your blower belts and change them every year.

Q. What's a ballpark figure to install a supercharger on an engine?

A. Just adding a blower to an already-modified racing engine is not the way to go. The engine and blower have to be engineered as a unit. Cams, induction system, compression ratio, engine displacement and many other factors have to be considered before the supercharger is bolted to the intake manifold. Just the components will easily run $4,500 for the supercharger, drive system, fuel injection or carburetion, custom manifolds, fuel pumps and related piping. This doesn't count all the custom work needed to fit the bits and pieces to the engine and around the frame. See the photos of the supercharged Yamaha V-Max elsewhere in this book for a good look at a custom installation on a bike that can light up the rear tire the entire length of the quarter mile.

Powerdyne Automotive Products (www.powerdyne.com) ∎

CHAPTER 13

Transmissions and Shifters

Transmissions

If you run a Suzuki, Yamaha or Kawasaki, filling your transmission requirements is a cinch. For assistance, call Orient Express (800-645-6521; www.orientexpress.com) or Fast by Gast (800-866-3880; www.fastbygast.com), tell them what you have, what class you are running, and they will set you up with the transmission. Choices range from replacement stock ratios with stronger gears, to undercut gears, automatics, and complete custom-made transmissions. The class you run will determine the type of transmission you can use.

Automatic transmissions come in two flavors: partial- and full-automatic. A partial-auto transmission has to have the ignition killed momentarily while one gear is disengaged and the next higher gear selected. The full-auto transmission does not need the ignition cut-out; instead, it holds the lower gear engaged while the higher gear is hooked up. This keeps the chassis from becoming unloaded and reduces lost time in shifting.

Undercut transmissions have the dogs on the gears undercut, or slightly cut back by a machine shop so that they stay in gear a bit better.

Billet transmissions, depending on who makes them, have all the major parts CNC-cut from stronger-than-stock billet steel.

You can have your transmission reworked, or buy one complete. Whether you choose a 3-, 4-, or 5-speed depends on the type of bike you have and its class. If you plan to run a fairly stock engine, then the factory-stock parts will hold up to a season or two of racing. If the bike has a few

miles on it—20,000 or more—then you should open the cases and rebuild the transmission.

On a bike with a non-unit transmission, such as a Harley Twin Cam, the transmission can be removed from the bike and modified without touching the engine. However, most imported bikes have their transmissions unitized with the engine and only a minor amount of work can be done on the transmission without a complete teardown. If your bike is one of these, you will have to take into consideration what shape the engine and transmission are in before tearing them down, because if you open the engine, at the minimum you will have to replace the rings and bearings. If you do that, you might as well go

Sputh, S&S and other companies make aftermarket cases for V-twin transmissions. They are 200% stronger than stock and can be fitted with many different gear ratios. *Sputh*

If you run a Suzuki, Orient Express will build you a set of billet gears for your 5-speed transmission.

The solution to the Hayabusa's transmission problems was provided by Fast By Gast (www.fastbygast.com) in the form of heavy duty parts. Second gear, third gear, and the output shaft were junked and Gast's racing parts installed. The gears were undercut, the shift forks replaced and all the parts slid onto a new set of industrial-strength bearings. Then the OEM clutch decided it couldn't take the torque and developed a bad case of the slips. Out came all the stock clutch parts and in went a multi stage lock-up unit built by MTC, a company owned by Top Fuel champion Tony Lang (www.mpsmall.com/mtc). The clutch is the secret weapon in getting the power to the ground.

After all that work, his 'Busa became the ultimate "street cleaner." It ran smoothly, could hardly be heard (the turbo acted as a big muffler), rode easily and, once the boost went positive, disappeared like Hans Solo's Millennium Falcon in warp drive.

Transmission Gears

Why use different numbers of gears in racing transmissions? It all depends on the type of engine and induction systems used. Top Fuel bikes rely on a combination of tire growth and final gearing to provide the needed ratios from the starting line all the way down the track; they sometimes run high-gear-only or two-speed transmissions. Larry McBride runs a B&J two-speed on his sub-six-second Top Fuel bike.

A turbo or heavily-nitrous bike likes a three-speed because the engine can pull harder with wide ratios. Most street bikes with five-speeds will cross the finish line in fourth gear. Fifth is an overdrive ratio and the engine has to pull harder to drive it, plus extra time is spent shifting. The five-speed automatics are different, though, and the bike's final gearing is set so the engine is right at red-line as the bike breaks the finish lights.

Four-speed transmissions, with the ratio of fourth the same as the ratio of fifth in a racing five-speed, are used in very-high-horsepower bikes to save the shift time going into fifth, and because the engine can pull better against a wide-ratio gear set.

for a big-bore kit, weld the crank, shot peen the rods, clean up the cases, open up an oil line or two, and let's not even talk about what to do with the head. Spend a lot of money.

So, you should make some decisions about both the engine and transmission long before you apply wrenches. If you're new to the sport, and plan on flogging your bog-stock Hayabusa for a race or six, you should be able to have some serious fun before you need to open it up.

I talked to a racer down at a meet in Palmdale, Calif. who was running a 'Busa with a turbo (he said it needed a bit more kick!) who said he'd run ten events in the last eleven months without doing so much as adjusting the valves. He even rode the bike around the pits on food runs.

He figured he had made 35 to 37 full-tilt-and-boogie runs with it—all in the low-9-second range—and his only major expense was tires. The bike *did* have a long swingarm, $3,500 turbo setup with intercooler, air shifter, undercut transmission, and a few other goodies, so it wasn't exactly a cheap proposition. He allowed that counting purchase price, he had a tad over $20,000 in the bike. He had run the bike a few times with the turbo and a stock set of gears in the transmission, but had a lot of trouble trying to make it shift properly and stay in gear.

The button just below the gauge operates the air shifter. It has a safety pin in it to keep from operating accidentally if the button gets hit or pushed at the wrong time.

One thing to be watchful for when pulling a lot of gear in a wide-ratio trans is detonation. After the 1000-ft mark, a 300-hp-or-better engine has built quite a load, producing copious amounts of heat under intense strain and it might start detonating. That's why high-power bikes such as turbo-nitrous Funnybikes have their black box set to take some of the advance out of the engine for the last 1-1/2 to 2 seconds of the run.

High Pressure Shifters

Shifting a drag bike by pulling in the clutch, lifting your foot and letting the clutch back out is a nice way to ride down the return road, but a slow way to race. Many close races are won or lost in less than .01 seconds. It takes .20 seconds to blink. It takes .44 seconds to foot-shift. Air shifters can cut shift time in half.

An air shifter consists of an air bottle with 120–160 psig, a solenoid, air hose, slave cylinder and linkage, momentary ignition kill switch, and a shift button. When you push the button, ignition is momentarily interrupted, the solenoid opens, air flows to the slave cylinder and the ram shoves the shift lever into the next gear. A spring in the cylinder returns the ram so it's ready for the next shift. Killing the ignition takes the load off the gears and lets the dogs shift into engagement.

Some air shifters are hooked into an automatic shift control that can be preset to shift at any rpm. This is more consistent than shifting by hand because it shifts at the same point every

Weismann Transmissions

Traction Products, Inc. (949-645-4064; gearboxes@hotmail.com) builds Weismann Transmissions for Pro Stock, Pro Mod and Funnybike classes. Their newest product is the Quickshift six-speed transmission that Chris Weismann has just finished for George Bryce's Star Racing Pro Stock Suzuki. They also build three- and four-speed transmissions for Suzuki and Kawasaki cases. They are electro-air shifted and represent a completely different approach to transferring power. There are no shift forks, bushings, barrels, bolted gears, thrust washers, shims, or foot shifters used with these transmissions.

Burnouts can be done in any gear and gears can be shifted during burnouts, saving wear on the engine. The throttle can be rolled on or off in any gear at any time without any problems. ∎

Star Racing uses this brand new Quickshift six-speed transmission in their Pro Stock Suzuki. *Weismann*

The only way to get good, fast shifts is with an air shifter. A tank, which can be part of the frame tubing, holds enough air pressure to shift through three to six gears simply by hitting a button. An ignition interlock can be set up on the same button to temporarily kill the ignition to unload the gears while shifting. This one's on a Harley.

When doing a burnout, the transmission must be in second or third gear. Remember to shift back to first after coming out of the box.

run. It can also work against you, should you want to short shift or hold the transmission in a lower gear longer.

Sometimes nitrogen is used in the tank because it holds a more consistent pressure through ambient temperature changes.

Another device that's useful for cutting reaction time—this time at the starting line—is a line lock. Bracket racers who need to stage at the same spot every run and not take the chance of rolling backwards, use an electrical lock on the rear wheel that's tied into the rpm control and releases at a preset rpm. This keeps the bike from rolling backwards out of the staging lights. It can be set to hold the rear wheel locked until your engine reaches clutch release rpm, then it releases the rear wheel exactly as the clutch starts to hook up.

CHAPTER 14

A Transfer of Power

Clutch

Here's where it helps to have a magician on the pit crew. Setting up a racing clutch takes equal amounts of knowledge, ability and prestidigitation to put just the right amount of power down to the asphalt at just the right time. A clutch is no more than a method of regulating power transfer from the engine to the transmission by means of friction devices.

Normal clutch construction consists of a fixed number of steel plates sandwiched between a fixed number of friction plates that are steel plates with some type of friction material similar to disc brake pad material coated on them. All the plates are held in a basket that is riveted to a gear that's driven through a primary chain or belt by another, smaller, gear on the end of the crank. The fiber friction plates have teeth on the outside that are engaged with a set on the inside of the basket, while the steel plates are toothed to a clutch hub connected to the transmission's main shaft.

The plates are forced together by clutch springs so that the inner and outer plates are driven at the same speed by the engine through the primary drive. When you pull on the clutch lever, you are counteracting pressure from the clutch springs, allowing the plates to disengage and letting the engine run while the transmission stays stationary.

Where the magic is needed is in the clutch engagement and release method and timing. If all we needed was to get the gears turning, a clutch could be just an off-on switch. Let out the lever and bam, you're moving. This wouldn't work on the street, because the engine would bog, or you

would have to feed so much power into the clutch that something else would have to give until the road speed caught up to the engine speed. Some aftermarket clutches work very much like this—nothing, nothing, nothing, BLAM—you're gone.

On a race track, applying too much power to the rear tire will do nothing but cause it to spin. Looks neat, all that smoke, but horsepower is being wasted making white swirls instead of doing work. A bit of tire spin is okay, but some high horsepower bikes can easily spin the rear tire—even a 14-inch slick—down the entire length of the track. Somewhere the power delivery has to be metered.

This is a complete replacement Pro Clutch for a V-twin motor. You can see the fiber/steel plate arrangement on the upper left. *Rivera Engineering*

This bike runs a centrifugal clutch that locks up as the revs climb. By changing the weights next to the clutch springs, lockup will occur at different clutch rotational speeds.

This is a custom manufactured clutch basket for a V-twin, but four-cylinder baskets look about the same. It will take instant, high-torque loads without expanding. It's available with different friction plates and various strength springs. *Rivera*

To meter power to the track you could feather the throttle, except that would break parts in the transmission or engine on turbocharged or supercharged bikes with automatics. Also, running at less than full throttle can keep the engine out of its power range and make it bog when you finally pin the throttle. This leaves only the clutch as a place to control power transfer. When you use an air shifter, and either kill the ignition between shifts, or run an automatic transmission, you engage the clutch fully to leave the line and don't touch it again until shutdown. So, feathering the clutch at the lever isn't an option. The clutch has to be able to slip until the track catches up to the motor. This is done by controlling clutch lockup.

Both Kawasaki and Suzuki clutches can use a centrifugal lockup mechanism that contains adjustable weights on the ends of engagement arms to exert more pressure against the clutch plates as the speed increases. They can be set to lock up at various rpm, your choice depending on track surface conditions such as the type of asphalt, the amount of rubber already laid down, horsepower, and a lot of other variables. You use the clutch lever at the start, but then the air shifter takes over and the lockup weights will hold the clutch plates engaged.

You will hear the term *slider clutch* in connection with racing clutches. This is almost the same thing as a lockup clutch except that no clutch lever is needed. Centrifugal force alone causes the clutch to lock up. A lot of racers set the clutch to start locking up at 4,500–5,000 rpm. Simply wind on the throttle and you're gone. These clutches work in conjunction with electronic step boxes that can be programmed to perform a multitude of functions with ignition advance, nitrous stages, and turbo boost, as the clutch plates engage. The first step on a lockup clutch can be set just below the starting line departure rpm, so that when you're waiting for the green light with the engine peaked on the first step, the clutch won't engage, but when the box is shifted into the higher setting and the revs climb, the clutch immediately hooks up.

High-horsepower bikes can slip a normal clutch all the way through the quarter, which slows speeds by as much as 5 mph and fries the friction discs harder than a McDonald's French fry left in the oil. For street bikes, the stock clutch plates will work adequately for occasional racing. Stronger springs are a good idea for racing, but they will create a stiffer clutch lever. But hey, you weren't planning on touring on the bike were you? It's easy to tell when the stock equipment is being overpowered. A clutch generates a lot of heat when it slips excessively. The smell of a burning clutch is one you won't forget. Stock plates can easily warp from the excessive heat generated by two or three runs.

If you're going to go drag racing, you can save yourself a lot of grief and install a racing clutch first thing. All bikes can benefit from a change to a billet clutch basket, but Kawasaki's stock clutch basket seems to be able to take the strain of a medium-hot engine without problems. I've seen a clutch let go and it isn't a pretty sight. Picture a chain saw spinning at 6,000 rpm right next to your leg (and other important items) and you get the idea.

If the drive plates in your clutch are aluminum, there's a major improvement available that beats going to steel plates. Aluminum akadized plates, going under the brand name "Cryoplates," use a cryogenic (ultra low temperature) process to deposit a coating on aluminum plates that greatly decreases wear and slows down warpage. They're 65% lighter than steel plates and the coating provides a ceramic-like barrier to heat transfer while still being able to hook up to the fiber plates without slippage. A set of plates runs $85 to $100, which ain't cheap, but if they work as advertised and knock up to .10 second off short times, they're cheap. The only caveat is to not use them against Kevlar fiber discs. They're available through Schnitz.

Starters

Most stock starters work on stock-compression engines quite well. However, on normally-aspirated fuel motors or other high-compression engines, they fall short, especially if the motor's already warm and it needs a start. The fix? Buy a high-torque starter. Simple, isn't it? Just spend money!

Some Pro classes allow you to remove the starter and use a remote starter. To do so, a hex nut is fitted to the drive side of the crank so an external socket can be mated to it. To accomplish this, a bearing support and/or adapter plate is

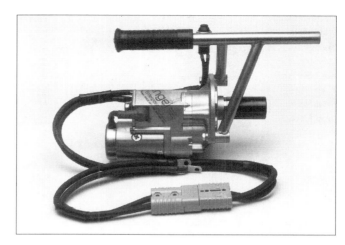

The remote starter runs from automotive batteries and is operated by the button on top of the grip bar. It's the only way to start a high compression fuel engine at the dragstrip. *Star Performance Parts*

A large bearing supports the starter nut and provides some external support for this Kawasaki's crank.

This V-twin is set up for a remote starter and air shifter. The shift lever is mounted so it can be reached easily by hand. The black box on the ground is a small battery charger, needed because the bike runs no alternator, which saves a few horsepower because of the loss of the charging power drag.

This remote starter uses two automotive batteries to provide the amps to spin a Top Fuel bike's engine. The fire extinguisher is a good idea.

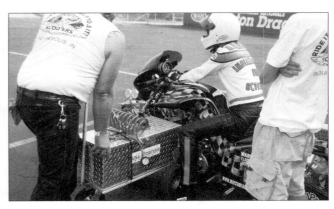

This start cart has everything in one package: air, batteries for the remote starter, and a few tools. It has a shaft on the front that hooks up with the V-Twin's crank. A high-compression fuel V-twin takes a lot of oomph to crank over.

fabricated to replace the sidecover. This also provides much needed additional support to the engine drive sprocket.

A remote starter uses up to two automotive-type batteries to turn over the engine. The engagement nut, or bolt, sticks through the cover, so that when it's time to fire the engine, you just switch on the ignition, prime the motor, crack the throttle, and place the starter socket on the crank.

Hit the button mounted on the starter's handle and away you go.

Lately, a lot of very fast bikes running in the 8-second bracket are turning up with factory starters, because the newer liquid-cooled high-compression (up to 13:1) engines had to have stronger starters to cope with the high squeeze. Must be part of the computer age; just push a button and go 8.89.

Here the remote starter is being engaged while the rider shoots gasoline into the carb by using a pressurized can that atomizes the gas for easier starts.

CHAPTER 15

Belts and Chains

Chains and Sprockets

Almost all new chain-driven street bikes run an O-ring chain. These are good things. They require very little lubrication, don't stretch, and seemingly never wear. They also take more horsepower to turn, and this is a bad thing. Use a standard, non-O-ring chain for drag racing. The Tsubaki 530 HQR solid roller chain works well with engines up to around 300 hp.

Were I to be fuelish, I'd go to an EK 630 "Top Fuel" chain. It's designed to handle up to 1200 hp, which ought to satisfy almost everyone except for Larry McBride or Jim McClure. Be sure to use only the master link made for the specific chain. If you use two master links with ten links between them, changing rear sprockets is made quite easy by simply removing the extra length of chain when you go to a smaller sprocket. It solves the problem of chain adjustment if there isn't enough take-up in the axle adjuster to accommodate a fixed-length chain.

Chain prices run $80 to $95 for Tsubaki 630 and $140 for a 130-pin EK 630. Chain life varies according to the horsepower it has to transfer to what size slick. An abrupt launch (is there any other kind?) with a Top Fuel bike can put a 6-inch whip into the trailing (lower) side of the chain which shows there's a whole lot of stretch going on when the torque hits. I watch for stretch, sprocket wear, roller drag, and evidence of heat. With the chain off the bike, run it through your hands in a horizontal direction. If any links stick or don't want to pivot, replace the chain. Use a non-greasy lube when you first mount the chain, only lube it once or twice, and then only lightly, then swap it out after 25–30 runs.

Generating lots of power isn't a problem. Getting it to the asphalt is. This bike spun its rear wheel all 1340 feet. A faster way down the track is either to take some power out of the engine, or set the clutch lock-up higher. His reaction time was .546 as shown on the Winston tower.

A minimum of 530-size chain is needed to transfer the tremendous power produced by a turbocharged bike. Fuel bikes need a 630 size to handle their 1,000+ hp engines.

The basic American V-twin primary power transmission. The crank drives a belt that turns the clutch basket. When the clutch plates are engaged, they drive the transmission behind the clutch. The starter gear is to the right and above the clutch. The engine goes 'round, the transmission turns and the bike moves forward. When you look at it this way, it's pretty simple engineering. Nary a computer chip in sight. *Rivera*

As for sprockets, aluminum saves the most weight. Steel transfers the most horsepower and lasts a while longer. Always change sprockets when you change the chain. Bigger rear sprockets will transfer more torque. Smaller front sprockets can bind the chain and break. Always check for binding by spinning the wheel by hand before you run it under power.

Sometimes mounting a slick will require moving the countershaft sprocket outboard for clearance. This is done by installing a bearing support, made by Kosman or D&G (both available from Schnitz). By moving the countershaft sprocket 3 to 5 inches to the left, a wider swingarm and rear slick can be fitted.

Rivera builds a primary belt drive conversion for most Harleys. It's cleaner and stronger than the stock chain setup, plus it is vibration-free compared to a chain, so on the street it's quieter. *Rivera*

Belt Drives

All new bikes from Harley-Davidson now have belt drive. The factory originally recommended replacing them at 30,000 miles, or sooner if conditions warranted. A quick repair spare belt was enclosed with every new bike for the first few years, but this practice was dropped when Harley found that the final drive belts were lasting over 60,000 miles. Now they just recommend that you check the belt and replace it when worn.

How about racing, though? How often should a belt be replaced? Or, should you go to the considerable expense of converting over to a chain? I've talked to a number of Harley racers running semi-street bikes and they say the belt doesn't seem to give any problems. Watch for anything unusual, like stretching abnormally, tooth chipping, cord fraying, holes or rock penetrations. Other than that, go race.

Getting the Shaft

Some bikes use driveshafts for final drive, and some of their owners would like to do a little racing just for fun. I've owned both BMW and Yamaha shaft drive bikes including the Yamaha Seca Turbo and the BMW K100 and boxer twins. I've also had the dubious pleasure of rebuilding a driveshaft in a Yamaha Venture Royale and the BMW twin.

My opinion is that shaft drives are just not strong enough to handle the violent loads of drag racing, and they take too much work to repair or rebuild them on a regular basis. German parts have never been noted for being cheap and Japanese shaft drive bits and pieces aren't far behind. Stick with chain- or belt-driven bikes for drag racing. If you want to run at Bonneville or El Mirage Dry Lakes, run a shaft without worries.

There but for a master link. Coming out of the burnout box, a Top Fuel V-twin parted company with this chain. The engine overrevved and the rev limiter shut it off half-way through the burnout. The silence was deafening. The master link split like it was made out of black licorice.

The transmission wasn't shifting into fifth, so they fired the bike in the pits and were running it through the gears. Jackstands under the wheelie bars make it easy to lift the rear wheel off the ground.

CHAPTER 16

Construction of a Pro Class Bike

In this chapter, we'll put it all together—using the information I've given you in Chapters 5 through 15.

Building a Pro Stock bike using off-the-shelf parts takes a modicum of mechanical ability, some decent work space and a beginning budget that will cover all the necessary parts. To put a Pro Stock bike on the track will take between $20,000 and $30,000. Costs for a Suzuki or Kawasaki Pro Stock bike appear in a chart later in this chapter. In reality, building any Pro bike for any sanctioning group will cost about the same unless you are building a fuel bike. I've chosen to describe the construction of a Pro

Stock bike because most racers have at least a general idea of what one is, and parts are readily available. You won't have to get involved with custom frame fabrication, engine mounts or supercharger/turbocharger plumbing. Everything I'll describe here will be the same with most Pro class bikes. I've left fuel bikes out of this discussion because of their complexity and cost. If you want to run a fuel bike, figure an increase of at least 50 percent to get it up and running, and a similar percentage to race it. The added cost and complexity make fuel bikes a bit more than first-time race bike builders need to tackle.

When you're at this point, the costs don't count. All the time, money, and hardship pale compared to lighting the fire on a fuel bike and making a six-second run.

Shin Akaike, #7032, a motorcycle shop owner, and Keiji Nakamura, #10, high school teacher, brought their Pro Drag bikes to Palmdale, CA to get some feeling for next year's series that they intend on running. Both bikes were built by Dave Earll, owner of Trac Dynamics.

The first step in building your Pro class bike is to collect all the necessary parts in one place. You can buy parts as you go along, but if you have everything available before you begin building, then the chances of the bike not being finished decrease. There are lots of unfinished projects rusting in garages.

One tool that's very important in initial assembly is a camera. Go to some races, take a lot of detailed photos of bikes in the same class as the one you plan to build. Take some close shots of details such as motor mounts, wiring, electronics mounting, shifter, fuel tank and feed, and, if the owner will let you, use a tape measure and record frame, engine, wheel, front end, and other dimensions. This will give you a good blueprint for your bike. It's very important to be able to visualize the completed bike, not just a collection of spare parts bolted together, before beginning fabrication. You might want to do a layout or sketch showing where everything is to be mounted. You don't need a blueprint, but some sort of plan will help keep you on the right track.

Beginning Fabrication

I've learned through past experience that the best way to begin assembly is to dummy everything together to check for fit and location. I'm going to assume you will be buying a chassis, not building one from scratch, so all the major parts should fit in their respective spots. The items you need to check are wiring placement, fuel lines, brake cables, hydraulic hose positioning, and placement of parts such as nitrous bottles and air tanks. Lay everything out and make sure you have all the required parts. Don't throw any shipping boxes away until you are one-hundred percent sure you won't have to return anything.

Begin by mounting the frame in a secure jig, preferably at waist height. Make sure it's sturdy enough to climb on and won't tip when shoving heavy parts such as engines into place. My work table is on lockable rollers and I turn it, rather than move myself around the bike. Whatever you decide, try to have the bike high enough to be able to see what you are doing without getting down on your knees or back.

Begin by mounting the engine in place. Just snug up the motor mount bolts. If you are using

Ny-lok nuts, only use them once at final assembly. Use a regular nut for mockup mounting. You will end up removing the engine a number of times before final assembly, so make it easy on yourself and don't tighten anything very much. If you don't have the racing engine yet, you can mockup the bike using a scrap block from a salvage yard. If you are building a non-unit-construction engine/transmission chassis, such as a V-twin, now's the time to install the transmission, check alignment between it and the engine and snug it down just tight enough to hold primary chain adjustment.

Next comes the rear axle (the frame is rigid and has no swingarm), rear sprocket, wheel and tire. Install the chain, which will have to be measured to fit, unless the frame manufacturer gives you the overall number of links. Adjust it properly and use a straightedge like a 1 × 2 aluminum I-beam to check for correct alignment between the countershaft sprocket and rear sprocket. If a straightedge is unavailable, eyeball the chain as it comes off the top of the rear sprocket and runs up to the countershaft sprocket. It should be parallel to the frame and not running with any slant. This is why you need a workbench. It makes checking things like alignment much easier. Make sure that everything rotates easily and there is no chain bind.

The next step is to mount the wheelie bar and get it at least close to final position. Chapter 5 shows you how to align the wheelie bar when the bike is on the track. Check the wheelie bar wheels for ease of rotation and put a little lube on their axle shafts. Mount the footpegs, rear brake master cylinder, lines and slave cylinder. Do the brake bleeding later, at the same time as the front brake. Install the header and pipe. (Some brackets might have to be heli-arced onto the frame. Don't gas weld anything!)

Now, let's turn to the front of the bike and hang the front suspension. Install the triple-clamps and bearings, and torque them to proper specifications. Mount the fork legs in their clamps and tighten them down; they won't be coming apart again. Bolt on the handlebars. Install the front wheel, tire, brake, and fender. Run the front brake lines up to the bars and install the brake lever (master cylinder if hydraulic). Don't

When estimating costs for a season, think what it takes to bring two bikes from Japan and have Trac Dynamics maintain them. The bikes alone represent over $75,000. Shipping (via JAL), travel expense for the team, transporter lease costs—one year will easily eat up $200k if all goes well.

The red and black tiles are laid down on the asphalt, providing a clean area to work, while adding a touch of class to this pit.

The straps around the cylinders will keep them in place should the engine cough. V-twins blow upwards, Japanese four-cylinders go down. Either direction is very expensive. Especially in a class like Top Fuel, you need to be independently wealthy, or find a sponsor with deep pockets. A season can, and will, eat up the better part of $350,000 if you want to run with the big dogs.

fill the cylinder with brake fluid until the bike is assembled for the final time. Mount all switches and controls, and the clutch lever if used. Mount the air tank and shifter. If you are running nitrous, now's the time to hang the bottle and run the lines to the intake manifold.

Depending on how you will run the bike, and your preference for controls, the electronics will have to be custom-made for your bike. Fabricating mounts will be up to you. Just make sure they don't interfere with any other parts and are away from heat. You can now hang the battery box and battery.

The wiring comes next. Wiring a bike is something of an art. After much trial and error, I've found a way that seems to be fairly easy and is not prone to error. When possible, I use color-coded wire, but this isn't always available. Lay out each wire from its control to its termination point. I add at least twenty percent to the length for Murphy's Law and label each end. Do this for every wire and when you are done, stand back and try to see a pattern to the wires. Then build them into a loom using either heat-shrink tubing or wiring wrap (available at electrical supply stores). When you're done, lay the loom on the

bike and check it for fit. I used to use crimp connectors for terminal connections, but one of them came loose at a bad time and now I solder all connectors.

Use the same wiring gauge and fuse size as used on your street bike. I recommend having a central fuse block, easily accessible. If wiring a bike is a bit intimidating for you, rather than take the chance of a burn down, find someone with electrical skills. Believe me, it's very easy to haywire something, and very discouraging to watch it burn. Install the fire extinguisher system and nozzles.

Install the fuel tank and unpainted fiberglass body. Sit on the bike and make sure all controls are within reach. Check for clearance around the body, especially with wiring and exhaust systems. When you are sure everything fits properly, take the bike apart again (you'll get good at this over the next few months) and paint or plate everything.

Now begin the final assembly. If you have all the parts and everything was properly pre-fit, then this stage should go easily. Take your time, work slowly and don't scratch the paint. I use masking tape and newspaper to protect any painted finish until everything is assembled. The first time you put the bike together for real shouldn't take more than three to four days. As your skill level and familiarity increase, you should be able to tear down and assemble the bike in one day. I've pulled a broken engine out of a drag bike in less than one hour and it was still almost too hot to touch when it was sitting in the van.

Testing

It's a good idea, even though the neighbors won't love you, to warm up the bike a few times at your workshop. Leave the body off so that any problems can be sorted out fairly easily. When you decide it's time to run, go to a low pressure event for your first timed runs. Don't show up at an NHRA or AMA/Prostar event where the pressures will be high. Run a couple of local events to set up the chassis and get the engine right.

Some tracks have testing and tuning days when there is no competition, just timed runs. These events are perfect for setting up a new rider and bike. First, make two or three slow passes, using no more than half-throttle. These runs will tell you if the bike wants to run straight and give you an idea of how it feels above 100 mph, but below a competitive speed. Believe me, your new racer will definitely feel different, run different, sound different, and perform different than anything you have ridden on the street. Be prepared for things to happen rapidly.

After you have sorted out the bike and yourself, it's time to make a couple of full-throttle-half-track passes. Again, this is to check handling and ensure proper control function.

Once you've made all these runs and worked out all the gremlins, take some time and run a wrench over every nut and bolt on the bike. Re-fuel and get ready to make some full-tilt-and-boogie passes. Don't try for speed, that will come as you progress. Try for smoothness and consistency. Learn how to do a proper burnout, then practice starts. The race is won or lost in the first couple of seconds. Get used to traveling over 150 mph in a quarter-mile.

Once all the parts are working correctly and you have a good grip on riding the bike, you can pay your fees and enter a pro event, but you had better be ready to run when the bike rolls off the trailer. Pro racing is intense, and you will have enough to do just trying to race that you sure don't need to be changing a clutch or swapping tires at a race. The most important ingredient at a race—especially a pro race—is yourself. If you don't have to worry about the bike, you can concentrate on becoming a good racer.

Costs

The prices shown here were current at press time. They may have changed by the time you read this, so I advise using them only as a rough guide to what parts will cost to build a Pro Stock or Pro Mod racer from the ground up.

These parts will just get the bike to operate under its own power. Operating costs will run about $1,500 per weekend. This covers wear and tear on parts, money toward an engine rebuild (rebuild cost ÷ number of runs = cost per run), tires and fuel. These are strictly operating costs for the bike. They don't include costs such as trailers, motels, meals, crew, entry fees, and so

Cost to Build a Pro Stock Drag Bike	
Parts	**Cost in Dollars**
Chassis, complete	$12,000–$15,000
Bodywork/paint	$760/$2000
Wheels, front/rear	$575/$1025
Tires, front/rear	$136/$205
Wheelie bar	$359
Engine (basic 8-second motor)	$6250–$8100 (new)
Wiring	$350
Clutch	$575
Transmission	$1360
Digital ignition	$700
Nitrous controller	$670
Timing retard	$277
Remote starter	$449
Kill switch	$65
Exhaust	$300
NOS system	$736
Induction	$740
Fuel cell	$153
Sprockets, counter/rear	$25/$74
Air tank, clutch and shifter	$720
Gauges	$340
Wiring, etc.	$350
Misc. (oil, fuel, rags . . . whatever)	$1500
TOTAL	$34,695

on. If your crew works for free (it helps if they're married to you), and you pack your own food, figure you can cut back on that figure by at least $10 to $20. Hey, no one said racing is cheap.

There's an old saying, "Speed costs money; how fast do you want to go?" Nowhere is it more true than in racing something powered by an internal combustion engine. The only other sport I am aware of that comes close is America's Cup Racing, and we all know that sailboats are just wet fiberglass containers into which you throw $100 bills.

But the time you spend racing is just the tip of the iceburg. For every weekend race in which the bike spends maybe 15 minutes running, you'll spend 100 hours in maintenance, repair, fabrication, transportation, and a whole lot of other things preparing for those 15 minutes.

Late News

As I was working on this manuscript (November, 2000) I heard that the hugely-successful team of Vance & Hines had just teamed up with Harley-Davidson and Screamin' Eagle to build a Pro Stock bike. The contract is open-ended and has no time limit, so I'd guess Harley is serious about seeing a V-twin on the winner's podium. Backed by Vance & Hine's abilities, Harley should soon need a larger trophy room.

Even Later News

Jackie Bryce at Star Performance Parts contacted me last week and asked me if there might be a place in this book for some photos of their new Star Racing Sportster. Sounds like the V-twin wars are heating up.

Star Racing has branched out a bit from racing Pro Stock Suzuki bikes. This is their Pro Stock Sportster, although you might be hard put to find any stock Sportster parts on the bike. The frame is made by Kosman, and all the engine parts are either fabricated in-house, or outsourced from aftermarket suppliers.

Sponsors

With the annual cost of a Pro Stock bike now approaching $100,000, money is a major factor limiting competition. I've learned the hard way that there's more talent than money running around. Getting a sponsor is rapidly becoming the only way to be competitive in the upper classes. No one races to lose, and no one wants to have to sell the kids and wife for a set of tires (wellll . . .) so some other source of money is needed.

When I was first getting into serious racing—80-hour weeks and *all* the paycheck—I hadn't learned the sponsor game yet and was trying to make a go on my own. The amounts of money I spent mean nothing today, mostly because it was so long ago that most of the coins had Roman emperors on them, but also because what was a lot of money to me might be less than zero to you. Suffice to say, if I had it I spent it.

Over the course of time, I managed to get the gas company, the phone company, the electric company, the water department, and several other creditors mad at me for not paying my bills. It wasn't that I didn't have the money—I was a journeyman plumber in what was fast becoming Silicon Valley—but at that time racing had a higher priority for me than my credit rating. The number of years it took to regain my good credit reminds me of the error of my ways.

Yep, it's better to find a sponsor to help pay the racing bills, and keep your personal finances on solid ground.

Big Game Hunting: Bagging the Elusive Sponsor

Where to start? How *do* you get someone else to part with his or her money instead of using all of yours? Here's what worked for me.

Here's where we all started: one rider, his own bike, T-shirt and tennis shoes, and the will to win. It's that easy.

This is where you end up when the big boys work a deal. Star Performance Parts and Angelle Savoie have Team Winston as a series sponsor. Whatever you may think about tobacco products, Winston has done a tremendous amount for drag racing.

First, I took a good look at the package I was trying to sell. I had a pretty good racing effort, operating out of a shop shared with four other car and bike crazies, and not sharing space with a garage full of dirty laundry. We had 3,000 square feet split five ways and shared all the expenses. I think this did more than almost anything else to aid our racing program. A visitor would see a clean area with painted floors and walls, lots of fluorescent lights, machine tools, welders and a whole group of very interesting machinery lying about. Everything from Lamborghinis to road racing sidecar bikes covered the floor at one time or another.

This well-equipped shop didn't come about at once, or at first, but it was an eventual outgrowth of a lot of years of garage racing. We had collectively acquired so much stuff that a shop became a necessity rather than a luxury. Split five ways, the operating costs and lease payments were quite reasonable. I think it's necessary to be at least at this level before going after big money. You may find sponsors at lower levels that will accept garage racing, but the serious money wants to see professionalism. Plus, a whole lot of selling yourself is smoke and mirrors. What do you think would impress a sponsor more: a

three-light-bulb garage with the kid's toys underfoot, or a clean, well-lighted shop dedicated to going fast?

Then I took a look at myself. Right! Long hair, Levis, T-shirt with "Support mental health or I'll kill you" emblazoned on the chest—and footwear? Hah!

Luckily for me, one of my better friends was a loan officer at a large bank. He enjoyed racing but wasn't really cut out for the greasy end of the game. (I think he slept wearing a Turnbull & Asser shirt and regimental tie. He once told me that he would rather go to work without his pants than tieless.)

After a bit of cajoling and basic ranting he managed to get across to me that what I was selling wasn't a race bike, wasn't the shop, wasn't the possibility of a trophy on the mantel; I was selling myself.

Selling myself! What a novel idea. Think a bit, though. What does a sponsor really want and get for his involvement? He sure isn't going to set his $1,500 Guy Laroche suit on a drag bike seat and make a pass. He probably will only come to the shop once or twice. He won't really understand more than 10% of what you're telling him. He will go to races. He will bring his business friends. To . . . See . . . You . . . Yes, he will enjoy the races, but if he's embarrassed by what "his" team looks like, rest assured the money will go away. Actually the money won't even appear unless you look the part of a successful competitor.

Selling Yourself

The first thing a potential sponsor is going to notice is your appearance. You need to look the part of a successful racer. Not that a tie and suit are necessary, though; wearing something that identifies you as a motorcycle racer is appropriate. Think white shirt and sponsor's jacket and some pants other than jeans. Be on time for any meetings and smile even if inside you're shakin' and quakin'. Show that you have confidence in yourself as a professional racer.

After the first sponsor-seeking meeting things will get much easier. You'll think about what you did right and wrong and adjust accordingly for your next presentation. It would be no end of help for you to take a couple of hours and prac- tice what you are going to say while looking into a mirror. Watch yourself and ask "would I give money to this person? Do I want him represent- ing me and my company?"

Write a script and practice. When I first went on a money search, I went so far as to tape myself before I met a single sponsor. Embarrassing! "Huh? Err. I dunno. Gimmie. Yeah. Huh? (Lots of times.) Don't got." And many other utterings just as crafty. People really don't listen to how they say something because they have been con- ditioned to talk in shorthand, use gestures, and not use complete sentences like I did right above. ("And many other . . . " has no verb.)

You will need to have a comprehensive biog- raphy. It should include a single page describing your background and education. Include a few photos (make them professional) of yourself and your current dragster.

The most important piece of paper in the bio will be a business plan. It will include your past accomplishments, current operations, and future plans. The last page should outline estimated costs and the amount of money you think the sponsor might provide. One way to estimate po- tential sponsorship money is to check what simi- lar sponsors are doing for other teams.

Lay out specific events such as public dis- plays, car shows, store openings and parades that you and the bike could attend and promote your sponsors. Request brochures and print media about their product or company that you could display. In the case of a potential motorcycle dealership sponsor, tell them you would be will- ing to display your bike in their showroom dur- ing the off-season.

Be sure all potential sponsors know how sup- porting *you* will benefit *them*. Explain how in- creased media coverage through a unique, highly visible race vehicle will help them increase busi- ness and profit.

Explain how their company name and logo will appear on the bike, the transporter and your leathers. If you need ideas, look at Star Perfor- mance's transporter and Pro Stock bike. Their Winston-sponsored team is about as professional as it gets. Their sponsorship didn't happen over-

Start at the bike shop where you spend most of your money. Even if the sponsorship is a 30% break on parts, it's a start. His saddlebag sports stickers from S&S, Russell, Star and others. All pay contingency money to first through third; there are lots of different ways to make money.

night, but was the result of years of racing and hundreds of hours of work.

Don't be afraid to ask for money, just be sure you have a plan for every dollar. You don't have to break down estimated expenses to the nearest buck, but you do need a chart showing outlay and projected expenses for at least one year.

If your potential sponsors show interest, a good way to set the hook is to invite them out to a race. Get them into the pits and up by the starting line to watch a few runs. If blood instead of water flows through their veins, they can't help but be- come excited watching you and others run. Be sure their tickets and pit passes are hand deliv- ered far enough in advance that they can allow for the time in their busy schedules. Remember, these are people who do something other than race.

Get to know the sponsor. What do they make, how do they market their product? What are the demographics of their market. A quick stop at the library can provide a lot of company infor- mation. If you are approaching a large company, find out who the media people are. This is espe- cially important in sending letters. By the way, do send letters. Using the mails instead of e-mail

Sponsor's stickers can go anywhere. Me, I'd like them, and my foot, a little farther from the pipe.

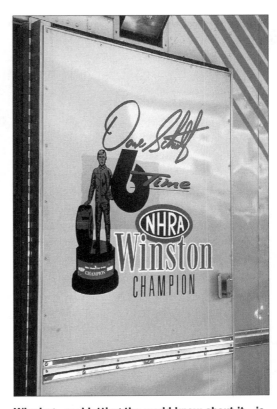

Winning—and letting the world know about it—is a good way to attract sponsors. This is on the door of a transporter and is a good, eye level way of telling the world who you are.

makes you come across as a lot more serious. Anyone can ask for money in an e-mail—it takes little skill and bears even fewer results. Send the letters and make the phone calls to a real person.

"Good morning, Jim Johnson please. This is Tom Murphy calling."

or

Jim Johnson
Media Director
Grace L. Ferguson Storm Door Company
NOT
Media Director
Grace L. Ferguson Storm Door Company
Dear Sir or Madam,

If you can't take the time, or don't have the ability to learn the names of the people from whom you wish to extract a small fortune, don't be surprised if they don't respond.

The same principals operate on a personal level. In order to sell another book, if I don't send a specific proposal to a specific editor, my letter probably won't even be opened; straight to the circular file it will go.

Make sure that a few days after the interview, you send them a hand written "thank you" note. Who knows, down the road a bit the company might change their mind about sponsorship, and if you left them with a good feeling, you might just get a phone call. It happened to me.

I'd made the circuit of potential sponsors for weeks, looking for a complete package sponsorship where the sponsor would cover the entire

cost of maintaining the team. More than one pair of shoes got worn out in the process of trying to sell myself past the front office and get to the people who make the decisions.

Nothing had happened and I decided to take my significant other on a short vacation. Because of my sponsorship-seeking schedule I hadn't been home for weeks if not months. She had casually mentioned to me that she almost mistook the mailman for me 'cause she was starting to forget what I looked like.

Remember Murphy's Law? Here I was, washing away my troubles on the beach at Ixtapa, Mexico, my suffering being tempered only by copious quantities of a concoction preferred by J. Buffett, when I was approached by a hotel employee with the urgent request to take a phone call of greatest importance.

You have to know the people in my shop to understand why I approached the phone with a

Even the sanctioning bodies have to pay their way. By being colorful and out in the open, they stand a better chance of getting a series sponsor.

bit of scepticism. They had gone to great trouble to rattle my cage in times past, and I didn't put it past them to have thought of some clever scheme to improve my R&R. Not this time.

Turns out a potential sponsor on whom I had totally given up had called the shop and wanted to speak to me *instanter* if not quicker. Now, getting a *larga distancia* conference call going between Ixtapa and Detroit was just about as easy as getting a mule to climb a ladder, but it finally was accomplished. In short order I was grabbing suitcases and yelling at my girlfriend to call the airlines. The low-hope sponsor had thought a bit and decided they wanted to involve themselves in racing for their product exposure and decided to go drag racing.

My girlfriend was quite interested in why I had interrupted our first long vacation for a bunch of stupid people who play Rambo on dirty motorcycles, and in no uncertain words ex-

pressed her displeasure at this turn of events. (I wonder what she's doing these days?)

Now, to believe the new sponsor couldn't wait to sort through the pile of sponsorship requests just to separate mine (and they got quite a few per month) from the dross would be wishful thinking, so I was quite interested in what had really happened.

A few months later I learned the actual process by which my name was selected for corporate largess. It seems that about the same time they were deciding to spread out their advertising budget, I had finally sat down and written some long overdue "thank you" notes. Total luck put my note on the decision-maker's desk about the same time the "Let's go Drag Racing" memo appeared. Their phone call followed, I left Mexico, and three months later I was under contract. Words can't describe my feeling when I got that first check.

Ditch Witch as a sponsor shows that you can go just about anywhere for help. You need a good plan and a portfolio of your victories when you approach a potential sponsor.

Where to Go

Don't limit your sponsorship search to motor-cycle-oriented businesses. Who would have thought a soap company like Tide (Procter & Gamble), or a discount company, K-Mart, would sponsor race vehicles? Make a list of business people you deal with. Talk up your dentist, doctor, nearby grocery store, Chinese restaurant, computer supply company, anyone you deal with and who knows who. Several small sponsors are just about as good as one big one.

Getting large checks makes racing much easier, but sponsors can help in many other ways. You will always need machine shop work. Oil gets used at a fantastic rate. The drag bike has to sit inside some sort of trailer. A big awning serves to keep the sun off and lets the awning manufacturer display his name in large letters. I even hit up a travel agency once. (Hey, at least it got me two tickets to Ixtapa.)

On the other hand, small sponsors sometimes take as much work as big sponsors. Plus, there's only so much room on the bike, your leathers and the helmet. Might as well start out to find a large sponsor if you think you have the necessary charm and ability to carry it off. But any sponsor is better than ruining your own credit to support your bad habits.

Sanctioning Groups and Classes

Most sanctioning bodies have pretty much the same rules for splitting up bikes into various classes: fuel or gas; blown or normally-aspirated; single-speed, two-speed or whatever fits in the box; Eliminator Dial-in or Heads-up; weight limit or cubic inch limits; and so on.

NHRA, AMA, IDBA, ADBA, IHRA, SEMDRA, Prostar, AHDRA—and others I've left out. There's a bunch. All these sanctioning bodies have written rules and regulations to divide bikes along generally the same classes. Several sanctioning bodies are specifically for Harley-Davidson motorcycles: ADBA, AHDRA, and others. The rules for ADBA are as follows and are similar for other groups. All ADBA classes are for pushrod 45-degree V-twin engines.

ADBA Classes

Fuel Classes

Top Fuel Two engines max, 175 ci absolute, nitro or alcohol, supercharged, turbocharged, injected or carbureted. Mid-six-second times at 200+ mph.

Pro Fuel Similar to Top Fuel except: single-speed, limited to 151.1 ci; two-speed, limited to 132 ci. Tire width, 12 inches. ET of mid-sixes with over 200 mph.

Pro Dragster Carbureted single-speed 122 ci engines. Low-sevens and 170+ mph.

Gas Classes

Pro Modified Carbureted, fuel injected, turbo or blown, alcohol or gas. Nitrous oxide al-

lowed. Blown engines (turbo or supercharged) with nitrous are limited to 122 ci. All others are held to 151 ci. High-sevens with 160+ mph.

Pro Stock Stock-appearing bikes, limited to gasoline and 160 ci. Must weigh 550 pounds at end of run. High-sevens with 160 mph.

Top Gas Normally-aspirated, unlimited displacement engines on gasoline. Large ci running low-eights and 150+ mph.

Super Modified Single engine, single carb big twin or Sportster engines. Rig and rider must weigh 5.1 pounds per cubic inch at end of run. Big twin engines between 84 and 120 ci. Sportster between 76 and 120 ci. Mid-eights with 150+ mph.

Atlanta Dragway is a very busy place, hosting AMA/Prostar motorcycle races and NHRA drag cars.

Modified Gas-only big twin and Sporty. Single engine, single carb. Big twin must weigh 575 pounds with 84 ci max. Sportster is 575 pounds with 76 ci max. Low-nine-seconds with 130+ mph.

Sportsmen Classes

Eliminator No limitations except for safety. Gasoline only. Dial-in eliminations, street registered bikes running low-elevens and 110+ mph.

SS/Buell Almost stock with bolt-in or bolt-on performance parts. Stock heads and cases. Stock bore and stroke. No machining of frame, engine, or head work. Low-tens and 120 mph. (This is the class for my nearly-stock Buell.)

SS/FL Buells with bolt-in or bolt-on parts, no machining or frame mods. Must run stock heads. Low-elevens and 110 mph.

SS/XL Same as SS/FL except a 3.5 in. bore allowed. Low-elevens and 110 mph.

AMA/Prostar Classes

Described below are the classes defined by AMA/Prostar.

Top Fuel – TF

This is the top of the heap in motorcycle (or car) racing. The bikes burn exotic fuels such as nitromethane and run pressurized induction systems that can boost ambient air pressure from 14.7 psi to upwards of 50 psi. Four-cylinder engine size is limited to 1700cc; however, most TF bikes are running motors closer to 1325cc and limiting the fuel to 90% nitro. Traction, not cubic inches, limits their performance. V-twin Top Fuel bikes run up to 170 ci motors. Engine/transmission design is totally open with the fastest racers running billet motors and custom transmissions. Any frame design is allowed. Clutch type and method of actuation is open. Bodywork is open.

All V-twin Top Fuel bikes must have a restraining strap around the engine cases and cylinders, because when a V-twin blows, the cylinders can go up with the force of a 20mm cannon. Inline four-cylinder engines blow downward, mandating a blanket/diaper below.

Getting across the finish line at 230 mph isn't as much a problem as stopping the bike in the limited length remaining. A single rear-wheeled vehicle running a 14.5×31 tire has very limited braking power. The front brake is a single rotor, but is capable of locking the front wheel at any speed and the narrow tire doesn't have a lot of braking ability, so the rear brake has to do a lot more work than it would on a street bike. Top Fuel dragsters stop with parachutes and a brake on each rear wheel. Right now, it is hard to imagine how to mount a chute effectively on a motorcycle, but if the speeds keep rising into the 250 mph bracket, someone will figure out how to mount one. Something like outriggers may be necessary, but this problem won't stop the fast guys for long.

Funnybike – FB

A lot of thought has been given to putting Funnybikes back into Top Fuel where they started. The biggest differences between the two classes is that Funnybikes are limited to using stock engine/transmission setups. Another difference between the two classes is that Funnybikes can run a wider variation of engine setups—nine—with Turbo/Nitrous or Turbo/Alcohol being the most popular. Rear wheel size is the same as Top Fuel. The stock crank must be used and this is a limiting factor when ultimate horsepower is sought. Funnybikes must also have bodywork that includes a gas tank, headlight, and rear fender. A fast Funnybike is 6.62 at 210 mph. The classes are:

FB/AB alcohol blown

FB/AG gas

FB/GI gas injected turbo

FB/GN gas nitrous turbo

FB/IA injected alcohol turbo, no nitrous

FB/IN injected nitrous, no boost

FB/TA turbo alcohol

FB/VN V-twin nitro

Pro Modified – PM

This is the hooligan class filled with 1500cc bikes with different engine/induction combinations, but dominated by nitrous oxide. They look a great deal like Funnybike machines. Normally aspirated, their ET is limited only by the 11-inch rear tire. Times run in the range of 6.70 and 201 mph. The classes are:

A/G A Gas

FX/IN Factory Experimental injected nitro

FX/N Factory Experimental nitrous

FX/T Factory Experimental turbo gas

V/N V-twin nitro

Pro Stock – PS

Similar to NHRA Pro Stock; heads up

Superbike – SB

This is a spin-off from the AMA's Superbike road race series. Wheelie bars are allowed, rigid rear suspension is the norm. Nitrous oxide rules the class, but turbo bikes like Mark Mosian's turbo Suzuki GSX-R 750 are becoming popular. Times are down in the 8.1 second range with Team Suzuki catching the top spots.

Streetbike Shootout – SBS

Stock appearing gas 750cc to 1300cc, nitrous and turbo, heads up

Sportsman Eliminator Classes – SE

There are five Sportsman classes with the first and fastest being Top Eliminator. Rules call for an aftermarket chassis, a 7-inch tire, 600-pound weight limit, and a turbo or nitrous but not both. The idea was to keep speeds down so that a non-pro competitor could run fast, but not be blowing through the lights above 190 mph.

The biggest reason to limit the speed through tire size was that too many accidents were happening on the top end, with the riders trying to get the bike slowed with too much front brake. However, this hasn't worked totally, because the record now is below 7.3 seconds and trap speed is over 190 mph. Just shows what can be done with a skinny tire.

Top Gas is one of three index classes in Sportsman class. Index racing has a set ET that the entire class must run at or above. Top Gas runs an 8.20 index and starts with a Pro tree. The first bike to the finish line without running under the index is the winner. Top Gas speeds easily exceed 160 mph and some of the "bad" bikes are capable of running 7.90 or better. Their brakes get a lot of use at the top end to keep from breaking out below 8.20. Sometimes you can see the bike nosedive as the rider clamps on the binders to stay above the index so he won't be disqualified.

The other two index classes are Super Comp with an 8.90 index, and Super Gas at 9.90. There have been other classes in the past, but with so many Japanese production motorcycles now capable of turning 9.90 out of the box, the classes were dropped. Actually, if you were to hang a set of wheelie bars on a 600 Supersport, it would have little trouble running competitively in Super Gas. The SE classes are:

T/E Top Eliminator; 7-inch slick, nitrous and turbo, no index

T/G Top Gas; 8.20 index, Pro tree

S/C Super Comp; 8.90 index, Pro tree

S/G Super Gas; 9.90 index, showroom/ Harley-type bikes

SS 600 Supersport; heads-up 1998 or newer, no index

Hot Rod Cruiser – HC

1998 or newer V-twin cruisers, no index

E.T. Bracket Classes

There are three ET classes, sometimes referred to as "Bracket" classes. These classes are a little hard to understand at first. The idea is to handicap the faster bike by staging the tree so there's a lag between the slower bike's green light and that of the faster bike. The winner is the one who runs closest to his or her dial-in time. To illustrate, each rider picks an ET to establish what their Dial-in time will be. This becomes the handicap between you and the other lane. For example, your Dial-in is 8.20. The other lane's Dial-in is 9.20. Therefore, you get a green light

1.00 seconds after the other lane gets theirs. Theoretically, both bikes will cross the finish line at the same time. This makes it possible to compete against bikes with faster or slower ETs than yours.

Pro ET – P/ET Starts with a .4 second full tree, max 12.99 dial in – Professional bracket racer. These guys are on the track simply for the money. Bracket racing pays contingency money along with prize bucks. A good rider (not necessarily the fastest) can make $15,000– $25,000 per year playing in this class. Pro ET pays $1,200 for a class win. In this class, sometimes the bike first off the line doesn't win. With a delayed start controlled by the tree, the faster bike leaves later, but catches and passes the slower bike down track for the win. The faster bike has to be careful, though, as he can run under his Dial-in while trying to pass the other bike.

Street ET – S/ET Street legal, .4 second full tree, max. 14.99 dial in. No wheelie bars, no trick electronics, the bike must be street legal. Only the first four places are paid, and not very much; no contingency money. This is a good class in which to learn to race, as the pressure is low and most of the racers are new at the game.

V-Twin ET Same as Street ET, but it's limited to V-twin-engined motorcycles. The average Street ET is 10.50 seconds; V-twins are at or above 14.50 seconds. The AMA wisely decided to separate the two classes because of their great speed difference. This way there aren't 150 mph bikes trying to run with 85 mph bikes.

International Drag Bike Association (IDBA) Classes

Street Shootout

600 Shootout

Kawasaki Showdown

Honda Showdown

Suzuki Showdown

Yamaha Showdown

H-D Showdown

Junior Drag Racer

Pro ET

Super Gas

Super Comp

Top Gas

Pro Street

Professional Motorcycle Racing Association (PMRA) Classes

F/B

T/G

S/C

S/G

Pro ET

Street ET

Street Bike Shootout

All Harley Drag Racing Association (AHDRA) Classes

ET

S/G

S/S

Street Eliminator

SEP - Screamin' Eagle Performance Parts

Pro Class Mod

Pro Class Pro Gas

Pro Class Pro Dragster

Pro Class Pro Stock

Pro Class Pro Fuel

Pro Class Top Fuel

Street Pro

Junior Class

National Motorcycle Racing Association (NMRA)

West Coast branch of AMA/Prostar

General Rules

All racing bikes must pass a technical inspection at the track. There are a few general rules that apply to all classes unless specifically noted. Some of these are shown in the table at right.

Pro Stock Rules

NHRA Pro Stock rules cover all types of bikes, but right now Suzuki, Kawasaki, and Yamaha hold the top places. Rules for Winston NHRA Pro Stock are covered on the next page, just to give you an idea where your bike would fit, not to give you specific parameters for racing. To be sure of what and how, get a rule book from the specific sanctioning body where you wish to race. The rules for different sanctioning bodies are just different enough that a bike fitting into one class in one body won't even come close to a similar class in another body.

A complete Pro Stock bike can easily cost $100,000 before it ever turns a wheel in competition.

General Rules

Ballistic Blanket. Required on any bike using nitrous. This year (2002) 600 SS and Street ET are the only classes where a blanket isn't required. The blanket must be AMA approved.

Catch Can. Mandatory on all but Street ET bikes. The crankcase breather hose must dump into a vented can. If the breather is plumbed into the header (it reduces crankcase pressure, but sucks oil; not for street usage), a secondary can must be used in case the engine grenades.

Coolant. Must not contain ethylene glycol or any antifreeze (it's slippery and almost impossible to clean off asphalt). The radiator must contain water only.

Cylinder Heads. Where permitted in class, aftermarket heads may be used if approved by tech. On air-cooled engines, fins may not be removed. The stock bolt pattern must be used. The stock cam must fit the head, and cam chain drive must be as stock.

Engines. Must be a Prostar-accepted stock-type engine designed for motorcycle use. Pro ET may use snowmobile engines. Any new design must have Prostar approval. All engines must be self-starting via an onboard starter or detachable electric starter. No push or roller starters allowed.

Supercharger. All blowers must be isolated from the rider by a steel plate not less than 1/8 inch thick that covers the entire top of the supercharger. A ballistic-type explosion blanket, meeting SEMA (Specialty Equipment Manufacturers Association) specs, may be substituted. Neither device is needed if the blower connects to the engine with clamp-on rubber hoses. "Sneeze valves" or "pop-off" valves are highly recommended.

Drive Train

Chain/Belt Guard. All bikes must run a guard that covers width and top of any chain or belt drive. Guards must be steel or aluminum if not OEM. Rear fenders and seats aren't chain guards.

Clutch. No bikes with engine-driven or lock-up clutches may be fired in the pits unless the rear wheel is elevated on a solid support and the front wheel placed against something solid (car, van, trailer). No load-bearing part of the clutch can be made from cast iron, or any cast material.

Brakes. Brakes must meet OEM specs, both front and rear. Brake lines must be OEM, steel or braided steel (highly recommended). The use of carbon fiber is prohibited.

Front Suspension. No rigid forks allowed. Tie-down straps no longer legal except in Street ET. Tubes may not extend more than 1-1/2 inches above fork crowns. Only hydraulic tubes allowed (Harley Springers have a hydraulic shock). Must use positive fork stops. One steering damper required (except Stock ET), and two are recommended.

Rear Suspension. Must be stiff enough so the frame will not bottom.

Frame Ballast. Must be securely mounted. No weight may be added below triple clamps on the forks. Weight cannot be added to the rider.

NHRA Pro Stock Motorcycle Specifications

Pro Stock Bikes. Must weigh no less than 600 pounds (550 for H-D and 575 for Suzuki) with rider aboard, and have a maximum wheelbase of 70 inches. Bikes must be 1993 or later model and retain their stock appearance, including a front fender, simulated headlight and tail light and manufacturer's identification on both sides. The engine and body make must be the same. All motorcycles must pass NHRA body inspection prior to competition.

Tires. The rear slick on a Pro Stock Bike is 10 inches wide and 26 inches in diameter and is designed specifically for motorcycle drag racing. (Mickey Thompson Performance Tires manufacturers the high-traction rear slicks preferred by today's riders. The front tire is a lightweight treadless design that aids in braking. Air pressure is 4 to 5 lbs in the rear and 30–32 psi in the front. Rear tires cost $175 and front tires cost $125.)

Transmission. Pro Stock transmissions are limited to six forward gears, though most competitors use five-speeds. The transmission is encased in the engine housing (except Harley-Davidson). The rider changes gears with an air shifter, which is handlebar actuated with a button. The seven-inch multi-stage, centrifugal lock up clutch uses 18 plates: nine fiber discs and nine steel floaters.

Rolling Chassis. A Pro Stock Bike chassis is made from 4130 chrome moly steel tubing. Though the wheelbase is limited to 70 inches, the wheelie bar, which is a critical chassis-tuning component, extends 130 inches behind the front axle. The rear is solid-mounted and the chassis includes an aluminum front fork, a swingarm, a one-quart fuel tank, handlebars, footpegs, and an engine mount. The cost of a rolling chassis and body is around $20,000.

Onboard Computer. Most bikes have an onboard computer system used primarily for data acquisition. Teams can monitor rpm, clutch slippage, rear-wheel spin, exhaust temperature, air/fuel ratio, and G-force levels. Computers run from $2,000 to $8,000.

Fuel. Pro Stock bikes may use only high-octane racing gasoline. The use of propylene oxide and/or nitrous oxide is prohibited. NHRA officials test and certify all fuels by chemical analysis. A Pro Stock bike uses one quart of fuel per quarter-mile run.

Engine. Pro Stock bike engines are limited to 1508cc (92 ci) for two-valve configurations and 1429cc (87.2 ci) for four-valve models. (This is the number of valves per cylinder.) Their dual-overhead-cam design allows them to rev to more than 13,500 rpm and produce between 292 and 305 hp. The two-valve engine uses eight spark plugs—two per cylinder; the four-valve uses four due to space limitations. The cylinder head is the most critical component of a Pro Stock Bike engine. Often, hundreds of hours of research and development go into making a single head.

Induction. A Pro Stock bike induction system consists of four gravity-fed, single-barrel carburetors (one per cylinder), which use metering rods that seldom require adjusting, and jets for fuel enrichment. Though virtually any stock engine is accepted, the overwhelming majority of Pro Stock bike racers use Suzuki or Kawasaki powerplants. A ready-to-run Pro Stock bike engine runs in excess of $25,000. (See note.)

Body. A modern Pro Stock bike is cloaked in an aerodynamically enhanced replica of the original, made from either fiberglass or a carbon fiber composite (very expensive, but lighter). The body has an air box that surrounds the carburetors and acts as a forced induction system. A standard Pro Stock Bike body also incorporates a two-step seat. After leaving the starting line, riders slide back from the lower portion to help improve weight transfer and reduce wind resistance.

Author's Note on Induction

This engine choice *might* be seeing a change. On one of my trips to an engine builder who uses nothing but Suzuki two-valve engines, I spied what looked like a V-twin engine in the assembly room. Now, this builder isn't known for his desire to run anything but winners, so I was somewhat surprised to see the V-twin parts. Conversation was a bit guarded, and photos a definite no-no, but from what little he said, I gathered that people wanted him to take a look at extracting horsepower from this type of engine by taking a different approach than others have used in the past.

He thought it was entirely possible to build a winning V-twin-powered Pro Stock Bike, and he's got a wall full of first place trophies, so . . .

Something will have to change in Pro Stock Bike, because the supply of air-cooled, two-valve Suzuki engine cases is limited. The four-valve just doesn't put out the power of the two-valve yet, plus it's liquid-cooled which puts more weight up high. Eventually, though, another powerplant will become dominant when the Suzuki cases dry up.

APPENDIX

Racing Organizations

All Harley Drag Racing Association (AHDRA)

3635 Reynolds Rd
P.O. Box 11845
Winston/Salem, NC 27116
336-924-2095
336-924-0072 Fax
E-mail: wsouthern@ahdra.com
Web site: www.ahdra.com

American Drag Bike Association (ADBA)

P.O. Box 1675
Owensboro, KY 42302
270-275-1762
Web site: www.americandragbike.com

AMA/Prostar

P.O. Box 18039
Huntsville, AL 38504
256-852-1101
256-859-3443 Fax
E-mail: info@amaprostar.com
Web site: www.amaprostar.com

International Drag Bike Association (IDBA)

3936 Raceway Park Rd.
Mount Olive, AL 35117
205-849-7886
205-841-0553 Fax
E-mail: IDBA@ix.netcom.com
Web site: www.idbaracing.com

International Hot Rod Association (IHRA)

9-1/2 East Main St.
Norwalk, OH 44857
419-663-6666
419-663-4472 Fax
E-mail: comments@ihra.com
Web site: www.ihra.com

National Hot Rod Association (NHRA)

2035 Financial Way
P.O. Box 5555
Glendora, CA 91740
626-914-4761
626-963-5360 Fax
E-mail: nhra@nhra.com
Web site: www.nhra.com

Professional Motorcycle Racing Association (PMRA)

3760 S Tyler Rd
Wichita, KS 67215
316-554-0139
Web site: www.pmra.net

For more information, schedules and race results: www.dragbike.com

Resources

Adams Performance

165 Log House Lane
Mooresville, NC 28115
704-663-1905

Alpinstar
AGV Sports Group Inc.

P.O. Box 378
Buckeystown, MD 21717
E-mail: info@accessoryinternational.com
Web site: www.AGV.com
800-777-7006
301-663-8950 Fax

Alumi-Trac (see Trac Dynamics)

Barnett Tool & Engineering

2238 Palma Drive
Ventura, CA 93003
805-642-9435
805-642-9436 Fax
E-mail: info@barnettclutches.com
Web site: www.barnettclutches.com

Bates Leathers

1663 E 28th St
Long Beach, CA 90806
562-426-8668
562-426-4001 Fax
E-mail: info@batesleathers.com
Web site: www.batesleathers.com

Bohn Body Armor

Action Stations, Inc.
166 Eaton Rd, Suite A
Chico, CA 95973-0201
888-922-9269
530-898-9188 Fax
E-mail: protector@bohnarmor.com
Web site: www.bohnarmor.com or
www.actionstation.com

CC Rider Racing

Connie and Marc Cohen
Harley Prostock rider (f)
Bristol, CT
E-mail: ccride@aol.com
Web site: www.ccriderracing.cc

Here's how to come out of the lights. Rolland Gibson brings his Pro Drag V-twin up for another run.

Competition Systems Racepack

Order from PR Factory Store:
11407 E 58th St
Raytown, MO 64133
800-878-3715
816-737-3715
816-358-7531 Fax
Web site: www.prfactorystore.com

Custom Chrome Inc.

16100 Jacquiline Ct
Morgan Hill, CA 95037
408-778-0500
408-782-6603 Fax
Web site: www.customchrome.com

Cycle Specialist

Larry "Spiderman" McBride
Newport News, Virginia
757-599-5236

Dainese
Bimoto bvba

Kortrijksesteenweg 241A
Sint-Martins-Latem
(near Ghent)
Belgium
B-9830
+32-(0)-9 281 0204
+32-(0)-9 281 0410 Fax
E-mail: dainese@dainese.be
E-mail: info@accessoryinternational.com
Web site: www.dainese.be

Dyna
Dynatek

164 S Valencia St
Glendora, CA 91741
626-963-1669
626-963-7399 Fax
E-mail: info@dynaonline.com
Web site: www.dynaonline.com

Dyno Jet Research

2191 Mendenhall Dr - Ste 105
North Las Vegas, NV 89031
Toll Free 1-800-992-4993
Web site: www.dynojet.com or
www.powercommander.com

Beyond the Edge

234 Franklin Ave #2
Nutley, NJ 07110
937-661-4138
Web site: www.dragbike.com

European Brake Corporation (EBC)

20314 131 Court NE
Woodinville, WA 98072
425-486-1244
425-485-7610 Fax
Web site: www.ebc-brakes.com

Fast By Gast

120 Industrial Drive
Grand Island, NY 14072
716-773-1536
716-773-7509 Fax
800-866-3880 Order line
E-mail: sales@fastbygast.com
Web site: www.fastbygast.com

First Gear
Intersport Fashions West Inc.

15602 Mosher Ave
Tustin, CA 92780
Toll Free 1-800-416-8255
714-258-2120
714-258-7511 Fax
E-mail: ifw.firstgear@thegrid.net
Web site: www.firstgear.com

Glass Werx (see Trac Dynamics)

Goodyear Tire & Rubber Co.

Corp. Headquarters
1144 E Market St
Akron, Ohio 44316
330-796-2121
330-796-2222 Fax
Web site: www.goodyear.com

Bassano Grimeca S.P.A.

40068 S Lazzaro Di Savena
Bologna-Via Remigia 42
Italy
+39-051 625 5195
+39-051 625 6321 Fax
Web site: www.bassanogrimeca.com

Hein Gericke
Intersport Fashions West

c/o Forzani Group Ltd
4141 Autoroute 440 Quest
Laval, Quebec H7P 4W6
CANADA
800-416-8255X312
E-mail: Info@accessoryinternational.com
Web site: www.intersport.com
Web site: www.gericke-usa.com

Hilborn Fuel Injection

22892 Glenwood Dr
Aliso Viejo, CA 92656
949-360-0909
949-360-0991 Fax
E-mail: service@hilborninjection.com
Web site: www.hilborninjection.com

Horsepower Express

963 Camden Ave
Campbell, CA 95008
408-866-1683
408-866-1457 Fax
Web site: www.powercommander.com/sitemap

Intersport Fashions West, Inc.

15602 Mosher Avenue
Tustin, CA 92780
800-416-8255 Ext 312

Joe Rocket brand
Outer Space Sports

3210 Jefferson Blvd
Windsor, Ontario N8T 2W6
CANADA
800-635-6103
519-945-8542 Fax
E-mail: joerocket@joerocket.com
E-mail: info@accessoryinternational.com
Web site: www.joerocket.com
Outer Space Sports is a division of
Marco Inc., Idaho Falls, ID 83404

Klotz Special Formula Products Inc.

7424 Freedom Way
Fort Wayne, IN 46818
800-242-0489
219-490-0490 Fax
E-mail: sales@klotzlube.com
Web site: www.klotzlube.com

Kosman Specialties

7706 Bell Rd; Unit E
Windsor, CA 95492
877-456-7626
707-837-0127 tech
707-837-8645 Fax
E-mail: sales@kosman.net
Web site: www.kosman.net

Koenig Engineering

1425 Maury
Demoines, IA 50317
515-244-1410
515-244-1148 Fax
E-mail: koenig@koenigeng.com
Web site: www.koenigeng.com

Kawasaki Green Team

P.O. Box 25252
Santa Ana, CA 92799-5252
800-661-7433 Dealers/products
949-460-5688 Consumer service
Web site: www.kawasaki.com

Lectron Carburetors (see Fast By Gast)

Mikuni American Corp

8910 Mikuni Avenue
North Ridge, CA 91324-3496
818-885-1242
818-993-6877 Fax
Web site: www.mikuni.com

Mr. Turbo

4014 Hopper Rd
Houston, TX 77093
281-442-7113
281-442-4472 Fax
E-mail: mrturbo@wt.net
Web site: www.mrturbo.com

Micro Systems Development Technologies Inc. (MSD)

1177 Park Avenue
San Jose, CA 95126-2911
408-280-1226
408-280-6868 Fax
E-mail: sales@msd.com
Web site: www.msd.com

Murdoch Racing Enterprises (MRE)

935 Harbor Lake Court
Safety Harbor, FL 34695
727-791-1321 Tech/information
800-237-7223 Parts/orders
727-791-9552 Fax
Web site: www.murdochracing.com

MTC Engineering

428 Shearer Blvd
Cocoa, FL 32922
321-636-9480
321-631-8804 Fax
E-mail: mtcpiston@aol.com
Web site: www.mpsmall.com

Mickey Thompson Tire

4670 Allen Rd
Stow, Ohio 44224
330-928-9092
330-928-0503 Fax
Web site: www.mickeythompsontires.com

Motonation

14168 Poway Road, Suite 205
Poway, CA 92064
877-789-4940
858-513-6285 Fax
E-mail: sales@motonation.com
Web site: www.monotation.com

Kushitani-US

3870 Del Amo Blvd. - Ste 507
Torrance, CA 90503
310-921-0133
310-921-1025 Fax
800-741-1725
E-mail: ron@kushitani.com
Web site: www.kushitani.com

Nitrous Express

4923 Lake Park Dr
Wichita Falls, TX 76302
940-767-7694
888-463-2781 Toll Free
940-767-7697 Fax
Web site: www.nitrousexpress.com

Orient Express

High Performance MC Components
81 Hanse Ave
Freeport, NY 11520
800-645-6521
516-546-5247 Fax
516-546-5232 Tech/sales
E-mail: sales@orientexpress.com
Web site: www.orientexpress.com

Performance Machine Inc.

8882 Martin Circle
LaPalma, CA 80823
714-523-3000
714-523-3007 Fax
E-mail: custserv@performancemachine.com
Web site: www.performancemachine.com

Pingel Performance

2072 11th Avenue
Adam, WI 53910
608-339-7999
608-339-9164 Fax
Web site: www.pingelonline.com

Powerdyne Automotive Products

104-C East Avenue K-4
Lancaster, CA 93535
661-723-2800
661-2802 Fax
E-mail: powerdyne@powerdyne.com
Web site: www.powerdyne.com

Precision Metal Fab Racing

952-496-0053
Web site: www.pmfronline.com

RC Components

373 Mitch McConnell Way
Bowling Green, KY 42104
270-842-9527
888-721-6495 Toll Free
E-mail: rcc@rccomponents.com
Web site: www.rccomponents.com

Race Visions

"Puppet" Jim Ditullio
350 Hinman Avenue
Buffalo, NY 14216
716-774-2755
Web site: www.racevisions.com
E-mail: racevisions@aol.com

Red Line Synthethic Oil Corporation

6100 Egret Ct
Benicia, CA 94510
707-745-6100
800-624-7958
707-745-3214 Fax
E-mail: redline@redlineoil.com
Web site: www.redlineoil.com

Rivera Engineering

12532 Lambert Rd
Whittier, CA 90606
800-872-1515 Toll Free
562-907-2600
562-907-2606 Fax
E-mail: info@riverengineering.com
Web site: www.riveraengineering.com

Russell Performance

2301 Dominguez Way
Torrance, CA 90501
800-416-8628 Tech
310-781-2222
310-320-1187 Fax
Web site: www.russellperformance.com

S & S Cycle

P.O. Box 215
County Highway G
Viola, WI 54664
608-627-1497
608-627-8324 tech support
E-mail: sscust@sscycle.com
Web site: www.sscycle.com

Schnitz Racing

222 N Third St
Decatur, IN 46733
800-837-9730
800-213-3244 Fax
E-mail: info@schnitzracing.com
Web site: www.schnitzracing.com

Shoei

3002 Dow, Ste 128
Tustin, CA 92780
714-730-0941
714-730-0942 Fax
E-mail: info@shoei-helmets.com
Web site: www.shoei.com

SIDI Boots (see Motonation)

Star Racing
Star Performance Parts

P.O. Box 1241
Americus, GA 31709
800-841-7827 orders
229-928-2321 Fax
E-mail: info@starracing.com
Web site: www.starracing.com

Stripbike.com

Safety Net Plus, Inc.
Dwight Drum
1007 Mandalay Dr
Brandon, FL 33511
813-653-2044
Gary Larsen
718 Bayside Blvd
Oldsmar, FL 34677
813-855-4387
Web site: www.stripbike.com

ThunderJet (see Dyno Jet)

Trac Dynamics

28042 Avenue Stanford
Valencia, CA 91355
661-295-1956
661-295-1672 Fax
E-mail: info@tracdynamics.com
Web site: www.tracdynamics.com

Traction Products (see Weismann Transmissions)

Trick Racing Gasoline

P.O. Box 248
Oakdale, CA 95361
800-444-1449
209-847-9726 Fax
Web site: www.trickgas.com

Vance & Hines

13861 Rosecrans Avenue
Santa Fe Springs, CA 90670-5019
562-921-7461
562-802-7466 Fax
E-mail: sales@vanceandhines.com
Web site: www.vanceandhines.com

Vanson Leathers, Inc.

951 Broadway
Fall River, MA 02724
508-678-2000
508-677-6773 Fax
E-mail: vanson@vansonleathers.com
Web site: www.vansonleathers.com

VP Racing Fuels

P.O. Box 47878
San Antonio, TX 78265
210-635-7744
210-635-7999 Fax
E-mail: vphq@aol.com
Web site: www.vpracingfuels.com

Ward Performance

587 Citation Drive
Shakopee, MN 55379
952-403-6740
952-403-6399 Fax
E-mail: info@wardperformance.com
Web site: www.wardperformance.com

Web Cam, Inc.

1815 Massachusetts Avenue
Riverside, CA 92507
909-369-5144
909-369-7266 Fax
E-mail: webcam@webcaminc.com
Web site: www.webcaminc.com

Weismann Transmissions
Weismann Marine

1728 Monrovia St
Costa Mesa, CA 92627
949-645-4064
949-645-2424 Fax
E-mail: gearboxes@hotmail.com
Web site: www.weismann.net

Wiseco Pistons

7201 Industrial Park Blvd
Mentor, Ohio 44060
800-321-1364
800-321-3703 Fax
E-mail: info@wiseco.com
Web site: www.wiseco.com

Index

About the Author

Tom Murphy started riding motorcycles in 1963. His first drag bike was a 1965 Triumph 500. Since then he's owned many racing bikes, but none so thrilling as the first one. He lives in Nevada in an area so rural that the bears still speak Spanish.

NOTES:

NOTES:

NOTES: